Actualities

Actualities of Aura

Edited by

Dag Petersson
Erik Steinskog

NSU Press

Published by: Nordic Summer University Press
Ljungåsvägen 6
SE-472 31 SVANESUND, SWEDEN
http://www.nsuweb.net

Produced by: Söderströms Förlag
Georgsgatan 29 A, 2 vån.
POSTBOX 870
FI-00101 HELSINGFORS, FINLAND
http://www.soderstrom.fi

Distributed by: Århus University Press
Langelandsgade 177
DK-8200 ÅRHUS, DENMARK
http://www.unipress.au.dk

Cover art by: Christa Puch Nielsen
http://www.dingdong–grafiskdesign.dk

ISBN: 91-88484-25-4

First published 2005

Printed by: Nord Print Ab, Helsingfors, Finland

07 06 05 04 03 02 01 00   10 9 8 7 6 5 4 3 2 1

CONTENTS

Acknowledgements

No book is the result exclusively of those mentioned on its cover. This volume is by no means an exception. Many people and institutions have supported this project by granting us the time and the money necessary to produce this book. Others have helped us with their invaluable skills and utmost generosity. And many have supported the project with their enthusiasm and good spirits. To all of you, we are forever grateful. In particular we want to name the following friends, colleagues and institutions for their support: The Aesthetics Study Circle and the Board of The Nordic Summer University; Roy Sellars and Dave Lee; Ulla Carlsson at NORDICOM; Tapani Ritamäki at Söderströms Förlag; Inger Fischer Jonge and John T. Lauridsen at The Royal Library in Copenhagen; Members and Board of the MODINET Research Centre; Erik Granly Jensen; Åsa Petersson; Christa Puch Nielsen, Ditte Vilstrup Holm. Thank you all for making this book possible.

Abbreviations

SW: Walter Benjamin, *Selected Writings*, vol. 1–4, eds. Marcus Bullock, Howard Eiland and Michael W. Jennings (Cambridge, Mass.: The Belknap Press of Harvard University Press, 1996–2003).

AP: Walter Benjamin, *The Arcades Project* (Cambridge, Mass.: The Belknap Press of Harvard University Press, 1999).

GS: Walter Benjamin, *Gesammelte Schriften*, eds. Rolf Tiedemann and Hermann Schwäppenhauser (Frankfurt am Main: Suhrkamp Verlag, 1991).

OGT: Walter Benjamin, *The Origin of German Tragic Drama* (London, Verso, 1998).

Corr. *The Correspondence of Walter Benjamin*, eds. Gershom Scholem and Theodor W. Adorno (Chicago: Chicago University Press, 1994).

Introduction

Collecting Twelve Studies of Walter Benjamin

Dag Petersson and Erik Steinskog

As Walter Benjamin began to collect materials in the French national library for the grand masterpiece he called *The Arcades Project*, he heard the painted leaves begin to rustle in the clear-blue ceiling overhead. By comparison, a more prosaic whisper from computers and servers could be detected as we set out to collect the contributions to this volume. Digital communications have in many ways done for the editing of this book what the library did for *The Arcades Project*, even if today's computer networks with their quickly evolving capacities for communication and information storage provide us with a quite different archive than the Parisian library Benjamin frequented in the 1930's. Digital technology has indeed facilitated and shaped other modes of writing as well as different conditions for editing; for us it has furthermore inspired new questions to pose about Benjamin's concept of aura.

Few have, like Benjamin, testified with a single concept to how technical developments dialogue with the limits of an era's modes of writing, perception and even thinking. Hence, the technology we are so involved with today, in all the facets and dimensions of intellectual labor, brings the actuality of his concept of aura to a state of critical concern. The historical tension between our digital archive and Benjamin's library must therefore not be obscured by an analogy of rustling leaves and humming hard-drives; much rather, we want the tension further strained by thinking spatially about collecting texts. Traditional library space—the space of reading rooms, collections and catalogues—enables a certain mode of literary experience with particular limits and possibilities. Digital space—the space of computed code, digital documents and interface mediation—produces a different mode that affects literary production, research and reading.

It is from the tension between those two modes that we think it is possible to assess a third space: one that, weaved into time, could once evoke an irreducible distance of aura. If film and photography meant the decay of aura and the destruction of its distance, does digital space reinstate it or does it change the meaning of aura? In the literature on new media, aura is still a commonly used concept for addressing what it is about our languages and bodies, about time and space that has changed, now that the modern mode of experience no longer fits with the world in which we live. But when the aura is employed as a useful concept today, it is never without an intrinsic ambiguity.

Looking back at September 2002, when we sent out the first call for papers into cyberspace, the event seemed neither auratic nor non-auratic, for as we later googled our cfp to see whereto its clones had spread, the sensation was rather that it had acquired a life of its own. But even if the term aura seemed unsuitable to describe that experience, several elements pertaining to it were indeed present: technical reproducibility, lack of an author identity, a struggle with words, an irreducible sense of distance and a gaze not returned. That the term aura seemed actual but inaccurate at the same time told us that if we were lucky, we had already produced an editorial situation very close to the research topic of the book. As the list of authors slowly took shape, we noticed a constellation of distances between contributors' names: some were well-known but most were not, some belonged to esteemed professors, others to less experienced scholars, some indicated a native English speaker, others an author with a different mother tongue, some emails came from Europe, others from the US, from Canada and Australia, some names were associated with the social sciences, others with the humanities, and so on.

As we received a very mixed group of potential contributors with different horizons for their analyses, the stage was set for an editorial experiment directly related to the aura. Could the texts form a micro-library over Benjamin's concept that would map the historical tensions between our digital archive and the library he once disappeared into? After the first deadline, when the received drafts had been eagerly read, it was no longer merely the names that revealed a spatial constellation; the various paths of argumentation, the theoretical architecture of each piece began to produce a dynamic space of its own, within and between the articles. Looking back at this developing heterotopy, it seems to have emerged less from the digital means of production than from complex literary processes that we identified as our task to steer responsibly. The emerging formation is illustrated on the front cover: it has no determinable center, yet there are centers identifiable by how the formation curves around them. If we imagine that these centers correspond to variations of the concept of aura, and if we think that the curving formations correspond to the articles' various modes of argumentation, then the heterotopy of this book is itself an actuality of aura.

Though the twelve studies of aura we offer here are very different from one another, we sense that they all benefit from being brought together. When two or more contributions intersect, for example while dealing with a particular passage in Benjamin, it is remarkable how their different approaches do not exclude one another, but often strengthen the alternative reading. This phenomenon is the editors' good luck; we could not have anticipated it, far less expected it or produced it. We think of those intersections and the many divergences as the result of our experiment. The kind of actuality of aura the editorial heterotopy reveals is a dynamic rhythm of reading. The experience of this rhythm is what the editorial strategy of this book contributes to the growing field of Benjamin research.

Copenhagen, December 17, 2004.

Fabricating Aura

The Face in Film

Graeme Gilloch

Engel sollen nicht sterben! [1]

As the papers in this collection amply demonstrate, 'aura' is one of Walter Benjamin's most intriguing and suggestive concepts. At the same time, it remains one of his most elusive. Aura refers to the sense of wonder, awe and reverence experienced by the onlooker or listener in the presence of a singular, authentic work of art; it refers to that "strange weave of space and time: the unique appearance or semblance of distance, no matter how close it may be," [2] to that uncanny sense of an inanimate thing returning the gaze cast upon it. [3] Aura is a highly enigmatic term for that which is itself tantalisingly intangible: the inscrutable, ineffable, inexhaustible potency of the artwork. Benjamin's nuanced understanding and evaluation of aura further complicates such indeterminacy. At different moments in his 1931 "Little History of Photography," for example, aura denotes the ominous gloom enshrouding the earliest photographs and from which the image seeks to free itself; [4] the intense individual quality of the subject, whose life is only ever partially captured by photographic portraiture; [5] and, the profound sense of recognition and reciprocity when our gaze is met by the sad eyes [6] of the photographed face. [7] Benjamin accentuates the last of these in his famous 1935–6 essay "The Work of Art in the Age of Its Technological Reproducibility," observing that it is in the countenances of those who were but are no more, in the faces of the dead, that aura finds a final resting place, in photographs distinguished by "their melancholy and incomparable beauty," [8] in images that will continue to haunt us. [9]

1

Notwithstanding such inconsistencies and Benjamin's frequently puzzling choice of metaphors—what is one to make of the idea that Eugene Atget's photographs "suck the aura out of reality like water from a sinking ship"?[10] —the gist of Benjamin's argument as to the contemporary fate of aura is familiar and requires only the briefest reiteration here. For him, the advent of cultural and artistic production and reproduction technologies in the modern period, most notably photography, film and sound recording, leads to the 'withering' or 'decay' of aura.[11] The hallmark of these new (mass) media is not simply that artworks can be reproduced—this has long been the case as Benjamin acknowledges[12]—but rather that reproducibility becomes the fundamental principle, the very *raison d'être* of contemporary cultural forms.[13] It no longer makes sense to speak of an original or authentic work of art as opposed to a fake or copy. For the first time one is confronted by a series of identical and wholly interchangeable images and objects, none of which can claim primacy. The singularity, uniqueness and exclusiveness of the auratic painting give way to the multiplicity, ubiquity and availability of the photographic print.[14] This has profound consequences: reproducibility liberates the artwork from its own ritualistic, magical origins. Whereas traditional art is or was grounded in the object's enduring 'cult value,' the new media are preoccupied with 'exhibition value,' that is, with the readiness and 'fitness' of the artefact, image or sound to be publicly seen and heard.[15] This has a political dimension: in displacing the notion of authenticity, the inherent reproducibility of film reconfigures and refunctions the aesthetic sphere. Benjamin notes: "as soon as the criterion of authenticity ceases to be applied to artistic production, the whole social function of art is revolutionized. Instead of being founded on ritual, it is based on a different practice: politics."[16]

Benjamin, then, is concerned with the final vestiges of aura in the modern age, with aura at the vanishing point, with aura seen 'at last sight.' This demise of aura—and of a host of other outmoded aesthetic categories like 'creativity' and 'genius'—is a function of technological reproducibility and constitutes a radical political advance.[17] Having said this,

2

however, it is important to note that other factors are at work in dispelling aura. Key technical features of the new media, as well as their inherent technological logic, are also significant. For example, in his "Work of Art" essay Benjamin points out how the actual processes of film production necessarily transform aesthetic practices, perceptions and experiences. Unlike theatrical performances presented on stage before a live audience, film acting involves a discontinuous series of mini-performances before the camera, mere fragments of acting subject to continual repetition and refinement. Scenes are shot sometimes in, sometimes out of sequence depending on a host of contingencies. For the actor there is no sense of continuity or completeness, no development of or identification with characters, no possibility of reciprocity or interaction with an audience. "As a result," Benjamin notes, "the aura surrounding the actor is dispelled— and, with it, the aura of the figure he portrays."[18] Furthermore, just as the action of the film is broken into a plethora of "episodes capable of being assembled,"[19] so, too, is the body of the actor as the camera zooms in and out for close-ups, focuses now on this particular gesture, now on that feature. The camera adopts, Benjamin claims, a probing, testing and critical attitude toward the actor, a perspective which the film's viewers subsequently make their own. They do not lose themselves in the intense concentration characteristic of auratic contemplation, but rather seek satisfaction in collective distraction.[20] In this way, Benjamin suggests, film enables the masses to "'get closer' to things"[21] and fosters a new critical expertise and class-consciousness.[22] Herein lies the medium's political significance and revolutionary promise.

Questions of technique are consequently crucial to aura's fate. What most interests me in this context is one of the more neglected aspects of Benjamin's thesis, namely, his recognition that certain photographic and cinematic techniques and strategies, both in the studio and outside, have been deployed and continue to develop, which ameliorate or offset the eradication of aura. These take the form, above all, of efforts to construct, manufacture or simulate aura, to produce auratic effects and experiences in the absence of aura. One is concerned here not with aura *per se*, but

3

rather with what one might term 'simulated' or 'artificial' aura. Of course, one must admit straight away that the notion of 'artificial aura' is a contradiction in terms—aura is, after all, that which attests to the authenticity, the genuineness, the uniqueness of the traditional artwork. Aura, genuine aura that is, cannot be fabricated—this is what makes it genuine. Nor can aura be restored—it is irredeemably liquidated by the logic of reproducibility inherent in new media. Artificial aura, though, refers to the spurious attempt to authenticate the inauthentic, to attach a sense of uniqueness to the commonplace, to maintain or manufacture a semblance of distance despite proximity. Artificial aura imbues objects and images with an 'air' of aura. It is not embedded in tradition but rather fabricated by various modern techniques, ones which, I suggest, run directly counter to what Benjamin and Siegfried Kracauer see as the essential critical imperatives of film and photography.

Benjamin observes how strategies to create artificial aura come to the fore as commercial and business interests intervene and increasingly control photographic and cinematic developments. In the case of photography, he notes how the 'magical' (genuinely auratic) qualities of the earliest photographs were rapidly supplanted by the mediocrity of the market: commercial and 'artistic' photographers producing sentimental portraits for the family album and pictures conceived in the image of paintings. As photographs became everyday commodities they disguised themselves as 'art.' Fanciful costumes, carefully staged poses before 'scenic' painted backdrops, and all manner of pillars, pedestals and drapery were brought in to lend the photographic image a sense of 'artistic,' painterly composition.[23] Commercial photographers increasingly sought to exploit new and more sophisticated techniques both in the studio (lighting, focus, shutter speed, etc.) and in processes of development (retouching, highlighting, tinting) to imbue pictures with a certain solemnity and grandeur, to intimate and imitate aura. Benjamin writes:

> After 1880 [...] photographers made it their business to simulate the aura
> which had been banished from the picture with the suppression of darkness
> through faster lenses [...]. They saw it as their task to simulate this aura

4

using all the arts of retouching, and especially the so-called gum print. Thus, especially in *Jugendstil* [*Art Nouveau*] a penumbral tone, interrupted by artificial highlights, came into vogue. Notwithstanding this fashionable twilight, however, a pose was more and more clearly in evidence, whose rigidity betrayed the impotence of that generation in the face of technical progress.[24]

The contrast between actual technological advance and the proliferation of techniques for regressive purposes is striking here. The fabrication of artificial aura—enfolding immobile figures in mysterious shadows, obscuring detail—occurs in opposition to the ever-increasing power of the camera to reveal and disenchant 'reality.' The genuinely radical promise of photography (and film)—the penetration and illumination of the world, the capturing of motion and life—is confounded by a predilection for the nebulous and an overwhelming sense of paralysis.

In the "Work of Art" essay Benjamin similarly recognises that capitalist control of film production ensures that the "revolutionary opportunities" afforded by the cinematic medium are misused "for counter-revolutionary purposes."[25] The burgeoning film industry "has an overriding interest in stimulating the involvement of the masses through illusionary displays and ambiguous speculations. To this end it has set in motion an immense publicity machine, in the service of which it has placed the careers and love lives of the stars; it has organized polls; it has organized beauty contests."[26] The withering of genuine aura occasioned by film is counteracted by the magical glitz and glamour of the Hollywood star system in which "the cult of the movie star" manages to preserve "that magic of the personality which has long been no more than the putrid magic of its own commodity character."[27]

Benjamin's comments on the film star here are interesting in a number of respects. The notion of the cultic itself is, of course, an echo of the ritualistic origins of the traditional work of art and stands in opposition to the progressive claims of exhibition value advanced by the new media. Moreover, in connecting the spurious "magic of the personality" with that of the "commodity character" Benjamin unambiguously links attempts to fabricate artificial aura with the notion of fetishization. Indeed,

5

as we will see, the artificial aura of the film star is predicated upon a fetishization of the image of the face. Far from fragmenting and testing the *physis* of the actor, camera techniques (most notably, the use of close-up),[28] forms of make-up and lighting combine to lend the star's face a special intensity, beauty and authority. The camera serenely marvels at the perfect, awe-inspiring countenance of the actor, constructs his/her visage as immaculate and incomparable. Importantly, however, this fabrication is not confined to the manipulations of the studio and editing suite. Benjamin also directs attention towards what one might understand as the discursive constitution of the movie star. Artificial aura is fabricated inter-textually: in advertising, lifestyle and fashion magazines, celebrity biographies, chat-shows, newspaper gossip columns and such like. From the outset the film star has been a multimedia phenomenon.

Indeed, it was one exemplary instance of this inter-textual process—an image combining fabricated authenticity, reproduction and reproducibility, the face of the film star, and commodity culture—which first directed my attention to the notion of artificial aura and set these reflections in train. A couple of years ago, an intriguing advertisement for gin appeared in a newspaper weekend supplement. It comprised a photograph (or still) of Audrey Hepburn juxtaposed with the picture of a model who had been posed in the same manner, and made-up, lit and photographed so as to resemble closely the Hepburn image. In a variation on a 'spot-the-difference' puzzle, the success of the advert relies on a deceptively simple process of recognition and evaluation. First, the face of Audrey Hepburn is identified as that of a genuine or real film star, as a figure possessing a unique quality, a special beauty, a distinctive 'charm.' Second, the face in the subsequent image is recognised as that of an impostor, it is an imitation, which, however similar, is clearly less beautiful, less charming than the original. As a counterfeit, this second face is fake, suspect, inauthentic, inferior and second-rate, "what's left" as the advertisement puts it. Only the real thing is good enough: Hepburn, Tuscan juniper berries, Gordon's gin.

In this advertisement we see that most common of contemporary

6

advertising ploys: the projection of the phoney "magic of the personality" onto the commodity. In this instance it is done, however, through an intricate play on notions of reproduction, originality and the copy. The face of Hepburn could be understood as an image of the reproducibility of images *par excellence*: after all, here we are presented with a photograph with an almost identical picture set beneath it, the whole composing an advertisement itself reproduced in a mass media publication.[29] What could be more bereft of aura than such an image? Moreover, according to Jean Baudrillard, the co-presence of an original and its double—the fundamental premise of the advert—is fatal for the former. One cannot survive the direct encounter with one's own doppelganger.[30] He warns:

> The double is an imaginary figure that, like the soul or one's shadow, or one's image in a mirror, haunts the subject with a faint death that has to be constantly warded off. If it materializes, death is imminent. This fantastic proposition is now literally realized in cloning. The clone is the very image of death, but without the symbolic illusion that once gave it its charm.[31]

And certainly the photograph of Hepburn itself has something of this "image of death" about it, for if film involves temporal flow, the motion of bodies, the dynamism of life, then the cinematic still presents temporal suspension, interruption, frozen action, still-life, death. In the gin advertisement we see the very imitation of the film still—the two images are set one above the other as if they were not two photographs different in time and space, but two frames on a film reel separated only by an instant, a tiny movement, an infinitesimal gesture. Here we see a photographic image haunted by another photographic image, a still by a still, a 'dead' image with a 'dead' doppelganger, a ghost with a ghost in tow.

How could such an advertisement suggest or exemplify artificial aura? The answer to this, and the success of the advert, lies precisely in our (almost) immediate recognition of the double as a double, in our ability to perceive both the similarity and the non-identity of the images and faces. By juxtaposing Hepburn's face with a 'non-Hepburn' face, the perfection and potency of this 'original' is emphasised by the co-presence

7

of the pale imitation, of the 'near-double.' The message is clear and un-
ambiguous: Hepburn cannot be duplicated. The doppelganger is defeated.
The ultimate image of reproducibility here points paradoxically,
deceptively to the impossibility of reproduction. It restores precisely those
distinctions between original and copy which film and photography, its
own media, have eradicated. Indeed, the advert is so constructed that in
distinguishing and privileging the face of Hepburn, the viewer takes this
countenance as the very incarnation of singularity itself, as the idea of
uniqueness, of the genuine *per se*. Hepburn's inimitable image is imbued
with an (artificial) aura.

How else might artificial aura be fabricated in relation to the film star
and, in particular, how might this centre on the portrayal of the star's
visage? The face of the star, of the actress in particular, has attracted the
attention of a number of critical cultural theorists and it is to their very
different 'physiognomical-philosophical' disquisitions that one may
fruitfully turn in seeking clues to answer such questions. In texts by Jean
Baudrillard, Roland Barthes, Siegfried Kracauer and Franz Hessel one
finds a series of parallel distinctions between the appearance of the face
of the star in early cinema—silent film and early talkies—and later
manifestations as sound and colour transformed the medium. For each
of these writers an emphasis upon rigidity and expressionlessness—the
frozen face, the face as 'dead'—is displaced by a concern with mobility
and mimesis—the charming or characterful face. They thereby provide a
series of telling contrasts suggestive of a number of cinematic techniques
initially utilised by the film industry to fabricate aura and foster that
"cult of the movie star" to which Benjamin draws our attention.

An Easter Island Statue
Baudrillard's reflections on the face of the star appear as part of his analysis
of the key concept of 'seduction,' a notion every bit as ambiguous and
elusive as aura. According to Baudrillard, the idol of the silent screen
and the first talkies constitutes the final instance of "collective seduction"[32]
in the modern epoch, an experience destined to be superseded by the

8

stupefied fascination attendant upon the contemporary Hollywood star and banal media personality. For Baudrillard, the extraordinary, enthralling countenance of the star of early cinema is characterised by its total artificiality and radical superficiality:

> The star is by no means an ideal or sublime being: she is artificial. She need not be an actress in the psychological sense; her face is not the reflection of a soul or sensitivity which she does not have. On the contrary, her presence serves to submerge all sensibility and expression beneath a ritual fascination with the void, beneath the ecstasy of her gaze and the nullity of her smile.[33]

Cold, frozen and "glacial"[34] this visage offers itself up as a blank, as the degree zero of expression:

> Artifice and non-sense, they are the idol's esoteric face, its mask of initiation. The seduction of a face purged of all expression, except that of the ritual smile and a no less conventional beauty. A white face, with the whiteness of signs consecrated to ritualized appearances, no longer subject to some deep law of signification.[35]

Wholly artificial, thoroughly inscrutable, utterly compelling, the fabricated face of the film star is a mask, an effigy, a fetish. In a memorable trope Baudrillard observes that such movie stars were and perhaps still are "our Easter Island statues."[36] For Baudrillard, as for Benjamin, this cultic aspect of the film star is bound up first and foremost with the veneration of the dead:

> The death of the stars is merely punishment for their ritualized idolatry. They must die, they must already be dead—so that they can be perfect and superficial, with or without their makeup. But their death must not lead us to a negative abreaction. For behind the only existing form of immortality, that of artifice, there lies the idea incarnated in the stars, that death itself shines by its absence, that death can be turned into a brilliant and superficial appearance, that it is itself a seductive surface.[37]

9

The dead face of the star is a fabrication, a source of artificial aura. Of course it also takes on those lingering traces of genuine aura Benjamin perceives in relation to the faces of the dead. Indeed, this is the ultimate combination: the dead face of the now dead, the death mask. Death–and above all, the untimely death of the young star–is the ultimate price paid for eternal stardom. After all, it is the images of those whose lives were tragically cut short, those serene countenances which appear blind to the hotel-room suicides, overdoses and car accidents for which they were destined, faces untroubled by the catastrophe which awaits them, but has already occurred for us, which exert the most compelling, melancholy power. The beautiful, youthful, doomed face is fixed for all time.[38]

Baudrillard names no names in his observations on the immaculate face of the actress, but his model can be guessed: Greta Garbo. It is Garbo's perfect, immortal face which preoccupies Roland Barthes, too. The screening in Paris of *Queen Christina,* a 1933 historical drama featuring Garbo as the eponymous Swedish sovereign who heroically relinquishes her throne for the love of the Spanish envoy Don Antonio (played by John Gilbert), provides the occasion for Barthes to contemplate the film's most remarkable and memorable visual element: Garbo's countenance. He writes:

> the make-up has the snowy thickness of a mask: it is not a painted face, but one set in plaster, protected by the surface of the colour not by its lineaments. Amid all this snow at once fragile and compact, the eyes alone, black like strange soft flesh, but not in the least expressive, are two faintly tremulous wounds. In spite of its extreme beauty, this face, not drawn but sculpted in something smooth and friable, that is, at once perfect and ephemeral, comes to resemble the flour-white complexion of Charlie Chaplin, the dark vegetation of his eyes, his totem-like countenance.[39]

What is particularly striking about *Queen Christina* is the way the film becomes an act of homage to this most inscrutable and imperturbable visage. The spectator is positioned as worshipper, not absent-minded examiner. White and powdery, Garbo's face is frozen within and framed by the snowbound Swedish landscape;[40] dressed in black, her face alone is illuminated by the flickering light from a candelabra she holds; supposedly contemplating the face of her lover in a mirror, it is her face which is doubled while his remains unseen; and, in the long closing shot of the film, Garbo stands on the bow of the ship transporting her and the body of her dead lover to Spain, staring into the distance, her face fixed like a ship's figurehead.[41]

Immutable, immobile, Garbo's face is seemingly "purged of all expression" or, perhaps, seems to express everything in a single, unyielding facial gesture. The face of Garbo is a mask, not the mask designed to conceal a secret, but rather the absolute mask of antiquity serving as the incarnation of an essence or ideal. As antiquity, the face of Garbo is the eternal, the immortal, the enduring visage, that half of art, to reverse Baudelaire's famous formulation, whose other half is "the ephemeral, the fugitive, the contingent."[42] Garbo's face is set in history, dressed in historical garb, but it appears without history, remains unchanged by events, oblivious of time, utterly impervious in its artifice to the natural history of the human *physis* as decay. As Barthes observes, Garbo famously hid herself in later life so that this image, this divine face remained always the same:

> She herself knew this: how many actresses have consented to let the crowd see the ominous maturing of their beauty. Not she, however; the essence was not to be degraded, her face was not to have any reality except of its perfection [...]. The Essence became gradually obscured, progressively veiled with dark glasses, broad hats and exiles: but it never deteriorated.[43]

For Barthes, Garbo's face constitutes permanent perfection, less the countenance of an actual living woman than the embodiment of the abstract "lyricism of Woman."[44] Timeless, total, transcendent–the face of Garbo is mythic.

Barthes concludes his fragment with a telling contrast between Garbo's face and that of, coincidently, Audrey Hepburn: "the face of Garbo is an Idea, that of Hepburn, an Event."[45] In contrast to Garbo's petrified visage, Hepburn's face is characterised by mobility, motility and mutability–

11

one is tempted to say, by *modernité*. It is a face which is "individualized," complicated, ludic—"woman as child, woman as kitten" as Barthes puts it. As Event, the face of Hepburn is not only subject to the temporal, but becomes its very expression, bearing lightly upon it the imprints, the traces of time. The faces of Garbo and Hepburn thereby come to articulate antithetical cinematic moments. They provide the definitive images of distinctive "iconographic ages," visual epochs characterised by different responses to representation of the human face on film: the time of "awe" and the subsequent era of "charm." If Hepburn constitutes the finest expression of the new facial language of charm, the face of Garbo represents the ultimate moment of awe, the last occasion when, Barthes observes, "capturing the human face still plunged audiences into the deepest ecstasy."[46] Garbo's countenance vanishes from the cinematic screen and disappears behind the wide-brimmed hats and sunglasses. *Queen Christina* finds Garbo on the brink of this departure. It offers the "lyricism of Woman" seen at last sight.

The themes and ideas presented by Barthes are prefigured to a remarkable degree in Siegfried Kracauer's 1933 fragment "*Greta Garbo*: *Eine Studie.*" Kracauer's concern, too, is with fathoming the unique quality of Garbo's countenance, its awe-inspiring (artificial) aura. For Kracauer, Garbo appears as the very incarnation of beauty:

> If Garbo were simply beautiful this would not account for the wonder of her worldwide fame. Certainly her beauty is a rarity. The way her stature harmonizes with her face, the way her features relate to each other: everything is so correctly and precisely arranged that no detail could be changed by so much as a millimetre. But there are other actresses ... who can lay claim to beauty [...] [Garbo] has no qualities, she is beauty itself.[47]

As a woman without qualities Garbo is not to be understood as an empty or vacuous figure—although, as Kracauer observes, "beauty and stupidity make common bedfellows."[48] Rather, Garbo's beauty, though wholly artificial,[49] is the fullest manifestation and expression of Woman as archetype. Garbo is:

the woman who is only ever a woman. The true secret of Garbo lies in the fact that she makes manifest a type that is not really a type at all, rather she represents the *genus* itself. [...] With other actresses one can usually guess origins and fate, or establish some particular characteristics and attributes they have made their own. They are women constituted in a particular way and their sphere of action is delimited accordingly. Garbo on the other hand, eludes any such determination. Her age constantly fluctuates, her nationality plays no role, her appearance changes from girl to child, and from child to lady. Just as she doesn't overact so, too, she has a special touch which could be entered in her repertoire: she is woman as such and nothing besides.[50]

Garbo is incapable of overacting, indeed of any imitation at all. As an Idea, Garbo cannot express, only embody other Ideas. Of her performance in *Grand Hotel* (1932) Kracauer writes:

It is so constructed that she not only embodies happiness as in this film but also pain, disappointment or self-sacrificing love. In truth her art concentrates on the portrayal of such fundamental conditions, ones not so much associated with a particular type of woman as with woman *per se*.[51]

Here is neither the identification of performer and character advocated by theatrical method acting, nor the dissociation of actor and role occasioned by the fragmentation of filmmaking. The character is instead wholly subsumed under the star. Garbo cannot pretend to be anyone or anything else, cannot stand for or stand in for any other. This serves as Kracauer's key point of contrast, not between the face as Idea and Event, but between the immutable and the imitative, between Garbo and a new kind of actress, the 'mimic' Joan Crawford. Crawford acts, Garbo appears. Whatever her supposed role, whatever her disguise, whatever her condition, Garbo "automatically refrains from all mimetic characteristics."[52] Garbo is, can only be, Garbo. Herein lies her greatness, herein her fundamental weakness.[53] In a brief and critical 1931 review of Garbo in the film *Anna Christie*, Kracauer observes:

13

> She plays a prostitute who drinks, smokes and has been around: but who
> really believes the depravity even when she says "Rubbish" so dis-
> paragingly and stares so blankly. Being an immaculate world ideal does
> not go unpunished, and the obligation to embody beautiful appearance
> sits uneasily with that of appearing as a physical being.[54]

The awe of Garbo gives way, not to the sublime quirkiness of Hepburn's
charm, but to the subtle nuances of Crawford's characterisation; the
countenance as beautiful "semblance" is displaced by the face as the
locus of "play."[55]

The Face Unfrozen

Such a transition is also to be found in an essay by Franz Hessel, one of
Benjamin's closest associates. Hessel's 1931 study *Marlene Dietrich: ein
Porträt* seeks to trace her early career and, in so doing, intriguingly suggests
how Dietrich moves between awe and charm/character, constructs herself
first in terms of one, then the other. Dietrich is not a moment of synthe-
sis between the ages of awe and charm, between Idea and Event, Archetype and Mimic, but rather constitutes and comports herself as the play
between them.

As with Barthes and Kracauer, Hessel's focus is on the expressivity
and/or immutability of the star's countenance.[56] Although Hessel does
identify the actress as an archetypical female figure,[57] his emphasis is on
the indeterminate and popular, rather than ideal and abstract, character
of Dietrich's beauty. He observes:

> With Marlene Dietrich it is difficult and dubious to emphasise the detail.
> In her own inimitable way she has become public property. [...] The effect
> the artist has is reminiscent of the enchanted doll of Persian fairytales,
> who has been crafted by carpenters, tailors, painters, priests and any
> number of master craftsmen; they dispute ownership of her, they ap-
> proach the Kadi, and he finds in her his lost wife. Whether she is playing
> a lady or a prostitute, a vanquisher or a victim, Marlene Dietrich always
> embodies a common dream, just like the heroine of one of her films, she
> is the woman one desires—everyone, the people, the world, time.[58]

The face of Dietrich, carefully crafted, becomes all things to all spectators. Hessel writes of Lola-Lola in *The Blue Angel*:

> The good-natured woman has the face everyone needs, for the director and magician the coolly familiar face of a colleague, for the blustering captain precisely what he has longed for during his voyage, for cheery Mazeppa with his banal chic the twinkling eye: "How about it then?"[59]

For Hessel, it is the ambiguity of Dietrich's features which is decisive, a daemonic quality evident in the following reflections on Dietrich's highly suggestive smile:

> With this smile Marlene Dietrich has conquered Europe and America. It is at once more divine and more vulgar than the smile of all her rivals. The smile of Greta Garbo is of fragile tenderness, evoking painful sympathy even if she appears to be happy, it is Christian, angelic. [...] Marlene Dietrich can smile like an idol, like the archaic Greek gods and at the same time appear harmless. One cannot reproach this smile. It is not malicious. And yet it can be the absorbing smile of Astarte, an expression of that that *Venus vulgivaga* whose sideline was as the goddess of death.[60]

This ambiguity is both the source and consequence of the distinctive mutability, the plasticity of Dietrich's face. Hessel's essay is concerned with how her career is marked by a pronounced transformation in the (re)presentation of her face. He observes how in her earlier roles—in *Die Frau, nach der man sich sehnt* (1929) for example—Dietrich's face is impassive and expressionless:

> Often she looks quite uninvolved, as if everything that was happening around her and because of her didn't affect her at all; it is not happening to her, it is merely taking place. And finally she takes the fatal shot aimed at her silently, as if even her own death were an event she was merely participating in.[61]

15

Dietrich's face here, like Garbo's immutable mask, remains always the same amid ever changing circumstances. This stony stoicism contrasts with her appearance in two films following *The Blue Angel*, her first Hollywood movies *Morocco* (1930)[62] and *Dishonoured* (1931):

> In a number of images from this new period a characteristic, an expression, comes ever more clearly to the fore [...]. It is a characteristic reminiscent of pre-Raphaelite painters. The contours of her cheekbones become clearer, the clear brow raises her eyebrows and emphasises the mysterious space between the eyes. And around her hair there spreads an aura, a fairy-tale glow. The transition of this slimmer, tenser figure from composure to animation becomes ever richer. Is this still our chic Lola?[63]

The penultimate sentence is unexpected and significant here. As a pre-Raphaelite portrait crowned by a fairy-tale aura, this new image of Dietrich nevertheless abandons awe and reinvents itself as animation. This 'coming to life' is such that, as Hessel emphasises, the unfolding of the dramatic action itself becomes wholly legible on Dietrich's face.[64]

Hessel then presents us with the indeterminacy and instability of the face and its image through time, with the possibility of the construction and reconstruction of the same countenance on different occasions as Idea, as Event, as Character.[65] Artificial aura is not simply manufactured in the studio, nor is it produced exclusively inter-textually as a discursive phenomenon. It is generated in the specific interplay and intersection of the object itself, the particular practices and techniques of mediation and, importantly, the context of spectatorship and reading. This notion of the legibility of the face, the degree to which it lends itself to interpretation, is an important insight. The auratic face 'does not permit itself to be read.'[66] This is not because its complexity renders it incomprehensible, but rather because sustained scrutiny brings nothing new to light. As Baudrillard insists, the star's frozen face is pure surface—there are no depths to be explored, no secrets to be discovered. This face tells us both everything and nothing in a single glance, at first sight. It has nothing to say—it simply appears—and thus stands in opposition to the expressive, the animated, the mimetic, the playful. If Garbo is the ultimate embodiment of this blank, monolithic indecipherability, her antithesis is perhaps not so much Hepburn, Crawford or Dietrich as Hector Mann, Paul Auster's fictional silent comic in *The Book of Illusions* (2002). To be sure, there is an important similarity—in his films Hector's visage remains "essentially still."[67] Yet this stasis is not an end in itself but rather serves a particular purpose: the face acts as a blank page upon which one may write, and the instrument of this inscription is the moustache, the "thin black line between Hector's nose and upper lip"[68] whose "antic gyrations"[69] are the true subject of the camera close-up. Auster writes:

> A twitching filament of anxieties, a metaphysical jump rope, a dancing thread of discombobulation, the mustache is a seismograph of Hector's inner states, and not only does it make you laugh, it tells you what Hector is thinking, actually allows you into the machinery of his thoughts. Other elements are involved [...] but the mustache is the instrument of communication, and even though it speaks a language without words, its wriggles and flutters are as clear and comprehensible as a message tapped out in Morse code.[70]

At decisive points in the narrative events are brought to a standstill. Then:

> The mustache launches into its soliloquy, and for those few precious moments, action gives way to thought. We can read the content of Hector's mind as though it were spelled out in letters across the screen, and before those letters vanish, they are no less visible than a building, a piano, or a pie in the face.[71]

Hector's films present us with the mimetic moustache, an ever-changing series of hirsute hieroglyphics, a countenance in continual communication with the audience. Nothing could be less like the ethereal Idea of Woman than this flippant face of Mann.

17

Concluding Reflections

This pun, however feeble, does bring us to the critical issue of gender and spectatorship. An obvious question, for instance, is whether one could replace Garbo's face with Rudolph Valentino's,[72] Hepburn's with Cary Grant's, and still speak of awe and charm, of 'the lyricism of Man,' of man as Idea and as 'kitten'? More importantly for us is this: if Dietrich's face is, as Hessel claims, constructed in the eye of the beholder, how then might differently positioned readers conspire in, or subvert, the fabrication of artificial aura? What is (il)legible and for whom? Here Barthes, Kracauer, Baudrillard and Hessel himself are called into question. Do their readings of the female star's face contribute to the critical disenchantment of modern mythologies, or do they simply serve as testimonies to the banality of the male gaze, voyeurism and scopophilia? Do they—albeit unintentionally—contribute to that very discursive constitution of artificial aura against which Benjamin warns? In short, are these male writers critics of the fetishized face or its unwittingly devotees? Indeed, are they not enthralled, captivated, entranced by the faces of Garbo, Hepburn and Dietrich just as easily and surely as the pompous, pathetic Professor Rath is seduced by Lola-Lola in *The Blue Angel*?[73]

Adequate answers to such questions would require another paper or even series of papers. It is nonetheless interesting to note how Andrea Weiss suggests alternative readings of Garbo and Dietrich by focusing on the sexual and gender ambiguities of their films: Garbo mannishly attired and initially mistaken for a boy by Don Antonio in *Queen Christina*, and Dietrich dressed in top hat and tails in *Morocco*.[74] Weiss contends that the prominent role of androgyny and cross-dressing as well as the eschewal of customary sexual mores and gender undercut conventional heterosexual expectations in these films' storylines and imagery. She argues persuasively enough for the possibility of a distinctive lesbian reading of both *Queen Christina* and *Morocco* which runs counter to preferred (male, heterosexual) interpretations. Weiss claims: "For lesbian spectators who saw Garbo in the early 1930s [...] Queen Christina will always be the lonely girl who dressed in male attire and refused to marry, and no

18

amount of heterosexual cover will ever change her."[75] Her emphasis on the identification of spectators with on-screen characters and the stars portraying them as a radical process of self-recognition and empowerment is not without its own problems, however. Although it might be understood as an exemplary instance of the kind of collective consciousness and expertise advocated by Benjamin, such a process of self-identification also suggests precisely that coherence of performance and bond of actor with role which film should fracture and disturb. Even seemingly radical readings against the grain of conventional cinematic interpretation are not immune to the artificial allure of the star, whether quintessential feminine beauty, inscrutable otherness, defiant female dissidence or subversive sexual alterity. Such ambiguities here only add to the mystique, Garbo's artificial aura.

The importance of reading should not distract us from the fact that, as intimated by Benjamin, artificial aura is first and foremost a matter of technique, technique in the service of capitalist ideology—the promotion of illusion, enchantment, myth, domination, profit. The reason for this is clear: artificial aura involves the more or less successful, but always highly conscious attempt to fabricate an experience that fundamentally contradicts the inherent logic and technological trajectory of the photographic and cinematic media. Artificial aura betrays the promise of the film medium in at least two ways. First, it involves forfeiting the possibility of penetrating and illuminating reality, the contemporary demand to bring objects closer to us and thereby qualitatively transform our experience of the everyday. Central to both Benjamin's and Kracauer's cinematic principles is that film is a privileged medium for disclosing that which escapes common visual perception, details and minutiae which although certainly present remain invisible to us because of their diminutive size, their speed and/or their gradualness. Close-up, slow motion and time-lapse photography open up to view an entire realm of "things normally unseen."[76] For Kracauer film reveals the manifold of unstaged "physical reality"; for Benjamin it discovers the "optical unconscious."[77] Indeed, in focussing on Hector Mann's playful moustache one might even say that

19

the camera succeeds here in making the unconscious, the inner life of the human subject, into an optical, legible phenomenon. Nothing could be further from this than the close-up that lingers upon the star's frozen face. Here we witness the zero degree of signification. Garbo becomes a blank page. Close up we are none the wiser—except for the salutary lesson that we will always remain at a distance no matter how close up the camera takes us. Close up we perceive the futility of the close-up.

Second, the fabrication of artificial aura involves a fundamental denial of mobility and mutability, of movement through time and space, of change and the succession of images, of transience and the traces left in the wake of passing. For both Benjamin and Kracauer motion pictures must be just that—images in and of movement. Accordingly for them film has an elective affinity with that most dynamic and vibrant of environments—the modern big city. Film corresponds to the jarring rhythm and swift tempo of the urban setting. In penetrating metropolitan reality film promises to capture the fluidity and flux of everyday life, the fleeting impressions and chance encounters of the street. Milling crowds, scurrying pedestrians, the staccato procession of traffic—these are the most cinematic of subjects.[78] The fundamental cinematic imperative for Kracauer is that film faithfully present the "flow of life,"[79] picturing people and things in flight, *en passant*. Indeed, Benjamin argues, wherever the city appeared paralysed or static—in the stale drabness of interiors, in the grey monotony of offices and factories, in the unbearable dreariness of drizzly Sunday afternoons—film will provide an explosive charge, blasting apart the oppressive atmosphere of stagnant spaces, hurling debris to far-flung places, sending us out, too, on myriad unforeseen trajectories.[80] For both writers the man with the movie camera must be a flâneur relishing and attesting to the modern metropolis in perpetual motion.[81]

In its continual twitchings and twirlings Mann's manic moustache is eminently cinematic, too. By contrast, is Garbo as frozen as the winter landscape. In the rigidity and fixity of her pose, the image of Garbo denies its cinematic qualities and aspires—vainly, absurdly—to another, supposedly more elevated status: portraiture, statuary. The face of the star as idol, as Easter Island monolith is fundamentally uncinematic. It offers itself up for contemplative immersion as a totality, impervious to the testing, fragmenting film camera. It is a manifestation of beauty wholly at the level of surface, impenetrable to the probing, curious lens, untouched by the passage of time. It confounds the demand for proximity and legibility. It resists the imperative for animation, for movement and mimetic play. It exhibits not the flow of life but the paralysis of death. The face of Garbo—and of Valentino, and the young Dietrich—is the Idea, not of Beauty, but of the uncinematic, of all that stands in opposition to the realisation of film's revolutionary potential, of the Idea of simulated aura. Not "crafted by carpenters, tailors, painters, priests"[82] but rather fabricated by make-up artists, lighting technicians, camera operators and film editors, the image of Garbo's face is the ultimate work of artifice in the age of technological reproducibility.

Notes

[1] "Angels should not die!" Anonymous epigram to Franz Hessel, *Marlene Dietrich: Eine Porträt* (Berlin: Das Arsenal Verlag, 1992), 1.

[2] Walter Benjamin, "Little History of Photography," in SW 2, 518. Compare Benjamin, "The Work of Art in the Age of Its Technical Reproducibility (Second Version)," in SW 3, 104–5.

[3] See Benjamin, *Charles Baudelaire: A Lyric Poet in the Era of High Capitalism* (London: Verso, 1986), 148.

[4] See Benjamin, "Little History of Photography," in SW 2, 517.

[5] See, for example, Benjamin's comments on the David Octavius Hill's photograph of Mrs. Elizabeth Hall, the "Newhaven fishwife." Ibid., 508–10.

[6] Benjamin observes how a photograph of Kafka aged six owes its auratic quality to the boy's "immensely sad eyes." Ibid., 515.

[7] Of such photographic subjects Benjamin writes: "There was an aura about them, a medium that lent fullness and security to their gaze even as it penetrated that medium." Ibid., 515–16.

[8] Benjamin, "The Work of Art," in SW 3, 108. In the same paragraph he also

writes: "It is no accident that the portrait is central to early photography. In the cult of remembrance of dead or absent loved ones, the cult value of the image finds its last refuge. In the fleeting expression of a human face, the aura beckons from early photographs for the last time."

[9] Perhaps the clearest example of this haunting quality is Roland Barthes' preoccupation with the photograph of his mother as a young girl in his *Camera Lucida* (London: Vintage, 1993).

[10] Benjamin, "Little History of Photography," in SW 2, 518.

[11] Benjamin, "The Work of Art," in SW 3, 104.

[12] Ibid., 102.

[13] Ibid., 106. Benjamin notes in this context that: "Film is the first art form whose artistic character is entirely determined by its reproducibility." Ibid., 109.

[14] Ibid., 106.

[15] See ibid., 106–7.

[16] Ibid., 106.

[17] Of course, Benjamin's comments regarding the enduring auratic qualities of early photographs seem to call this into question. Interestingly, the "magical value" of Karl Dauthendey's self-portrait with his fiancée is a consequence of the "most precise technology." Benjamin, "Little History of Photography," in SW 2, 510.

[18] Benjamin, "The Work of Art," in SW 3, 112.

[19] Ibid., 113.

[20] See ibid., 119.

[21] Ibid., 105.

[22] See ibid., 116.

[23] Benjamin recalls his own humiliating experience as "a parlor Tyrolean, yodelling, waving our hat against a painted snowscape, or as a smartly turned-out, standing rakishly with our weight on one leg, as is proper, leaning against a polished door jamb." Benjamin, "Little History of Photography," in SW 2, 515.

[24] Ibid., 517.

[25] Benjamin, "The Work of Art," in SW 3, 113.

[26] Ibid., 114.

[27] Ibid., 113.

[28] The cinematic close-up is of special importance here: it is the very technique that ought to bring the face of the star closest to us, and yet it so often forms the principal means by which a sense of reverential distance is evoked.

[29] Benjamin insists that "the reproduction [*Reproduktion*] as offered by illustrated magazines and newsreels, differs unmistakably from the image. Uniqueness and permanence are as closely entwined in the latter as are transitoriness and repeatability in the former." Benjamin, "The Work of Art," in SW 3, 105.

[30] In *The Consumer Society: Myths and Structures* (London: Sage, 1998), Jean Baudrillard develops the notion of death and the doppelganger in his reflections on the early German silent film *The Student of Prague*. In this screenplay, cobbled together from a variety of sources including elements from Goethe's *Faust* and Dostoevsky's *The Double*, a young impoverished student sells his mirror image to the Devil. This image then appears as the student's double, his terrible identical twin, whose malevolent and eventually murderous antics bring shame and disgrace. The student retreats into hiding to plot his revenge. He finally confronts and shoots the impostor only to discover that in so doing he actually has killed himself. Baudrillard uses this tale to comment on the alienation experienced in commodity culture, but the notion of the double, the clone, also appears here and elsewhere as a sinister, haunting figure, the spectre of death.

[31] Baudrillard, *Seduction* (New York: St Martin's Press, 1990), 168.

[32] Ibid., 94.

[33] Ibid., 95.

[34] Baudrillard writes: "The great stars and seductresses never dazzle because of their talent or intelligence, but because of their absence. They are dazzling in their nullity, and in their coldness—the coldness of makeup and ritual hieraticism." Ibid., 96.

[35] Ibid.

[36] Ibid.

[37] Ibid., 96–7.

[38] It is Barthes who best articulates this notion in his discussion of Alexander Gardner's 1865 photograph of Lewis Paine, a picture taken just prior to Paine's execution for attempted murder: "The photograph is handsome, as is the boy: that is the *studium*. But the *punctum* is: *he is going to die*. I read at the same time: *This will be* and *this has been*; I observe with horror an anterior future of which death is the stake." *Camera Lucida*, 96.

[39] Barthes, *Mythologies* (London: Paladin, 1973), 56.

[40] In his collection *Kino. Essays, Studien, Glossen zum Film* (Frankfurt am Main: Suhrkamp Verlag, 1974), Siegfried Kracauer also points to the relationship between snowscape and Garbo's face. Writing of a scene in *Gösta Berlings Saga*, he notes how: "as the sleigh drives and drives, fresh excitement is continuously created by the pale glow of the snow, by Garbo's face in the sleigh and by the movement of the reins across her face," 36. Andrew Britton, in "Stars and Genre," in *Stardom: Industry of Desire* ed. Christine Gledhill (London: Routledge 1991), notes that the film seeks "to make the spectator's experience of Garbo's face the analogue of Christina's experience of the landscape," 289. In light of this, Benjamin's understanding of the experience of aura in terms of that of a landscape is not insignificant.

23

[41] For this shot, the film's director, David Mamoulian, apparently told Garbo: "I want your face to be a blank sheet of paper." (cited in Marcia Landy and Amy Villarejo, *Queen Christina* (London: BFI Publishing, 1995), 34.

[42] Charles Baudelaire, *The Painter of Modern Life and Other Essays* (New York and London: Da Capo / Phaidon Press, 1986), 13.

[43] Barthes, *Mythologies*, 57.

[44] Ibid.

[45] Ibid.

[46] Ibid., 56.

[47] Kracauer, *Kino*, 38.

[48] Ibid., 39.

[49] Garbo's beauty is that of "constructed nature." Ibid.

[50] Ibid., 40.

[51] Ibid., 41.

[52] Ibid., 42.

[53] Kracauer writes: "When she plays pronounced types or intermediate emotions, Garbo's effect is ever weaker." Ibid.

[54] Ibid., 140.

[55] In a footnote to the "Work of Art" essay Benjamin notes how these two poles of mimesis, 'semblance' and 'play' are conditioned by the contemporary crisis of aura: "the decay of the aura in works of art is matched by a huge gain in the scope for play [*Spiel-Raum*]. This space for play is widest in film. In film, the element of semblance has been entirely displaced by the element of play." SW 3, 127.

[56] Hessel also pays attention to Dietrich's distinctive (singing) voice and Berlin accent. See *Marlene Dietrich*, 10 and 13.

[57] Hessel notes that the French extol Dietrich as "woman *per se*, the woman who manifests her original being in contemporary form." Ibid., 7.

[58] Ibid., 8.

[59] Ibid., 9.

[60] Ibid., 9–10.

[61] Ibid., 19.

[62] Hessel writes: "Her appearance in *Morocco* seems to mark the beginning of something quite new. It is as if an apparently immutable idol with a fixed smile were suddenly coming to life. The eye which looked through people and mirror into the unknown suddenly stays transfixed on a face, and human suffering draws the feature anew." Ibid., 26.

[63] Ibid., 25.

[64] Hessel observes: "The drama of this love is played out in slight changes in her face." Ibid., 27.

[65] Hence for Barthes, Hepburn can appear as charm, as the antithesis of awe, while for the reader of the magazine advertisement, Hepburn's face constitutes the very Idea of the original, of the auratic.

[66] This expression is invoked by Edgar Allan Poe in his story "The Man of the Crowd." The enigmatic face of the stranger fruitlessly pursued by the narrator "does not permit itself to be read." Edgar Allen Poe, *The Fall of the House of Usher and Other Writings* (London: Penguin, 1986), 179. This tale fascinated Benjamin, see *Charles Baudelaire*, 48 and 126

[67] Paul Auster, *The Book of Illusions* (London: Faber and Faber, 2002), 30.

[68] Ibid., 29.

[69] Ibid., 30.

[70] Ibid., 29.

[71] Ibid., 30.

[72] See Miriam Hansen, "Pleasure, Ambivalence and Identification: Valentino and Female Spectatorship," in *Stardom*, ed. Gledhill. As Hansen points out, in the 1953 essay *"Visage et Figure"* Barthes ascribes the cult of Valentino to the "aura of his face," 276.

[73] This question is posed—and answered in the negative—by Manfred Flügge in his "Afterword" to the Dietrich study. See in Hessel, *Marlene Dietrich*, 36–8.

[74] Andrea Weiss, "A Queer Feeling When I Look at You: Hollywood Stars and Lesbian Spectatorship," in *Stardom*, ed. Gledhill.

[75] Ibid., 298.

[76] Siegfried Kracauer, *Theory of Film. The Redemption of Physical Reality* (Princeton, NJ: Princeton University Press, 1997), 46.

[77] Benjamin, "The Work of Art," in SW 3, 117.

[78] On film's predisposition for portraying the urban crowd, see for example Kracauer, *Theory of Film*, 50–51.

[79] Ibid., 71.

[80] See Benjamin, "The Work of Art," in SW 3, 117.

[81] See Kracauer, *Theory of Film*, 72.

[82] Hessel, *Marlene Dietrich*, 8.

The Politics of Aura and Imagination in Benjamin's Writings on Hashish

Tara Forrest

The immediate reality of the surrealist revolution is not so much to change anything in the physical and apparent order of things as to create a movement in men's minds.

(Surrealists' Declaration of January 27, 1925)[1]

In a letter to Gershom Scholem written in July 1932, Benjamin recounts with disappointment a list of projects which—due to the prolonged precariousness of his financial situation—remain untouched or uncompleted. He writes that among the books which "mark off the real site of ruin or catastrophe" is "a truly exceptional book about hashish." "Nobody," he cautions Scholem, "knows about this [project], and for the time being it should remain between us."[2] However, while Benjamin's plans for a book on hashish appear concretely for the first time in this letter, as early as 1919 he had expressed an interest in exploring the psychological effects produced by hashish and opium. Inspired by Charles Baudelaire's writings on the topic in *Artificial Paradise* (which were written in the 1850s)[3] Benjamin's interest lay in examining what the effects of these drugs could "teach us philosophically."[4]

It wasn't, however, until some eight years later in December 1927 that Benjamin began the first of a series of experiments with hashish that continued sporadically over the next seven years. His first experiment (and several which followed) was undertaken under the supervision of Doctors Fritz Fränkel and Ernst Joël (both of whom Benjamin had known from his days in the Berlin Youth Movement).[5] In 1926 Fränkel and Joël

26

(who jointly ran a clinic for drug addicts in Berlin) published an article on the psychopathological effects induced by hashish intoxication in "*Klinische Wochenschrift*." The range of effects outlined in this article (which include a heightened perceptual acuity, the experience of an expansion of space, the "derangement of one's sense of time [*Zeitsinn*]," a return to the infantile, and the frequent activation of memory)[6] were to feature significantly, not only in Benjamin's own writings about the effects induced by the drug, but also in his delineation of the significance of auratic experience. As I will show in this essay, the contours of Benjamin's conception of auratic experience—and the important role which it occupies in relation to his analysis of the significance of both mimetic perception and the functioning of involuntary memory—grew out of his experiences while under the influence of hashish,[7] even though his analysis of the political significance of auratic experience wasn't developed in his writings until some years later.

While Benjamin did not transform or incorporate his writings on hashish into a book-length study, the protocols he wrote while under the influence of the drug, as well as a number of more formally constructed pieces, were published posthumously in 1972 under the title *Über Haschisch*.[8] As Benjamin claims in a letter written to Scholem in January 1928: "[These writings] may well turn out to be a very worthwhile supplement to my philosophical observations, with which they are most intimately related, as are to a certain degree even my experiences while under the influence of the drug."[9] While the ideas explored in Benjamin's writings on hashish are intermeshed with those developed in his childhood reminiscences, and in his essays on Marcel Proust, and photography (which were also written during this period),[10] the most significant influences shaping his conception of the radical experiential effects induced by hashish intoxication were Baudelaire's *Artificial Paradise* and the writings of the Surrealists.

Benjamin's "burning interest"[11] in Surrealism during this period was, as Peter Osborne has pointed out, fuelled by its "contribution to the expansion of the idea of political experience,"[12] at a time when the capacity for experience had been significantly diminished. The extent of Benjamin's interest in the writings of the group can be gauged from his 1935 letter to Theodor W. Adorno, in which he reflects upon the impact Louis Aragon's 1926 Surrealist narrative *Paris Peasant* had had upon him when he first came upon the book in the late 1920s.[13] "Evenings," Benjamin writes, "lying in bed, I could never read more than two to three pages by him because my heart started to pound so hard that I had to put the book down."[14]

Although Aragon's magical descriptions of the *Passage de l'Opera* in *Paris Peasant* are not explored by Benjamin in any detail in his 1929 essay "Surrealism: The Last Snapshot of the European Intelligentsia,"[15] it is nonetheless clear that Aragon's book had a significant impact, not only on the development of the radical conception of intoxication which emerges from this essay, but also on Benjamin's analysis of the political significance of the perceptual and experiential effects induced by hashish intoxication. "To win the energies of intoxication [*die Kräfte des Rausches*] for the revolution," Benjamin writes, "is the project on which Surrealism focuses in all its books and enterprises. This it may call its most particular task"[16] –the significance of which can be traced to the manner in which the perceptual effects induced by hashish intoxication provide access to the "image space"[17] that both Benjamin and the Surrealists associate with the activation of involuntary memory.

In the opening pages of *Paris Peasant*, the image spaces opened up by the intoxicated gaze of its narrator are revealed as he strolls through the wondrous aquarium into which the *Passage de l'Opera* has been transformed. Attracted by a sound emanating from a shop that sells walking canes, the narrator's attention is drawn to the "greenish, almost submarine light" radiating from the window display, the contents of which are suddenly transformed into images from his childhood. "It was," he recounts, "the same kind of phosphorescence that, I remember, emanated from the fish I watched, as a child, from the jetty of Port Bail on the Cotentin peninsula."[18] The canes–which "possess[ed] the illuminating properties of creatures of the deep"–"floated gently like seaweed." While some time later—as he gazes through the window of a beauty salon—the sight of a woman's "remodelled coiffure" metamorphosises into "a great maroon insect."[19] These experiences of contiguity—or similarity—across time are, however, not isolated incidents, but the mark of the renewal of the capacity for perception and imagination which—for both Aragon and Benjamin—are hallmarks of Surrealist experience.

In an important fragment in *One-Way Street* (in which the relationship between perceptual renewal and this rejuvenation in the capacity for imagination is rendered more clear) Benjamin argues that the significance of the latter rests upon the extent to which it "subserves the past."[20] The "faculty of imagination," he writes, is

> the gift of interpolating into the infinitely small, of inventing, for every intensity, an extensiveness to contain its new, compressed fullness—in short, of receiving each image as if it were that of the folded fan, which only in spreading draws breath and flourishes, in its new expanse, the beloved features within it.[21]

The impressions evoked by such images (which Aragon's narrator finds manifested in objects and materials as diverse as telephone switchboards, drinking straws, lamps, and the wickerwork of armchairs)[22] activate an experience of the past in the present which Benjamin describes as a "*profane illumination*"—that is, "a materialistic, anthropological inspiration, to which hashish, opium, or whatever else can give an introductory lesson."[23]

The political significance of this inspiration (which the Surrealists associated with dreams and practices such as automatic writing, hypnosis, and drug taking) is rendered more clear when read alongside André Breton's analysis of the highly circumscribed character of modern existence in his 1924 *Manifesto of Surrealism.* "Experience today," Breton writes,

> paces back and forth in a cage from which it is more and more difficult to make it emerge. It too leans for support on what is most immediately expedient, and it is protected by the sentinels of common sense. Under

29

the pretense of civilization and progress, we have managed to banish from the mind everything that may rightly or wrongly be termed superstition or fancy; forbidden is any kind of search for truth which is not in conformance with accepted practices.[24]

For Breton the most significant side effect of this diminution in the quality of experience is the breakdown of the capacity for imagination and, with it, the waning of the ability to envision a different kind of existence. He argues that the capacity for imagination (which "knows no bounds" in the realm of children) is only exercised "in strict accordance with the laws of an arbitrary utility." Because it is "incapable of assuming this inferior role" for a prolonged period, he claims that it "generally prefers to abandon man to his lusterless fate" in "the vicinity of [his] twentieth year."[25] For Breton this abandonment has dire consequences for those whose lives are characterised by emptiness and atrophy, because he argues that it is the "imagination alone" which "offers [...] some intimation of what *can be*."[26]

In this context, Surrealism's role is to rid the mind of the "cancer" which "consists of thinking [...] that certain things 'are,' while others, which well might be, 'are not,'"[27] through the rejuvenation of the imagination and, with it, the activation of an encounter with the unconscious. "For this," Breton writes, "we must give thanks to the discoveries of Sigmund Freud," on the basis of which the imagination is able to reassert itself.[28] Like Proust, Breton argues that it is only through the mobilisation of an individual's past and present[29] (through the "connection established under certain conditions between two things [...] which would not be permitted by common sense")[30] that the limitations of the conscious mind could be obliterated, opening up a space in which one's capacity for imagination could once again assert itself. As Benjamin stresses in both the preparatory notes for his essay on Surrealism and the essay itself, the Surrealists are concerned "with experiences, not with theories"[31] and "the showplace of [their] revelation is memory."[32]

In a similar vein to his analysis of Proust's delineation of the functioning of involuntary memory, Benjamin claims that it is only in a heightened state of moodiness or intoxication that these experiences can become manifest.[33] "Breton and Nadja," he writes in "Surrealism,"

> convert everything that we have experienced on mournful railway journeys [...], on Godforsaken Sunday afternoons [...], in the first glance through the rain-blurred window of a new apartment, into revolutionary experience [*Erfahrung*], if not action. They bring the immense forces of "atmosphere" concealed in these things to the point of explosion.[34]

Similarly, Breton argues that just as the intensity and duration of a spark are enhanced in rarefied gases, the atmosphere created by Surrealist practices is particularly conducive to the activation of involuntary memory.[35] "The mind which plunges into Surrealism," he writes, "relives with glowing excitement the best part of its childhood. [...] From childhood memories, and a few others, there emanates a sentiment of being unintegrated, and then later of having gone astray, which I hold to be the most fertile that exists."[36] Quoting Baudelaire, Breton claims that these explosions of memory cannot be willed, but rather "come to [man] spontaneously, despotically. He cannot chase them away; for the will is powerless now and no longer controls the faculties."[37]

Both the dissolution of the will and its precipitation by a range of different factors are the central features of Baudelaire's analysis of the experiential effects induced by hashish intoxication in *Artificial Paradise*.[38] As in Joël and Fränkel's study of the effects induced by the drug, Baudelaire argues in *Artificial Paradise* that central among these factors is the derangement of perception ushered in by hashish, in which one's experience of the dimensions of time and space is expanded to "monstrous proportions."[39] He argues that it is through this process of expansion that a heightened sensitivity becomes apparent in each of the senses: "One's ear perceives near-imperceptible sounds in the very midst of the loudest tumult" and under the "magnifying mirror" of hashish, objects and spaces take on "strange appearances."[40] In a passage which foreshadows Benjamin's analysis of the "magical correspondences" evoked by language in his essays on mimesis,[41] Baudelaire claims that "[e]ven grammar—sterile grammar" is transformed by hashish into a form of "evocative witchcraft;" "words come to life, wrapped in flesh and bone— the noun, in all its substantive majesty; the adjective, transparent garb that dresses and colors it like glaze; and the verb, angel of motion, that sets the sentence moving."[42]

Although Baudelaire refers to this intoxicated state as hallucinatory, he is careful to distinguish his use of the term from the manner in which it is employed by physicians. Hallucination in its strict sense, Baudelaire argues, is characterised by a sense of self-sufficiency, insofar as the experience that it designates is sealed off from, and is therefore not influenced by, external conditions. Put simply, the person who hallucinates will see things and hear sounds which in reality do not exist, while the hallucinations induced by hashish intoxication are fuelled by the surroundings in which one finds oneself.[43] In a passage which evokes Benjamin's fascination with the plant photographs of Karl Blossfeldt,[44] Baudelaire claims that the hashish eater "endu[es] all the external world with an intensity of interest": The "hue of a blade of grass," the "shape of a trefoil," the "gleaming of a dew-drop" and "the quivering of a leaf"[45] each take on the most striking appearance when viewed under the "magic glaze" of hashish.[46]

As per the Surrealists, Baudelaire argues that concomitant with this increase in sensitivity comes the enhancement of one's capacity to perceive similarities between things which would ordinarily be conceived of as disparate: "Sounds are clad in color, and colors contain a certain music," "musical notes become numbers" and analogies (which "attack, pervade, and overcome the mind") "assume an unaccustomed vividness."[47] However, as Benjamin states in "Convolute J" of *The Arcades Project*, it would be a mistake to conceive of these experiences as "a simple counterpart to certain experiments with synesthesia."[48] In keeping with his analysis of Proust's delineation of the significance of the impressions evoked by involuntary memory, what is significant for Benjamin about these correspondences is not the sensory connections themselves, but the medium of memory through which these sense impressions become intermingled.

32

In "Convolute J" Benjamin argues that memory in Baudelaire's writings is

> possessed of unusual density. The corresponding sensory data correspond
> in it; they are teeming with memories, which run so thick that they seem
> to have arisen not from this life at all but from some more spacious *vie
> antérieure*.[49]

It is the shards of this *vie antérieure* which the hashish eater glimpses in the images, thoughts, and feelings which—under his or her intoxicated gaze—"surge up and are projected with the ambitious energy and sudden flare of fireworks" which "like the explosive powders and coloring chemicals of a pyrotechnic display, [...] blaze up and vanish in the darkness."[50]

Auratic Experience and Involuntary Memory

The political significance of Benjamin's fascination with the "intermittent visitations"[51] of memory evoked by hashish intoxication (and the practices of the Surrealists more generally) is rendered more clear when read alongside Benjamin's analysis of the atrophy of modern experience in his 1939 essay "On Some Motifs in Baudelaire." Central to Benjamin's delineation of this decline in the capacity for experience is his analysis of the destruction of the aura—the significance of which can be traced to the important role auratic experience occupies in Benjamin's analysis of the conditions which would lay the ground for the creation and sustenance of a desire for "a better nature."[52]

In both "The Work of Art in the Age of Its Technological Reproducibility" and "On Some Motifs in Baudelaire," the concept of the aura emerges as the mark of an experience born of a non-reified relationship between man and nature. "We define the aura," Benjamin writes in the "Work of Art" essay,

> as the unique apparition of a distance, however near it may be. To follow
> with the eye—while resting on a summer afternoon—a mountain range on
> the horizon or a branch that casts its shadow on the beholder is to breathe

the aura of those mountains, of that branch. In the light of this description, we can readily grasp the social basis of the aura's present decay.[53]

In "On Some Motifs in Baudelaire," Benjamin argues that this experience of distance (which is of a temporal order) designates "the associations which, at home in the *mémoire involontaire*, seek to cluster around an object of perception."[54] He claims that "[i]nherent in the gaze [...] is the expectation that it will be returned by that on which it is bestowed. Where this expectation is met [...] there is an experience [*Erfahrung*] of the aura in all its fullness."[55] Thus, to experience the aura of something

> we look at means to invest it with the ability to look back at us. This ability corresponds to the data of *mémoire involontaire*. (These data, incidentally, are unique: they are lost to the memory that seeks to retain them. Thus, they lend support to a concept of the aura that involves the "unique apparition of a distance."[56]

If the image of someone gazing at a mountain range on the horizon enables us to "readily grasp the social basis of the aura's present decay," as Benjamin argues in his analysis of Baudelaire, it is because "the expectation aroused by the gaze of the human eye" in this image is "not fulfilled" under the conditions of modernity.[57] In contrast to the mood of tranquillity which permeates this image, Benjamin argues that life in the modern city–from the structure of newspapers and crowds, to the organisation of production line labour–is everywhere permeated by a sense of shock and collision. Influenced by Georg Simmel's analysis of the psychological effects of urban living (as elaborated in his 1903 essay "The Metropolis and Mental Life")[58] Benjamin argues that the proliferation of shock in the modern city results in the decrease in one's capacity to assimilate external stimuli by way of one's experience (*Erfahrung*).[59]

In "On Some Motifs in Baudelaire," Benjamin argues that this decrease in the capacity for experience is linked to the role consciousness plays as a "protective shield" guarding the organism from "excessive energies at work in the external world."[60] Drawing on Sigmund Freud's analysis of the psychological effects produced by shock in *Beyond the Pleasure Principle*, Benjamin states that "[t]he greater the shock factor in particular impressions, the more vigilant consciousness has to be in screening stimuli; the more efficiently it does so, the less these impressions enter long experience [*Erfahrung*] and the more they correspond to the concept of isolated experience [*Erlebnis*]."[61]

For Benjamin "the special achievement of shock defense is the way it assigns an incident a precise point in time in consciousness, at the cost of the integrity of the incident's contents."[62] This process not only turns the incident into "an isolated experience [*Erlebnis*]," but in doing so "sterilize[s it...] for poetic experience [*Erfahrung*]."[63] "Experiences," Benjamin writes elsewhere, "are lived similarities." "What is decisive here is not the causal connections established over the course of time" (which characterise the kind of experience designated by the term *Erlebnis*),[64] but rather "the capacity for endless interpolations into what has been."[65] While "a lived event is finite—at any rate, confined to one sphere of experience [*des Erlebens*]; a remembered event is infinite, because it is merely a key to everything that happened before it and after it."[66]

In "On Some Motifs in Baudelaire" both the inability to assimilate data by way of one's experience, and the decline in one's capacity to draw on one's experience, are embodied in Benjamin's description of the factory worker, whose relationship to both the product of his or her labour—and time more generally—exemplifies the isolated "perpetual present"[67] which defines Benjamin's conception of *Erlebnis*. In contrast to the emphasis on practice which is central to the art of craftsmanship (in which the capacity to draw on one's experience is essential to the development of one's practice), Benjamin argues that production line labour makes "a speciality" out of a "lack of any development." "The unskilled worker," he writes, "is the one most deeply degraded by machine training. His work has been sealed off from experience" because "practice counts for nothing in the factory."[68]

Expanding on this idea Benjamin argues that the factory worker's experiences can be compared to those of the gambler (a familiar figure in both *The Arcades Project* and Baudelaire's poetry).[69] While production line labour certainly lacks the "touch of adventure" central to the appeal of gambling, Benjamin argues that gambling is nonetheless marked by the same sense of "futility" and "emptiness" borne of an "inability to complete something—qualities [which are] inherent in the activity of a wage slave in a factory."[70] "The hand movement of the worker at the machine," he writes,

> has no connection with the preceding gesture for the very reason that it repeats that gesture exactly. Since each operation at the machine is just as screened off from the preceding operation as a *coup* in a game of chance is from the one that preceded it, the drudgery of the labourer is, in its own way, a counterpart to the drudgery of the gambler. Both types of work are equally devoid of substance.[71]

This passage is significant because it allegorises the temporal structure of modern experience as encompassed by Benjamin's definition of *Erlebnis*. In contrast to the experience of contiguity across time which is central to his understanding of auratic experience (*Erfahrung*), *Erlebnis* designates the experience of a series of self-contained, isolated, and finite moments; each of which is screened off from those preceding it by the "process of continually starting all over again" upon which the temporal structure of *Erlebnis* is based.[72]

If Benjamin is drawn to Baudelaire's poetry then it is not only because of the manner in which he gives voice to this degeneration in the capacity for auratic experience,[73] but because of the way in which he invests these self-contained, finite moments with "the weight of long experience [*Erfahrung*]"[74] through his evocation—in the form of the *correspondances*—of an experience of time which exists outside of the "homogenous, empty time"[75] characteristic of *Erlebnis*. These *correspondances* (which emerge when the perception of something in the present evokes an impression of the past with which it is unconsciously associated) are, Benjamin writes, the "data of recollection."[76] They are moments of "completing time" which are "not marked by any immediate experience [*Erlebnis*]."[77]

For Benjamin, the significance of these *correspondances* (which in Baudelaire's poetry are associated with the evocation of the glimmer and density of certain colours, images of trees, masts, oarsmen, the flavour of fruit, dazzling sunlight, the sensation of heat, and the chant of boatmen) lies not in the particular content of the recollected memories (many of which would appear to derive from Baudelaire's voyage across the Indian Ocean at the age of 20).[78] Rather, what is significant for Benjamin about these *correspondances* is the extent to which the opening up of time provoked by involuntary memory provides a space within which the remembering subject is able to envision the possibility of a different kind of relationship to his or her environment, and with it, the possibility of a different kind of existence. "In reality," Benjamin writes in his notes for "On the Concept of History," "there is not a moment that would not carry with it *its* revolutionary chance—provided only that it is defined in a specific way, namely as the chance for a completely new resolution of a completely new problem [*Aufgabe*]."[79] It is precisely in these moments—in which the "empty passage"[80] of time as *Erlebnis* is torn asunder by the experience of the past in the present—that the political significance of Benjamin's delineation of auratic experience manifests itself.

Imagination and Mimesis

In Benjamin's writings on hashish, the experience of the past in the present associated with the *correspondances* is evoked by a heightened sensitivity to one's surroundings. In "Hashish in Marseilles", for example, Benjamin writes of the extraordinary tenderness toward his environment induced by the drug: "It was not far from the first café of the evening, in which, suddenly, the amorous joy dispensed by the contemplation of some fringes blown by the wind had convinced me that the hashish had begun its work."[81] Baudelaire, too, expresses a similar sentiment: "[A] new sharpness—a greater keenness—becomes apparent in all of the senses. The senses of smell, sight, hearing and touch alike participate in this development."[82]

What is significant about this increase in sensitivity described by both

37

Benjamin and Baudelaire is the extent to which it is attributed to the freeing up of one's experience of time induced by hashish intoxication. For the hashish eater, Baudelaire writes, "the dimension of time" is "abolished completely."[83] While Benjamin—in his "*Protokoll des Haschischversuchs vom 11. Mai 1928*"—claims that a "complete disorientation of the sense of time *[Zeitsinn]*" characterises his experience—the significance of which he corroborates by quoting the observations of Ernst Joël (with whom he undertook the experiment): "I have miscalculated the time. [...] My watch is going backwards."[84]

As per his analysis of Baudelaire's poetry, it is in this loosening up of one's experience of time that Benjamin locates the possibility for the rejuvenation of auratic experience. The connections between the perceptual and experiential capacities of the hashish eater and auratic experience are drawn most suggestively in Benjamin's description in "Hashish in Marseilles" of the hashish eater as a "physiognomist."[85] Although he is referring specifically, in this essay, to the hashish eater's capacity for recognising—in a crowd of unfamiliar faces—facial characteristics reminiscent of friends and acquaintances, as revealed in his notes on the effects of the drug in *The Arcades Project*, this capacity is not limited to the observation of human faces, but extends to the manner in which the intoxicated gaze of the hashish eater animates face-like qualities inherent within objects and spaces. In "Convolute M," Benjamin argues that—for the hashish eater—everything develops a face: "[E]ach thing," he claims, "has the degree of bodily presence that allows it to be searched—as one searches a face—for such traits as appear. Under these conditions even a sentence (to say nothing of the single word) puts on a face."[86]

What is significant about these comments in the light of Benjamin's analysis of the decline in the capacity for experience is the extent to which this perceptual capacity is rendered synonymous with the definition of a non-reified, auratic form of experience outlined in "On Some Motifs in Baudelaire." "Experience of the aura," Benjamin writes, "arises from the fact that a response characteristic of human relationships is transposed to the relationship between humans and inanimate or natural objects. The person we look at, or who feels he is being looked at, looks at us in turn."[87] Thus, to recapitulate a point made earlier: "To experience the aura of an object we look at means to invest it with the ability to look back at us. This ability corresponds to the data of the *memoire involontaire*."[88]

In a similar vein to Benjamin's analysis of the image spaces opened up by the writings and practices of the Surrealists, the conception of involuntary memory outlined in Benjamin's writings on hashish revolves around the involuntary production and recollection of images:

> As this very evening proved, there can be an absolutely blizzard-like production of images, independently of whether our attention is directed toward anyone or anything else. Whereas in our normal state free-floating images to which we pay no heed simply remain in the unconscious, under the influence of hashish images present themselves to us seemingly without requiring our attention. Of course, this process may result in the production of images that are so extraordinary, so fleeting, and so rapidly generated that we can do nothing but gaze at them simply because of their beauty and singularity.[89]

In "Convolute M," this increase in the activation of involuntary memory is associated with the enhancement of the hashish eater's capacity for recognising similarities–the significance of which is traced in the analysis of mimetic perception outlined in Benjamin's 1933 essays "Doctrine of the Similar" and "On the Mimetic Faculty."

In "Doctrine of the Similar," Benjamin argues that "[i]nsight into the realms of the 'similar' is of fundamental significance for the illumination of major sectors of occult knowledge"[90] –the significance of which is demonstrated, not in the content of the similarities themselves, but in the replication of the processes through which such similarities are manifested. Benjamin claims that this capacity for recognising similarities (which is a "a weak rudiment of the once powerful compulsion to become similar and also to behave mimetically"[91]) has been significantly attenuated in modern times–resulting in a "perceptual world" which "contains only minimal residues of the magical correspondences and analogies that were

39

familiar to ancient peoples."[92] These correspondences—which the ancients traced in the constellations of stars with which the "spirits and forces of life were shaped in accordance"[93]—extended significantly beyond the limited confines within which modern man is able to recognise similarity: "The similarities perceived consciously—for instance, in faces—are," Benjamin writes, "compared to the countless similarities perceived unconsciously or not at all, like the enormous underwater mass of an iceberg in comparison to the small tip one sees rising out of the water."[94]

In "The Lamp" (which served as a preliminary draft for the ideas discussed in "Doctrine of the Similar")[95] Benjamin argues that one of the few realms within which what was "the natural heritage of mankind in its early stages" can be found today, is in the play of children.[96] "Children's play," he writes in "Doctrine of the Similar," "is everywhere permeated by mimetic modes of behaviour, and its realm is by no means limited to what one person can imitate in another." Particularly adept at both recognising and producing similarities, "[t]he child plays at being not only a shopkeeper or teacher but also a windmill and a train"[97] in a realm which is free from what Breton describes as the "imperative [of] practical necessity."[98] For Benjamin, it is by remaining loyal to that "animistic" relationship to the world of nature and things (which is both a mark of the life of the ancients and the hallmark of auratic experience) that the "liberating" dimension of childhood play manifests itself.[99]

In "Convolute M" Benjamin argues that the "category of similarity, which for the waking consciousness has only minimal relevance," also "attains unlimited relevance" for the person intoxicated by hashish.[100] In "Myslovice-Braunschweig-Marseilles," for example, he recounts the story of a man, who—in a late night search for chocolate prompted by the "pangs of hunger" occasioned by the drug—is beckoned by the contents of a barber shop which have been transformed into confectionary products: "Only now," he writes, "did I realize that the hashish had begun to work, and if I had not been alerted by the way in which boxes of powder had changed into candy jars, nickel trays into chocolate bars, and wigs into cakes, my own loud laughter would have been warning

40

enough."[101] While in his experiment of May 11, Benjamin describes the "curious mimetic anticipations" which dominate both his and Ernst Joël's experience of the drug. Joël, for his part, transforms the corner of a writing table into a "naval base, coal station, something between Wittenberg and Jüterbog"—the significance of which, he notes, can be traced to a childhood memory.[102] While under Benjamin's intoxicated gaze, an oven metamorphoses into a cat, a writing table into a fruit stall, and "the creases in [his] white beach trousers" into "the creases of a burnous."[103] When Joël takes a biscuit, Benjamin offers him a light,[104] and while his cousin Egon Wissing is talking, Benjamin's "apprehension of his words [is] instantly translated into the perception of colored, metallic sequins that coalesce [...] into patterns" (like "the beautiful colored knitting patterns" in the *Herzblättchens Zeitvertreib* Benjamin had loved as a child).[105]

Although the image spaces opened up by hashish intoxication are, in Benjamin's writings, often associated with memories of the hashish eater's childhood, what is significant is not so much the particular content of these memories, but rather the extent to which the experience of childhood in the present evoked by involuntary memory rejuvenates the capacity for perception and imagination that Benjamin, Baudelaire, and Breton each associate with childhood. Citing his own re-encounter as an adult with sounds such as the "dull pop with which the flame [lit] up the gas mantle" in his childhood home, and "the jangling of [his] mother's keys in her basket"[106] as examples, Benjamin argues that it is through the recollection of childhood memories that one's capacity for mimetic perception can be reignited.[107]

Central not only to Benjamin's, but also to Baudelaire's and Breton's analyses of the radicality of childhood perception and cognition is not only the child's heightened mimetic capacity for recognising and producing similarities, but the extent to which the child's capacity for imagination is not limited by what the adult world deems appropriate and/or possible. "Imagination," Baudelaire writes, "is not fantasy," but "a virtually divine faculty that apprehends immediately, by means lying outside philosophical methods, the intimate and secret relation of things,

41

the correspondences and analogies."[108] It "decomposes all creation and with the raw materials accumulated [...] it creates a new world, it produces the sensation of newness."[109]

In *Artificial Paradise* Baudelaire argues that, "if we were wise," we would harness this "bubbling over of imagination" occasioned by the effects of the drug in order to derive not only "the certainty of a better life," but also "the hope of attaining it through daily exercises of our will."[110] His concern, however, lies with the danger that the image spaces opened up by hashish intoxication could be experienced not as catalysts for action, but rather as spectacles conceived of as ends or paradises in themselves. For Baudelaire it is the dissolution of the will occasioned by the drug which is responsible for this development. For while this dissolution opens up a space within which the imagination can flourish, he argues that it also guards against "the ability [of the hashish eater] to profit by it."[111] According to Baudelaire, "[i]f a man can instantly procure all wealth in heaven and earth by taking a teaspoon of jelly, then he will never seek to acquire the slightest fraction of it by working. And our most urgent need is to live and work! [...] Indeed, what point is there in working, toiling, writing, creating anything at all, when it is possible to obtain Paradise in a single swallow?"[112]

For Benjamin, a similar shadow is cast upon the writings and practices of the Surrealists by what he describes as their "inadequate, undialectical conception of the nature of intoxication."[113] He argues that the "histrionic or fanatical stress on the mysterious side of the mysterious"[114] (which reveals itself, at times, in the writings of the Surrealists) is not politically productive in itself. Rather, what is productive is the "fruitful, living experience that allowed these people to step outside the charmed space of intoxication"[115] by bringing the experiences of the past in the present occasioned by Surrealist practices to bear on the exigencies of the present situation.[116] The task, Benjamin writes in "Surrealism," is "to discover in the space of political action the one hundred percent image space."[117] This space will not "be measured out by contemplation,"[118] but is borne out of a rejuvenation of the capacity for auratic experience—the significance of which lies in the extent to which both the experience of the past in the present which it designates—and the renewal of the capacity for imagination with which it is associated—can serve as a catalyst for the creation and sustenance of a desire for a different kind of existence.

Notes

[1] Anonymous declaration furnished by Raymond Queneau and quoted in Maurice Nadeau, *The History of Surrealism* (Middlesex: Penguin Books, 1978), 114. Nadeau claims that this declaration, which was published as a tract in 1925, has not—to his knowledge—been reprinted.

[2] Benjamin, letter to Gershom Scholem, July 26, 1932, in Corr., 396.

[3] Charles Baudelaire, *Artificial Paradise: On Hashish and Wine as Means of Expanding Individuality* (New York: Herder and Herder, 1971).

[4] See Benjamin, letter to Ernst Schoen, September 19, 1919, in Corr., 148.

[5] For Benjamin's comments on his reacquaintance with Fränkel and Joël, see his letter to Scholem, January 30, 1928, in Corr., 323.

[6] Fritz Fränkel and Ernst Joël, "Der Haschisch-Rausch: Beiträge zu einer experimentellen Psychopathologie," in *Klinische Wochenschrift*, Nr. 37 (1926), 1707–9. A long quote from this article appears at the beginning of Benjamin's "Hashish in Marseilles," in SW 2, 673–79.

[7] This observation is confirmed by the editors of Benjamin, SW 2. See "Chronology," 827.

[8] *Über Haschisch: Novellistisches, Berichte, Materialien*, ed. Tillman Rexroth (Frankfurt am Main: Suhrkamp, 1972). A selection of Benjamin's writings on hashish has been published in English translation in SW 2: "Main Features of my Second Impression of Hashish," 85–90; "Hashish, Beginning of March 1930," 327–30; "Myslovice-Braunschweig-Marseilles," 386–393 and "Hashish in Marseilles," 673–79. Materials included in *Über Haschisch* not included in this volume include the "*Crocknotizen*," and most of the material from the "*Protokolle*." See *Über Haschisch*, 57–61 and 65–143 respectively. This material is also included in GS VI, 558–618.

[9] Benjamin, letter to Scholem, January 30, 1928, in Corr., 323.

[10] See "A Berlin Chronicle," in SW 2; "Berlin Childhood around 1900," in SW 3; "On the Image of Proust," and "Little History of Photography," in SW 2.

[11] Gershom Scholem, *Walter Benjamin: The Story of a Friendship* (Philadelphia: The Jewish Publication Society of America, 1981), 134.

[12] Peter Osborne, "Small-scale Victories, Large-scale Defeats: Walter Benjamin's Politics of Time," in *Walter Benjamin's Philosophy: Destruction and Experience*, eds. Andrew Benjamin and Peter Osborne (London: Routledge, 1994), 63.

[13] The first mention of Aragon in Benjamin's correspondence appears in a letter to Hugo von Hofmannsthal, June 5, 1927, in Corr., 315.

[14] Benjamin, letter to Theodor W. Adorno, May 31, 1935, in Corr., 488. As Bernd Witte has noted, Benjamin also translated a number of sections from *Paris Peasant* which were published in *Literarische Welt* in 1928. See *Walter Benjamin: An Intellectual Biography* (Detroit: Wayne State University Press, 1997), 91.

[15] Benjamin, "Surrealism: The Last Snapshot of the European Intelligentsia," in SW 2, 207–21.

[16] Ibid., 215 and "Der Sürrealismus: Die Letzte Momentaufnahme der europäischen Intelligenz," in GS II, 307.

[17] Benjamin, "Surrealism," in SW 2, 217.

[18] Louis Aragon, *Paris Peasant* (London: Pan Books, 1987), 36–37.

[19] Ibid., 36 and 54.

[20] Benjamin, "Main Features of my Second Impression of Hashish," in SW 2, 89.

[21] Benjamin, "One-Way Street," in SW 1, 466.

[22] Aragon, *Paris Peasant*, 94.

[23] Benjamin, "Surrealism," in SW 2, 209.

[24] André Breton, "Manifesto of Surrealism," in *Manifestoes of Surrealism* (Ann Arbor: University of Michigan Press, 1972), 10.

[25] Ibid., 4.

[26] Ibid., 5.

[27] André Breton, "Second Manifesto of Surrealism," in *Manifestoes of Surrealism*, 187.

[28] Breton, "First Manifesto," 10.

[29] André Breton, *Communicating Vessels* (Lincoln: University of Nebraska Press, 1997), 122

[30] André Breton, "Ascendant Sign," in *Free Rein* (Lincoln: University of Nebraska Press, 1997), 104. Quoted in Ruth Brandon, *Surreal Lives: The Surrealists, 1917–1945* (London: Papermac, 2000), 449.

[31] Benjamin, "Surrealism," in SW 2, 208.

[32] Benjamin, "Zum großen Aufsatz über Sürrealismus," in GS II, 1021.

[33] For a more detailed account of Benjamin's analysis of the significance of Proust's delineation of involuntary memory, see my essay "Benjamin, Proust, and the Rejuvenating Powers of Memory," in *Literature and Aesthetics*, vol. 12 (November 2002), 47–62.

[34] Benjamin, "Surrealism," in SW 2, 210; see also GS II, 300.

[35] Breton, "Manifesto of Surrealism," 37.

[36] Ibid. 39–40. This passage, when read in full, bears a number of similarities to Benjamin's description of involuntary memory in "Aus einer kleinen Rede über Proust, an meinem vierzigsten Geburtstag gehalten," in GS II, 1064. See also Adorno's account of the significance of the Surrealists' attempts to uncover childhood memories in "Looking Back on Surrealism," in *Notes to Literature: Vol. 1*, ed. Rolf Tiedemann (New York: Columbia University Press, 1991), 88.

[37] Breton, "Manifesto of Surrealism," 36

[38] The roots of Baudelaire's fascination with the drug can be traced back to his involvement in the 1840's with the *Club des Hachichins*, a group of artists and writers (including Gérard de Nerval, Honoré de Balzac, Eugéne Delacroix, and Dr. Jacques-Joseph Moreau) who would meet in Paris to take, and discuss the effects of the drug. See Claude Pichois and Jean Ziegler, *Baudelaire* (London: Vintage, 2002), 128–29, and Sadie Plant, *Writing on Drugs* (London: Faber and Faber, 2001), 41–42. As Edouard Roditi argues in his introduction to Baudelaire's *Artificial Paradise*, it is also likely that Baudelaire experimented with the drug as a young man; see *Artificial Paradise*, xv.

[39] Baudelaire, *Artifical Paradise*, 70.

[40] Ibid. 43 and 54.

[41] See, for example, "Doctrine of the Similar," in SW 2, 695.

[42] Baudelaire, *Artificial Paradise*, 69. See also Aragon's discussion of the manner in which words can function as mirrors in *Paris Peasant*, 103.

[43] In "Der Haschisch-Rausch: Beiträge zu einer experimentellen Psychopathologie," Joël and Fränkel also make a distinction between the images induced by hashish and hallucinations proper. See 1708.

[44] Benjamin's analysis of the plant photographs of Karl Blossfeldt was written in 1928 in the midst of his experiments with hashish. See "News about Flowers," in SW 2, 155–57.

[45] Baudelaire, *Artificial Paradise*, 65. Baudelaire is quoting Edgar Allan Poe here, although he does not cite the source.

[46] Ibid., 68.

[47] Ibid., 54–55.

[48] Benjamin, AP, 367 [J79,6].

[49] Ibid.

[50] Baudelaire, *Artificial Paradise*, 72.

[51] Ibid., 34.

[52] In [J76,1] Benjamin claims that "[t]he decline of aura and the waning of the dream of a better nature—this latter conditioned on its defensive position in the class struggle—are one and the same." AP, 362.

53 Benjamin, "The Work of Art in the Age of Its Technological Reproducibility (Third Version)," in SW 4, 255.

54 Benjamin, "On Some Motifs in Baudelaire," in SW 4, 337.

55 Ibid., 338.

56 Ibid.

57 Ibid., 339.

58 Georg Simmel, "The Metropolis and Mental Life," in *Simmel on Culture–Selected Writings*, eds. David Frisby and Mike Featherstone (London: Sage Publications, 1997).

59 Benjamin, "On Some Motifs in Baudelaire," in SW 4, 315.

60 Benjamin, quoting Freud, in ibid. 317.

61 Ibid., 319.

62 Ibid.

63 Ibid., 318. "The *mémoire voluntaire*," Benjamin writes in *The Arcades Project*, "is a registry providing the object [or incident] with a classificatory number behind which it disappears. 'So now we've been there.' ('I've had an experience.')" AP, 211 [H5,1]. In a letter to Adorno, May 20, 1940, Benjamin "trace[s] the roots of [his] 'theory of experience' to a childhood memory." "My parents," he writes, "naturally took walks with us wherever we spent our summers. There were either two or three of us children. The one I have in mind is my brother. After we had visited one of the obligatory tourist attractions around Freudenstadt, Wengen, or Schreiberhau, my brother used to say, 'Now we can say that we've been there.' This statement made an unforgettable impression on me." Corr., 629.

64 Benjamin, "Experience," in SW 2, 553.

65 Benjamin, "A Berlin Chronicle," in SW 2, 603.

66 Benjamin, "On the Image of Proust," in SW 2, 238. I have modified the English translation of "*ein erlebtes Ereignis*" as "an experienced event" to "a lived event" because the translation of *erlebtes* as "experienced" is confusing in this context. See "Zum Bilde Prousts," in GS II, 312.

67 I have borrowed this description from John McCole's analysis of Benjamins's conception of *Erlebnis* in *Walter Benjamin and the Antinomies of Tradition* (Ithaca: Cornell University Press, 1993), 262.

68 Benjamin, "On Some Motifs in Baudelaire," in SW 4, 329.

69 See, for example, Baudelaire's poem "The Clock" in *The Flowers of Evil* (Oxford: Oxford University Press, 1998), 160–61.

70 Benjamin, "On Some Motifs in Baudelaire," in SW 4, 330.

71 Ibid.

72 Ibid., 331.

73 See, for example, Baudelaire's delineation of the experience of time characteristic

of modernity in "The Clock" and in his prose poem "The Double Room" in *Baudelaire in English*, eds. Carol Clarke and Robert Sykes (London: Penguin, 1997), 237–39.

74 Benjamin, "On Some Motifs in Baudelaire," in SW 4, 343.

75 Benjamin, "On the Concept of History," in SW 4, 395.

76 Benjamin, "On Some Motifs in Baudelaire," in SW 4, 334.

77 Ibid., 332–33.

78 See, for example, "Exotic Perfume," "Head of Hair," and "The Dancing Serpent," in *The Flowers of Evil*, 48–49, 50–53, and 56–59. For a detailed account of Baudelaire's voyage, see Chapter 9 of Claude Pichois and Jean Ziegler, *Baudelaire*, 74–81.

79 Benjamin, "Paralipomena to 'On the Concept of History'," in SW 4, 402.

80 Benjamin, AP, 351 [J69,5].

81 Benjamin, "Hashish in Marseilles," in SW 2, 678.

82 Baudelaire, *Artificial Paradise*, 54.

83 Ibid., 61. See also 21, 22, 24, and 70.

84 "Walter Benjamin: Protokoll des Haschischversuchs vom 11. Mai 1928," in *Über Haschisch*, 84, and GS VI, 572. The feeling that "the chronological order" has been freed up also features in Benjamin's account of Ernst Bloch's experiment with hashish in "Bloch's Protokoll zum Versuch vom <14. Januar 1928>." See *Über Haschisch*, 78, and GS VI, 568. See also Benjamin's analysis of "the hashish eater's demands on time and space" in "Hashish in Marseilles," in SW 2, 674.

85 Benjamin, "Hashish in Marseilles," in SW 2, 675.

86 Benjamin, AP 418 [M1a,1]. In "Hashish in Marseilles," Benjamin (quoting Karl Kraus) states that the phrase, "'The more closely you look at a word, the more distantly it looks back'–appears to extend the optical," 678. See also Benjamin's comments about the manner in which his surroundings "wink" at him in "Main Features of My Second Impression of Hashish," in SW 2, 88, and "First Sketches" in AP, 841 <O°, 5>.

87 Benjamin, "On Some Motifs in Baudelaire," in SW 4, 338.

88 Ibid.

89 Benjamin, "Hashish, Beginning of March 1930," in SW 2, 328–29.

90 Benjamin, "Doctrine of the Similar," in SW 2, 694.

91 Ibid., 698.

92 Benjamin, "On the Mimetic Faculty," in SW 2, 721.

93 Benjamin, "The Lamp," in SW 2, 691. See also Benjamin, "On Astrology," in SW 2, 684–85.

94 Benjamin, "Doctrine of the Similar," in SW 2, 695.

95 See the translator's note to the "The Lamp," in SW 2, 693.

96 Benjamin, "The Lamp," in SW 2, 691.

97 See Benjamin, "Doctrine of the Similar," in SW 2, 694 and "On the Mimetic Faculty," in SW 2, 720.

98 Breton, "Manifesto of Surrealism," 4.

99 See Benjamin, "Toys and Play," in SW 2, 100.

100 Benjamin, AP, 418 [M1a,1].

101 Benjamin, "Myslovice-Braunschweig-Marseilles," in SW 2, 390.

102 Benjamin, "Protokoll des Haschischversuchs vom 11. Mai 1928," and Ernst Joël, "Protokoll zu demselben Versuch," in Über Haschisch, 83, 86 and 90. See GS VI, 571, 573, and 576.

103 See Benjamin, "Hauptzüge der ersten Haschisch-Impression," in Über Haschisch, 67 and GS IV, 559, and "Myslovice-Braunschweig-Marseilles," in SW 2, 392.

104 See Benjamin, "Protokoll des Haschischversuchs vom 11. Main 1928," 83 and GS VI, 571.

105 Benjamin, "Hashish, Beginning of March 1930," in SW 2, 328.

106 Benjamin, "The Lamp," in SW 2, 692.

107 "Modern man is transported into this very force field [of mimesis] by memories of his childhood." Ibid.

108 Baudelaire, "Further Notes on Edgar Poe," in Selected Writings on Art and Literature, ed. P. E. Charvet (London: Penguin Books, 1992), 199. Benjamin also quotes this passage in "Convolute J," AP, 285 [J31a,6].

109 Baudelaire, "The Salon of 1859–Letters to the Editor of the Revue Française," in Art in Paris: 1845–1862, Salons and other Exhibitions, ed. Jonathan Mayne (Oxford: Phaidon, 1981), 156. Benjamin also includes this passage in AP, 290 [K34a,2]. See also Baudelaire's analysis of the radicality of childhood perception and cognition in "The Painter of Modern Life," in Selected Writings on Art and Literature, 398, and Benjamin's analysis of the "renewal" of existence accomplished by children in "Unpacking my Library: A Talk about Collecting," in SW 2, 487.

110 Baudelaire, Artificial Paradise, 34 and 57.

111 Ibid., 81.

112 Ibid., 26.

113 Benjamin, "Surrealism," in SW 2, 216.

114 Ibid.

115 Ibid., 208.

116 "The point," as John McCole has argued, "was not to revel in the ecstasy of a complementary world but to return with a sharpened sense for the realities of the world that lie […] this side of the charmed circle." Walter Benjamin and the Antinomies of Tradition, 226.

117 Benjamin, "Surrealism," in SW 2, 217.

118 Ibid.

Transformations of Readability and Time

A Case of Reproducibility and Cloning

Dag Petersson

> The past has left images of itself in literary texts, images comparable to those which are imprinted by light on a photosensitive plate. The future alone possesses developers active enough to scan such surfaces perfectly. Many pages in Mariveaux or Rousseau contain a mysterious meaning which the first readers of these texts could not fully have deciphered.
>
> (André Monglond)[1]

In February 1940, while taking notes for what would be his last finished text ("On the Concept of History"), Walter Benjamin singled out the passage above from André Monglond's historical tome *Le préromantisme français* (1930). True to his own theoretical prescriptions, Benjamin then carefully crafted a new context for the citation.[2] In a fragment entitled "The Dialectical Image" he added to it the following methodological remarks: "The historical method is a philological method based on the book of life. 'Read what was never written,' runs a line in Hofmannsthal. The reader one should think of here is the true historian."[3] This somewhat mysterious juxtaposition was then reformulated in more accessible terms in the finished text:

> Articulating the past historically does not mean recognizing it "the way it really was." It means appropriating a memory as it flashes up in a moment of danger. Historical materialism wishes to hold fast that image of the past which unexpectedly appears to the historical subject in a moment of danger. The danger threatens both the content of the tradition and

49

those who inherit it. For both, it is one and the same thing: the danger of becoming a tool of the ruling classes. Every age must strive anew to wrest tradition away from the conformism that is working to overpower it.[4]

For many of today's able disputants of Benjamin, passages like this have been received as a welcome opening toward a new, politicized cultural theory. But some politically attentive readers of Benjamin, such as the Italian philosopher Giorgio Agamben, have convincingly argued that a straightforward appropriation of Benjamin's theory today in fact reinvigorates the dangers of mythologization that Benjamin pointed out some sixty-five years ago.[5] Following Agamben's lead, Benjamin's philosophy is not immediately available for our time and a politically invested Benjaminian scholarship today is still something to be constructed. This text will reflect on the possibilities for such a theoretical construction, along with some related difficulties.

In order not to succumb to, but to use a moment of danger, Benjamin instructs his future readers to turn its violent forces into an augmented ability to recognize the past. The historical knowledge thus produced will not slowly accumulate, but suddenly flash up in a revolutionary moment. In early 1940 the sensation of danger in Paris (which had been Benjamin's home for seven years) was imminent. The completion of "On the Concept of History" in early May 1940 coincided with the German invasion of Belgium, the Netherlands and France. These military advances forced Benjamin into exile for the second time; in 1933 he had fled Germany and now he was preparing to escape Europe for the United States.

Although a historical circumstance of crucial importance, one should remember that if today's Benjaminian scholars want to "wrest tradition away from conformism" in the sense Benjamin advocated for the true historian in "every age," we would have to begin by assessing the dangers of our own time. We would then be forced to realize that it is not merely as a past context that the dangers of war relate to Benjamin's instruction. Twentieth-century history, to which Benjamin's philosophy belongs as a most challenging prism, ought to be dialectically experienced with the fullness of our present abilities and not reconstructed or restaged in its supposedly proper past context.

Yet, if we dare this assertive claim today, we must also confront a banal methodological question that makes the reading of Benjamin even more complicated: following Benjamin's instructions to the letter, can our time's production of dialectical images still be compared to photography, as in the Monglond quotation, or would not our time call for a different image with another structural form? Such a question admittedly begets a somewhat speculative entry into Benjamin's writings, yet it is one that demands a very concrete inquiry: How historically determined is Benjamin's philosophy of history? If, as he says, a "resolute refusal of the concept of 'timeless truth' is in order,"[6] how historical is the truth of his true historian? To put it differently: if we were able today to read what was never written, to what extent would our philological efforts yield insights that would change our capacity to read? It seems unlikely that a photographic historiography would still have potentials to affect today's global politics of war in any sense similar to that in which Benjamin hoped the aesthetics of film would be "useless for the purposes of fascism,"[7] not least because the moment of danger today may be less that of becoming a tool of the ruling classes than becoming a class ruled by its own technical tools and visual technologies.[8]

It is in order to pursue these questions that Benjamin's logic of readability and time will be discussed here. Readability will be understood as a historically mutable category that determines the capacity of language to read itself. By turning our time's readability to Benjamin's methodology and begin by focusing on the term reproducibility, this text will identify a moment of danger in the readability of genetically designed or cloned life.

The Authenticity of Truth
It has often been repeated how in the "Work of Art" essay, Benjamin used photography to discuss the political implications of mass reproduced art. Benjamin wrote:

> To an ever-increasing degree, the work reproduced becomes the re-
> production of a work designed for reproducibility. From a photographic
> plate, for example, one can make any number of prints; to ask for the
> "authentic" print makes no sense. But as soon as the criterion of authen-
> ticity ceases to be applied to artistic production, the whole social function
> of art is revolutionized. Instead of being founded on ritual, it is based on
> a different practice: politics.[9]

It is also well rehearsed that in the same essay Benjamin termed authenticity the "nucleus" (*Kern*) of the artwork and that he concluded: "The
authenticity of a thing is the quintessence of all that is transmissible in it
from its origin on, ranging from its physical duration to the historical
testimony relating to it. Since the historical testimony is founded on the
physical duration, the former, too, is jeopardized by reproduction, in
which the physical duration plays no part."[10] From Benjamin's position,
the advent of modern photography coincided with both a new mode of
reading and a collapse of the authoritarian notion of artistic originality.
In that double sense photography corresponded to an event Benjamin
called the withering of aura, affecting the being of art, perception, language
and history.

The changes that this decline of the aura brought about—also in the
areas of economy, social conditions and politics—have been thoroughly
debated for decades.[11] But remarkably few analyses have been explicitly
attentive to how the auratic decline impacts on the possibility of being
historically true to Benjamin's philosophical language. This is somewhat
surprising, as historical fidelity to Benjamin and a historical aura in decline
immediately appear to be incongruous moments. When the aura declines,
so does the power of historical authenticity and originality, and that does
certainly not exclude the philosophical writings of Benjamin. The problem
of Benjamin's authenticity can, however, be easily solved by saying that
to read Benjamin is an experience aiming 'to read what was never written.'
In the preface to the second edition of "Berlin Childhood around 1900"
Benjamin indeed welcomes the capacity of his images to take on a fate
beyond his control: "No customary forms await them yet, like those

that, over the course of centuries, and in obedience to a feeling for nature, answer to remembrances of a childhood spent in the country. But,
then, the images of my metropolitan childhood perhaps are capable, at
their core, of preforming later historical experience."[12] Contemporary
with this text, from spring 1938, is a fragment intended for an introduction
to a book on Baudelaire. Here Benjamin forcefully rejects the desire to
seek for the truth at the historical source:

> Of course, one is tempted to pursue "the matter in itself." In the case of
> Baudelaire, it offers itself in profusion. The sources flow as abundantly as
> one could wish, and where they converge to form the stream of tradition,
> they flow along between well-laid-out slopes as far as the eye can reach.
> Historical materialism is not led astray by this spectacle. It does not seek
> the image of the clouds in this stream, but neither does it turn away from
> the stream to drink "from the source" and pursue the "matter itself" behind
> men's backs. Whose mills does this stream drive? Who is utilizing its
> power? Who dammed it? These are the questions that historical materia-
> lism asks, changing our impressions of the landscape by naming the forces
> that have been operative in it.[13]

In short, Benjamin reminds us that neither as writers nor as readers can
we be sure that a text stays true to its word, or even remains identical to
itself over a period of time. A critical dilemma for Benjamin scholars is
then how, if at all, we can read his philosophy truthfully, and from what
common grounds we can agree to judge or evaluate our readings, when
the philosophy itself has invalidated any stable and determinable truth-
value, both at its source and at its destination.

How to learn to read what was never written when there is truth only
in a text thus read? Could not this zen-like aporia be solved simply by
reproducing Benjamin's mode of reading and reflect it back onto his
own texts? Perhaps it could, but then at the same stroke that would
necessitate mistrusting the original meaning of his methodological
writings. As the historical method must also be dialectically worked over,
the real question becomes this: is it possible, or advisable, after Benjamin,
in whatever time or circumstance, to rely on the same strategies for

approaching history that Benjamin invented for reading—say, Baudelaire? In other words, can we faithfully analyze and transpose Benjamin's mode of awakening into our own time and trust to it for a similar awakening to our history and a reading of—say, Benjamin? If we do, then we must be ready to face what appears to be another, similar aporia of truth: if one is true to Benjamin's materialist historiography, then not only will Benjamin vanish as its source but the truth-character of Benjamin's truth will also appear to have changed. The more faithful Benjamin's readers are to his method, the more does that method's potential for truth void itself. This explains why the truthfulness of our accounts becomes inevitably more indeterminable the closer to Benjamin we read. Ironically, Benjamin himself appears to be almost unreadable.

The possibility of overcoming these aporias should be sought in what upholds them, and that brings us to Benjamin's notion of time. Immediately, one should notice that Benjamin's immanent philosophy employs a concept of truth that is neither itself eternal, nor the result of an eternally valid system of thought. Benjamin's system (if it is one) operates from what he calls differentials of time: "On the differentials of time (which, for others, disturb the main lines of the inquiry), I base my reckoning."[14] As any notion of a timeless truth is renounced, and eternity—as another fragment from *The Arcades Project* puts it—"is far more the ruffle on a dress than some idea," Benjamin's truth is legitimized as truth only by being "bound to a nucleus of time [*Zeitkern*]."[15] This does not mean that truth is relative to a temporal development of knowledge: knowledge does not determine truth and truth does not determine knowledge; truth is only determined by the temporal nucleus which permeates knower and known alike. Hence, in order to approach the above aporias, one might suggest that today we live in a different kind of time than did Benjamin, tied differently to a changed nucleus and not merely further down the same stretch of time. In that case, it is easy to see that any symmetrical transposition of Benjamin's method into our time would be a disservice to his philosophy. Benjamin's truth cannot be our truth—but less because things have changed than because time itself has changed. "Each 'now,'" he wrote, "is the now of a particular recognizability. In it, truth is charged to the bursting point with time. (This point of explosion, and nothing else, is the death of the *intentio* which thus coincides with the birth of authentic historical time, the time of truth.)"[16]

The Time of Truth

In order to describe the time of truth that Benjamin presents as a differential (never as a *Zeitgeist*), one may forward the hypothesis that in opposition to a strong tradition in modern western philosophy, Benjamin understood time as derived from something more fundamental than itself. Instead of considering time an *a priori* form of intuition (Kant), an absolute negative of existence (Hegel), or the essence of Being (Heidegger), Benjamin sees time as a function relative to what he calls adamic language and messianic time. Hence, rather than considering time in the customary three, mutually exclusive tenses, past, present and future, Benjamin distinguishes between different types of relations between pasts, nows and futures. Most famously, he argues: "For while the relation of the present to the past is purely temporal, the relation of what-has-been to the now is dialectical: not temporal in nature but figural [*bildlich*]."[17] It must be noticed here, that Benjamin is often remarkably inconsistent when it comes to the relation between words and concepts. For example, when he writes: "The present determines where, in the object from the past, that object's fore-history and after-history diverge so as to circumscribe its nucleus,"[18] it is here as well a question of a dialectical relationship between a now and what-has-been, although the choice of words ('present' and 'past') would indicate a temporal relationship, given the former quotation. Yet what is really important about juxtaposing these two fragments, other than their verbal inconsistency, is the connection that appears between dialectical history and the notion of a temporal nucleus.

The temporal nucleus is what enables a dialectical relation between what-has-been and the now. The task is to analyze the structure of this dialectics. If Benjamin allows time to be a function of adamic language and messianic time (which remains to be shown), there is nothing to

55

keep us from supposing that, for the nucleus it is time as a passing that is the object for the dialectical relation. If time is dialectically divided in and for itself, recognizable as other to itself and opposed to itself so as to be relieved (*aufgehoben*) into a new form, then those developing moments cannot occur in time but only in another kind of environment, which, hypothetically, would be the adamic language and messianic time. There, in the initial dialectical moment, time as a nucleus recognizes that it is naturally incongruous with empty or homogeneous time. However, since it cannot deny the existence of a past, a new relation between what-has-been and the now takes form: an image appears. But the image and empty time cannot simply unify, so the nucleus considers time a multiplicity in every instant; time has thus intensified and is no longer a mere extension. At certain critical moments time will be about to explode. This, as Benjamin indicated above, releases the time of truth. In "On the Image of Proust" he notices a formation of eternity that corresponds to this time.

> Ramón Fernandez rightly distinguished between a *thème de l'éternité* and a *thème du temps* in Proust. But Proust's eternity is by no means a platonic or a utopian one; it is rapturous. [...] The eternity which Proust opens to view is intertwined [*verschränkte*] time, not boundless time. His true interest is in the passage of time in its most real—that is, intertwined—form, and this passage nowhere holds sway more openly than in remembrance within and aging without.[19]

Intertwined time is a time of truth: not a timeless eternity but a released time differential that prevails in the quasi-phenomena of remembrance and aging. Earlier in the essay on Proust, Benjamin writes that as opposed to an experienced event, a remembered event is "infinite, because it is merely a key [*Schlüssel*] to everything that happened before it and after it."[20] When later in the essay, Benjamin refers to another intertwining, this time of roads in Combray which turns the narrator's childhood landscape around like a gust of wind, the instant of mnemonic confusion is similarly what makes "a whole world age a lifetime."[21] In other words,

Proust's intertwining of times and their expression as remembrance or aging are to Benjamin eminently dialectical experiences of a time of truth. The pressing question is then: how can one truthfully communicate that experience?

What Benjamin refers to as the "key"—a remembered infinite event—has a corresponding language, a *Schlüsselsprache*, which is the intricate code language, the linguistic courtesy codex that is used among the upper classes. If one learns to turn the phrases right, the keys of this language open cabinets (what Benjamin elsewhere calls *Schränke*) containing potential images of what-has-been.[22] In his Proust essay the key provides access to images of social formations and life conditions that only exist in time differentials specific for a given class. Just as the key of remembrance is infinite—for it presents all that happened before and after the event—the code language is equally infinite in the sense of being a linguistic matrix for all that a certain class is able to express. The lower classes mime the upper classes' endless chatter and Proust mimes their miming; thus he reveals their time differentials in a language of truth—the language spoken only by language itself. Proust's narrator becomes a linguistic subject in Benjamin's philosophical critique, capable of enlisting the mimetic faculty of language in order to appropriate the key language of the upper classes and to conjure up the true images of their lives. Proust is nothing but a secret agent miming their language and assuming the temporal experience that belongs to it: "Ortega y Gasset was the first to draw attention to the vegetative existence of Proust's characters, which are planted so firmly in their social habitat, influenced by the position of the sun of aristocratic favor, stirred by the wind that blows from Guermantes or Méséglise, and inextricably enmeshed in the thicket of their fate. This is the environment that gave rise to the poet's mimicry."[23]

The consistent emphasis in this passage on a slowly growing, floral temporality may be juxtaposed to a rarely noticed fragment from *The Arcades Project*, in which Benjamin claims that one must not kill time like a gambler, but charge it like a battery as does the flâneur; yet there is a third type that synthesizes these two, namely the critic who waits, charges

57

time and passes off the energy of time in a different form.[24] For example, the anecdote of Proust waiting at the residence of Princesse Clermont-Tonnerre under the pretext of needing some medication he has left at home, at an address he elaborately but imprecisely describes to the attending courier—this shows how Proust's mimetic language charges time with waiting, so that its energy may be released in Benjamin's language as an image of Proust: "Proust's most accurate, most conclusive insights fasten on their objects the way insects fasten on leaves, blossoms, branches, betraying nothing of their existence until a leap, a beating of wings, a vault, show the startled observer that some incalculable individual life has imperceptibly crept into an alien world."[25]

"On the Image of Proust" rests upon an intimate relationship between Benjamin's faculty of mimesis and a dialectical structure of time. In order to begin to unlock the previously described aporias in Benjamin's historical method, it is important to describe how this relationship works in historical terms. In a passage from "On the Concept of History," Benjamin distinguishes between historicism and materialistic historiography in terms similar to the Proust essay's difference between boundless time and intertwined time. While time in historicism is an empty form to be filled with historical events, for the materialist, "what is historically understood contains time in its *interior* as a precious but tasteless seed."[26] Elsewhere, Benjamin uses similar terms to dissociate himself from Hegelianism:

> On the dialectical image. In it lies time. Already with Hegel, time enters into dialectic. But the Hegelian dialectic knows time solely as the properly historical, if not psychological, time of thinking. The time differential in which alone the dialectical image is real is still unknown to him. Attempt to show this with regard to fashion. Real time enters the dialectical image not in natural magnitude—let alone psychologically—but in its smallest gestalt.[27]

For the dialectical materialist, time differentials condition the dialectical images. Benjamin's historiography navigates from the changing values of these differentials rather than from major happenings in time.[28] As a political activist, the historical materialist looks out for instances which with retroactive force cause a deviation from the norms with which the ruling classes write history.[29] Yet, what makes such an instance recognizable as filled with the powers of a time differential is a "secret index" from the past, "by which it is referred to redemption."[30] The index leads past instances to become images, but "the historical index of the images not only says that they belong to a particular time; it says, above all, that they attain to legibility only at a particular time."[31]

The index is itself always 'not yet.' This is not the same as asserting that the index is a timeless being. Rather, it is always not yet a being, and thus not within the flow of either time or history—and neither is it eternal nor is it timeless. The index is a singularity of waiting that points the historical event to its redemption by saying that it can become readable; the index itself is a pure potentiality.

For Benjamin, it is language that is pregnant with the past event, but what determines the event's moment of birth into history is its index. When the index responds to a temporal tension, the event will become recognizable as a dialectical relation: "it is the present that polarizes the event into fore- and after-history."[32] Only then can it begin being dialectically identified as an historical image in now-time. This is Benjamin's reversal of the Hegelian logic. Instead of a dialectical opposition between two moments whose relief (*Aufhebung*) into a third moment marks the progress of history in time, Benjamin opposes the fore- and after-history of an event and relieves that into a dialectical image. Yet, although an event becomes readable only in its 'now of recognizability,' the event has had a previous tendency or desire to manifest itself—determined not by its self-understanding but by the degree to which its index can lead it to "bring the present into a critical state."[33] However, the index is not an impulse towards the event's realization: it remains a pure adamic potentiality for its expression.[34]

Since therefore both the nucleus of time and the index are two purely potential elements that determine the recognizability of the image, we cannot know them. As elements that change our capacity to know,

59

Benjamin suggests that they can only be conceptualized as "splinters that marble a now-time.[35] This model would be consistent with my hypothesis that the time of truth is determined by adamic language and messianic time, and it suggests furthermore that the mode of expression of dialectical materialism is messianic in the sense of being based upon a redemptive judgment. The historian may redeem a past event as an image, but the redemption of all time differentials can only befall the Messiah on Judgment Day.[36] The primary condition for dialectically redeeming an event is to read the tensions of its time differentials, which, when intensified enough, need a shock of arrested thought to unfold as a monad:

> Materialist historiography [...] is based on a constructive principle. Thinking involves not only the movement of thoughts, but their arrest as well. Where thinking suddenly comes to a stop in a constellation saturated with tensions, it gives that constellation a shock, by which thinking is crystallized as a monad. The historical materialist approaches a historical object only where it confronts him as a monad. In this structure he recognizes the sign of a messianic arrest of happening, or (to put it differently) a revolutionary chance in the fight for the oppressed past.[37]

To read what was never written is to read this 'sign of a messianic arrest,' recognizable only in the monadic relation between the historical object and crystallized thought. But how may the materialist historian shock anything by stopping to think? Such a question misunderstands everything: to stop thought is not to quit thinking. The flow of thought may be compared to the flow of the stream of tradition cited earlier. To stop one's thought is not the same as surrendering to some mysterious immediacy: Benjamin suggests that thinking, always within a constellation pregnant with tensions, can halt itself in the seemingly natural flow of time. The arrested thought thus holds or carries an image of that flow, like swirls of turbulence appear after an obstacle in a river. That image is blasted out of historicism's empty time by the monadic relationship between thought and historical object.[38] To think is not only to move forward but also "to brush history against the grain."[39] The birth of such an image is its *Erlösung*, its redemption. It must therefore be stressed that what is to be redeemed are the forces named in adamic language; Benjamin understands the unredeemed past event as a configuration of force:

> The fore- and after-history of a historical phenomenon show up in the phenomenon itself on the strength of its dialectical presentation. [*Die Vor- und Nachgeschichte eines historischen Tatbestandes erscheinen kraft seiner dialektischen Darstellung an ihm selbst.*] What is more: every dialectically presented historical circumstance polarizes itself and becomes a force field in which the confrontation [*Auseinandersetzung*] between its fore-history and after-history is played out. It becomes such a field insofar as the present instant [*Aktualität*] interpenetrates it. And thus the historical evidence [*historische Tatbestand*] polarizes into fore- and after-history always anew, never in the same way. And it does so at a distance from its own existence, in the present instant itself—like a line which, divided according to the Apollonian section, experiences its partition from outside itself.[40]

This passage describes the process that Benjamin calls actualization: "historical materialism which has annihilated within itself the idea of progress,"[41] and translating it from German is not a task to be envied. For one thing, Benjamin does not say "its own existence" in the last sentence, because what elsewhere has been called 'what-has-been,' 'the past event' and here, *der historische Tatbestand*, does not exist in itself. Therefore, what is described in this quotation is the becoming-image of a past event as it comes to exist for the first time. Rather than saying "its own existence" Benjamin simply puts it: "*Und er tut es außerhalb seiner, in der Aktualität selbst.*"[43] The historical evidence (*der historische Tatbestand*) of which he here speaks (or perhaps rather, the historical 'fact' of the adamically named forces) is polarized, not in its own self-presence, but literally "outside its own (instant), in the instant itself." What is worth emphasizing is that when Benjamin splits the being of the historical fact between "its own (instant)"—the virtual instant only grammatically referred to by *seiner*—and "the instant itself"—actually stated with the word *Aktualität*—he effects a bifurcation *in* language that corresponds to a bifurcation between a now-time and its temporal deferral. The deferred experience intrinsic to the word *Aktualität* is then described in the rest of the sentence with the image of the Apollonian section, which becomes something of a messianic *Schlüsselsprache* for Benjamin's philosophy of history. Such a redemptive language marks an infinity other than Proust's remembrance: it points to the forces of the past event itself, always divided as a potential image.[43]

Infinitely Deferred Judgment Day–Transformed and Secularized
Returning to questions posed earlier, we may now ask whether the dialectical "One-Way Street" toward messianic redemption remains the necessary path for a dialectical materialism inspired by Benjamin, or whether we should rather be concerned with trying to find an alternative form of image–if for no other reason than because the stream of our post-modern tradition resembles more a delta or a marshland than a river. A fragment from "Convolute N" in *The Arcades Project* provides a significant clue to how Benjamin's messianism could be read productively in our time: "My thinking is related to theology as blotting pad is related to ink. It is saturated [*vollgesogen*] with it. Were one to go by the blotter, however, nothing of what is written would remain."[44] This analogy is "chiasmically formulated" as Rebecca Comay puts it,[45] meaning that it performs an equation resting on an undetermined third, in this case, "what is written." Like the previously analyzed passage on *Aktualität* expressed a chiasmus between time and language at the heart of Benjamin's materialistic theory, this blotting pad image describes his theory's relation to theology as a chiasmus of finite and infinite writing. Theology has saturated his mystic writing pad with its substance, but only after that substance has been repeatedly shaped into finite letters or traces. Thought, as it were, comes after writing, when the blotter sucks up the wet mirror images of the traces, adding ink trace to ink trace with every actualization of time. However saturated with old dry ink, the blotter is still in use and thus its wet palimpsest configuration is a mutable image of what can be read, quoted, translated, etc. This is Benjamin's virtual text, between the finite and the infinite, of which the latter is illegibly full

of time. Were one to "go by the blotter" and try to decipher the infinite potentiality, one would assume the Messiah's vantage point over history. We would read from God's remembrance, which, as Benjamin recognizes both in "On the Concept of History" and in "The Task of the Translator," we cannot do.[46]

The unredeemable dialectics between an infinite writing (infinite potentiality that does not remain) and its limited preservation in redeemed but finite images (that are actually legible) does not contradict Benjamin's openness in "Berlin Childhood" toward a different future readability. The virtual text constantly changes. To put it negatively: the actual images of Benjamin's childhood—to the extent that they are messianically written and hence redeemed—are only lifted out of history and rendered no longer readable as long as the precondition for a true historian is still to read what was never written. The argument I wish to propose with the blotting pad image is that by not closing the chiasmus between finite and infinite writing, Benjamin tells us that nothing is ever written, that the virtual text is always open, constantly reproduced on the pad without an aura. Benjamin asks of us to learn to read our virtual text, to make readable the constellations appearing when we alter our normal way of thought; read carefully, he suggests that his images may change our readability, not that if we learn his readability his images will yield us the authentic truth of history. However, an index always points a historical fact to its actualization, making that fact no longer quotable in the same way after its redemption. But the time nucleus of Benjamin's images differs from the time nucleus of today, and therefore are our truth potentials different. As a consequence a dialectical image is never properly redeemed in the sense of having returned to its true adamic self. In short, everything I have argued so far comes down to this: the event we may recognize as the 'historical fact' of Benjamin's philosophy (the time differential that releases our time of truth) tells us that the mode of reading produced by our virtual text must be measured against the forces we experience as a moment of danger. A provocative result of this analysis is that the image-structure Benjamin so often refers to as 'the flash' is probably useless to us: it only works critically in relation to a strong current of tradition that forcefully moves forward in a unified direction. Now, for us, that tradition has lost nearly all of its former power.

I have suggested that reading Benjamin today is more like exploring a swamp than damming a stream. This too has its dangers for there are other forces at play in the marshes and it is easy to loose one's way. Images from a bog differ from those in a stream and our thought has to map them rather than trying to stop the flow of time. The following could serve as an exercise: in "One-Way Street" is a fragment that together with the blotting pad might help us begin mapping the image of writing: "If the smoke from the tip of my cigarette and the ink from the nib of my pen flowed with equal ease, I would be in the Arcadia of my writing."[47] Link to this fragment the analogy between ink and theology, and nothing becomes more able to keep a writer from his ideal landscape than theology. For a cartographer of Benjamin's marshlands, the exclusion from Arcadia is conditional for sustaining his philosophy's horizons: understanding that Benjamin's art of criticism would die in Arcadia is the outcome of a secular judgment already implicit in his writings.[48] The theology that kept him from Arcadia was a badly needed resistance, an Other that ensured the happiness of his thought: "the idea of happiness is indissolubly bound up with the idea of redemption,"[49] he proclaimed. For the cartographer today, the dialectical images Benjamin thereby produced put up a more joyful confrontation than theology. Happiness today belongs to mapping the images rather than photographing them, and maps have a different way with historical correspondences: a map of all citations would still not amount to Judgment Day. To deconstruct the latter, we could simply consider its dialectical fore- and after-history in terms of a polarization between an always already—a "*weak* messianic power"[50] and an always not yet—the "gateway in time through which the Messiah might enter,"[51] and find in its highest tension the secular notion of now-time that Gilles Deleuze once termed 'Chronos,' the limited, yet infinite time of a living present.[52] Yet, Deleuze's Chronos cannot be represented dialectically: it can emerge from all the dialectics at a standstill, but it cannot be reduced to them. An image of Benjamin's swamp today, based on the temporal nucleus of Chronos, could be found in the movement-images of film or in digital pictures, capable of morphing in cyclic rhythms and in infinite supplementarity. Judgment Day is no longer the final effectuation of a complete, ruinous history; after Benjamin, several scholars have happily redeemed eschatology itself.[53] The dialectics between 'always not yet' and 'always already' ends dialectical teleology and in its stead puts an unrepresentable multitude of cycles: an "eternal return as the return of the Same," as Deleuze puts it in *The Logic of Sense*, with the same reference to Nietzsche that Benjamin also often used, albeit in tense relation to Blanqui's *L'éternité par les astres*.[54] Today, the notion of a virtual singularity has maintained its Nietzschean conceptualization of force relations most notably in the reception of Michel Foucault, but as his historical formations are not dialectical images but statements and tableaux, to those belong a different conceptualization of thought: rather than a messianic arrest, thought is pure life.[55] Compared to photographs, digital images are, as Catherine Waldby has pointed out, remarkably alive.[56] They do not circumscribe the unliving, the mourned or the mortified as photographs have always done—instead, they affirm vitality and the joyful intoxication of a constant alterability.

When the index and the temporal nucleus of Benjamin's philosophy resurface in Foucault and Deleuze's writings as historically mutable singularities, we do not care to ask what Benjamin really meant or what we can deduce from his writings; we care instead about investigating our force fields, and the 'secret index' in his language produces a historical backdrop against which they can become legible and visible. Benjamin's lesson to us is to keep our eyes on the changing capacities of our virtual language and, as Foucault has added, on the changing capacities of our bodies.

Potentialities of the Clone
The map over Benjamin's marshlands shows a virtual plane of matter and function; it is what Deleuze and Félix Guattari call an abstract machine.[57] In his book *Foucault*, Deleuze explains this concept in more

65

detail: "It is an almost mute and blind machine, even if it is what makes us see and what makes us speak;" "the diagram, or the abstract machine is a map of force relations, a map of density, of intensity [...]." "If its effects actualize, it is because the relations of forces, or of power, are nothing but virtualities, potentialities, unstable, evanescent, molecular and defined only by possibilities, the probability of interaction [...]."[58] A potential intensity declares what can be done: in Benjamin's terms, recognizability declares the limits of recognition; readabilty declares the limits of reading, and reproducibility declares the limits of reproduction.

Today's recognizability of what Benjamin called the disintegration of aura makes it appear with different kind of reproducibility: something I choose to call 'cloning.' In a textbook on genetics, Benjamin Lewin defines cloning in terms of what it can do: "Cloning a fragment of DNA allows indefinite amounts to be produced from even a singular original molecule. (A clone is defined as a large number of cells or molecules all identical with an ancestral cell or molecule.)"[59] The language of Lewin's definition, with its chiasmic relation between "produced from an original" and "identical with an ancestral," suggests a strong functional affinity between cloning and Benjamin's technical reproducibility. Cathryn Vasseleu has recognized this correspondence:

> The mechanism of reproductive technology, as analysed by Walter Benjamin, can be characterised by its displacement of the "originality" of the unique, and the erasure of the difference between original and reproduction. The intention of a genetic biologism is ultimately the eradication of the unaccountable differences inherent in the reproductive capacity of living beings, and the production of an infinite reiterability of the biological sameness of living things.[60]

It is not only in the biological sense that the term cloning names the technical reproducibility of our times; one may also speak of internet clones like viruses, worms and spam mails, and corporate clones such as brands, trademarks and business format franchises. To compare the reproducibility of these clones with Benjamin's photographic reproducibility, the crucial question is not what clones are but how they proliferate. A comparative analysis of potentialities requires a description of their reproductive processes in order to identify the most creative difference.

If the technical reproducibility of photography does away with the original, it is only because it forms generations with hordes of siblings. ("To ask for the 'authentic' *print* makes no sense." [Emphasis added.]) Photographic negatives age and successive generations of prints from the same aging negative may actually differ. As historical objects, photographs have a certain patina and as commodities their wear-and-tear partially determines their market value. It is important to realize that not only reproducibility, but also material preservability determine the photograph's historical exhibition value—a claim to which art photography's dramatically increased exchange value lends sufficient support.[61]

The photographic process may easily be understood idealistically (as in the Monglond quatation), that is, as a process whereby a purely informal idea (the world as it is) mediates itself through light and shapes the unstable matter of the chemical emulsion into an analogical imprint. The morphogenetic processes of biological reproduction can hardly be explained in similar terms. As Howard Pattee and Stuart Kaufmann have suggested, the processes of cell reproduction in eukaryotic organisms require a different distinction between materiality and form.[62] To explain this we notice that the language code of DNA determines both its own auto-reproduction and the reproduction of the body's proteins (via RNA). Hence DNA information relates to two irreducibly different materials: its own base pairs and external amino acids. But since DNA functions as a dynamic matrix for the morphogenetic processes that determine the production of both itself and of proteins, genetic information cannot be understood as an ideal or abstract entity that is mediated in chemical materiality for its form's preservation. As genetic information is inseparable from matter and processuality, the traditional notion of inert matter formed to sustain abstract information is not very helpful.

Critics of so-called hylomorphic information theories (e.g., Gilbert Simondon, N. Katherine Hayles or Ilya Prigogine) have abandoned the

67

traditional opposition between active form and inert matter and suggest, conversely, that matter spontaneously generates and regulates morphogenetic processes from a complexity of variables intrinsic to itself.[63] Matter is considered a potentiality in the sense that it harbors the force fields that determine these morphogenetic processes. When this model is applied to the biological processes of sexual reproduction, the notion of a necessary genetic threshold between generations disappears. This seems an extremely productive tension between cloning and photographic reproducibility. That the generation, as a concept, loses its self-evidential naturalness is indeed something that affects the question of morphogenesis. (Jacques Derrida would say: "who is the mother?"[64]) But how should this be understood? Basic genetics teaches us, that as an instruction key for both auto-reproduction and reproduction of RNA strands that will determine the production of protein chains, DNA sequences (like genes or chromosomes) reproduce themselves by splitting up lengthwise and copying their order of base molecules. But since the readability of the DNA is lodged in the code itself (e.g. in codes for where to begin and end, when to open the helix and when to cut), reading must be understood differently than a dialectical process: it involves replication, transcription and translation of the code's materiality.[65] To put it brief-ly, DNA reproduces by spontaneously executing its own morphogenetic processes: matter produces form by reading itself.

The total genome of an organism is the DNA that is present and identical in each cell nucleus (except in the organism's reproductive cells). The information it carries is not preserved anywhere in some original, archived DNA string from which all the others are copied. Likewise, during normal mitotic cell reproduction the individual configuration of base pairs in the double helix does not preserve itself in a durable substance, but is instead preserved by its own morphogenetic process, in its act of replication. DNA subsists in the act of being read; it lives as long as it reads itself. But a specific kind of reading produces reproduction cells. Through what is called a meiotic cell reduction and division, chromosomes of a haploid reproduction cell are made genetically open for fertilization, that is, capable of merging with a set of chromosomes from a foreign reproduction cell. This process of meiosis consists of several reading phases that in the end serve to grant enough genetic variation in the offspring—and to ensure that its genome is irreducible to the configuration of its parent's chromosomes. We still do not know exactly what it is that makes a fertilized egg cell begin reading itself, although it seems clear that at no point is there an abstract piece of information that sustains itself in ideal form.

When cloning an organism like the sheep Dolly, biologists take advantage of the fact that DNA subsists through auto-reproduction. Instead of a spontaneous coupling of two reproduction cells from two individuals, scientists take out a 'sleeping' cell nucleus from a starved, quiescent donor cell and insert it into an enucleated oocyte taken from a different organism. Placed inside the womb of a surrogate mother, the embryo may, if conditions are right, grow into a clone. If successful, the cell nucleus donor is then simultaneously a parent and an identical twin to the clone. In order for this to be conceptually possible science must conceive of genetic information as a language whose reading is rather a material process of reproduction than a dialectical production of meaning. Deleuze calls this a production of sense, and to it belongs a politics of strength that is not motivated by a dialectical response to danger. In one of the very rare passages where Deleuze argues normatively, he identifies as a pressing political task that of producing sense:

> It is thus pleasing that there resounds today the news that sense is never a principle or an origin, but that it is produced. It is not something to discover, to restore, and to re-employ; it is something to produce by a new machinery. [...] It suffices that we dissipate ourselves a little, that we be able to be at the surface, that we stretch our skin like a drum, in order that the 'great politics' begin. An empty square for neither man nor God; singularities which are neither general nor individual, neither personal nor universal. All of this is traversed by circulations, echoes, and events which produce more sense, more freedom, and more strength than man has ever dreamed of or God ever conceived. Today's task is to make the empty square

69

circulate and to make preindividual and nonpersonal singularities speak—in short, to produce sense.[66]

Comparing this call for political action with the one quoted from Benjamin at the beginning, we find a number of discrepancies. Rather than responding to a moment of danger, Deleuze emphasizes the good news; rather than returning to history we ought to change our bodies and minds; here with Deleuze we must not recognize anything, understand this or that, or even take action or arms against an enemy as long as we manage to circulate the 'empty square' and make the singularities speak.

Although cloning is nothing new, and the world has probably seen reproduction by cloning since before sexual reproduction evolved on the planet, the technology that enables stem cell research, designed life and genetic forensics has opened a Deleuzean empty square. If there is any danger in that for us humans, it is that this square is too wide, that it lets too many "unbounded singularities" in at once.[67] But what is a danger for some is an opportunity for someone else, wherefore the production of sense is always good, only we cannot know in advance for whom.[68] What is bad, on the other hand, is to regulate the singularities according to an individual's present needs. Hence, stem cell research must be a good thing but to patent a genetic sequence is most certainly not. Deleuze's great politics is not Marxist or leftist or even ideological; it is a politics that want to expand the limits of what the world's bodies and minds can do. To the extent that Benjamin's philosophy suggests a Deleuzean reading today, not in spite of their differencies, but because of them, a good reading of Benjamin must be more faithful to his philosophy's desire to become different from itself than to his instructions about how this transformation should come about.

Conclusion
While the dramatic increase in technical reproducability was for Benjamin a power with which to challenge the orders of authencity and originality, cloning involves a quite different way to unsettle the politics of

70

reproduction. To the extent that the stream of tradition has become a marsh or a desert,[69] cloning does not inherit the battle over originality or authenticity. Cloning is busy fighting other struggles—often tied to rights of use—which is at least one reason why the concept of aura is no longer equally critical and certainly not immediately re-actualizable.

Today's redundancy of the concept of aura in Benjamin's sense is a direct consequence of an altered time structure. The time differentials that Benjamin so masterfully actualized with his 'dialectics at a standstill' produce today a theory of nesting time cycles—what Deleuze, in *The Logic of Sense* and elsewhere, termed Chronos. As I have tried to show, this change does not imply a turning away from Benjamin; it is a way to improve reading him, knowing that the messianism of his dialectical historiography has its own transmutation of readability 'coded' in itself. Intrinsic to its logic is that dialectics has to transform whenever it becomes capable of expressing its own potential fulfillment. The force field of Benjamin's dialectical materialism has changed: no longer does it support individual cycles of deferred recognizability—today it enables a dynamic and mutable entrainment of functional cycles, and their rhythmic relations provide a new composition of now-times. As entrained temporal cycles, a new kind of time-scale can be measured from the increases and decreases of a body's changing rhythms. In *Intensive Science and Virtual Philosophy*, Manuel DeLanda has suggested that this dynamic polyrhythmics of time oscillations may itself be responsible for a morphogenetic process: "if embryonic development occurs in parallel, if bundles of relatively independent processes occur simultaneously, then *new designs may arise from disengaging bundles*, or more precisely, from altering the duration of one process relative to another, or the relative timing of a start or end of a process. This evolutionary design strategy is known as *heterochrony*."[73] It is with concepts like these that Benjamin's most profound analyses of technology, art and social formations can become readable for a powerful historical materialism that faces the challenges of global economies, digital communications and political hegemony.

71

Notes

1   André Monglond, *Le Préromantisme français* (Grenoble: Editions B. Arthaud, 1930), vol 1, quoted in Walter Benjamin, AP, 482 [N15a,1], and, in a slightly different English translation, "Paralipomena to 'On the Concept of History'," in SW 4, 405.

2   "To write history thus means to *cite* history. It belongs to the concept of citation, however, that the historical object in each case is torn from its context." Benjamin, AP, 476 [N11,3].

3   Benjamin, "Paralipomena," in SW 4, 405. For an extensive comment on this quotation, see the "Editor's Introduction" in Giorgio Agamben, *Potentialities*, ed. Daniel Heller-Roazen (Stanford: Stanford University Press, 1999), 1. See also Agamben's chapter "Benjamin and the Demonic" in the same volume, especially 158.

4   Benjamin, "On the Concept of History," in SW 4, 391.

5   See Agamben, "Time and History: Critique of the Instant and the Continuum," in *Infancy and History: Essays on the Destruction of Experience* (London: Verso, 1993).

6   Benjamin, AP, 463 [N3,2].

7   "In what follows, the concepts which are introduced into the theory of art differ from those now current in that they are completely useless for the purposes of fascism." Benjamin, "The Work of Art in the Age of its Technical Reproducibility (Second Version)," in SW 3, 102. Emphasis removed.

8   Perhaps Paul Virilio is the one who has expressed this risk in the most convincing way: "I personally fear we are being confronted by a sort of pathology of immediate perception that owes everything, or very nearly everything, to the recent proliferation of photo-cinematographic and video-infographic *seeing machines*. Machines that by mediatizing ordinary everyday representations end up destroying their credibility." Paul Virilio, *Open Sky* (London and New York: Verso, 1997), 90.

9   Benjamin, "The Work of Art," in SW 3, 106. Emphasis removed.

10   Ibid., 103. These passages are identical in all three German versions of the essay.

11   For recent anthologies dedicated to the present readability of aura, see *Benjamin's Blind Spot: Walter Benjamin and the Premature Death of Aura*, ed. Lise Patt (Topanga: The Institute of Critical Inquiry, 2001); *Mapping Benjamin: The Work of Art in The Digital Age*, eds. Hans Ulrich Gumbrecht and Michael Marrinan (Stanford: Stanford University Press, 2003).

12   Benjamin, "Berlin Childhood Around 1900," in SW 3, 344.

13   Benjamin, "Addenda to 'The Paris of the Second Empire in Baudelaire'," in SW 4, 63–64.

14   Benjamin, AP, 456 [N1,2].

15   Ibid., 463 [N3,2].

16 Ibid., 463 [N3,1].
17 Ibid.
18 Ibid., 476 [N11,5].
19 Benjamin, "On the Image of Proust," in SW 2, 244.
20 Ibid., 238.
21 Ibid., 244.
22 I refer to the stocking-game image that appears both in "Childhood in Berlin" and in "On the Image of Proust." Specifically, what I want to highlight is the relation in German between, on the one hand, the key and the cabinet in the fragment "*Schränke*" from the first version of "Berliner Kindheit" (rewritten and retitled in the later version as "*Der Strumpf*"), and on the other hand the notion of a language key unlocking images of *verschränkte Zeit* in the essay on Proust. See GS IV, 283–87 and VII, 416–17.
23 Benjamin, "On the Image of Proust," in SW 2, 242.
24 Benjamin, AP, 864 [O°,78].
25 Benjamin, "On the Image of Proust," in SW 2, 242.
26 Benjamin, "On the Concept of History," in SW 4, 396.
27 Benjamin, AP, 867 <Q°,21>.
28 Ibid., 456 [N1,2].
29 Benjamin, "On the Concept of History," in SW 4, 391–92.
30 Ibid., 390.
31 Benjamin, AP, 462 [N3,1].
32 Ibid., 471 [N7a,8].
33 Ibid., 471 [N7a, 5].
34 The event's desire to be actualized, and the now that polarizes the fore- and after-history of the event are two moments that dialectically determine each other. This demands a means of expression that Benjamin terms adamic: it names the historical tension within the dialectical relation, but does not sublate it. In "On Language as Such and On the Language of Man" in SW 1, 62-74, adamic language manifests itself as pure naming. Mimesis is the language form that releases the tension named by adamic language. Its object is to actualize the dialectical tension in a now. The materialist appropriates a messianic language of judgment in order to redeem the event as an image. See also the fragment "Antithesis Concerning Word and Name" in SW 2, 717–19.
35 Benjamin, "On the Concept of History," in SW 4, 397
36 Ibid. 390. For an analysis of the political force in Benjamin's notion of the messianic, see Giorgio Agamben "Benjamin and the Demonic," especially 151-54.
37 Benjamin, "On the Concept of History," in SW 4, 396. A fragment in *The Arcades Project* explicates the historical moment of recognition from a dialectically opposite

73

point of view–the object's own monadic structure; see AP 475 [N10,3].

[38] Note that the crystallization of the monad does not precede the encounter in any temporal or causal manner. Materialist reading is not interpretation–it is construction, or montage. See AP, 458, [N1,10].

[39] Benjamin, "On the Concept of History," in SW 4, 392.

[40] Benjamin, AP, 470, [N7a,1]; *Das Passagen-Werk*, in GS V, 587–88 [N7a,1]. This quote may be compared to a passage from the Proust essay: "It took Proust to make the nineteenth century ripe for memories. What before him had been a period devoid of tension now became a force field in which later writers aroused multifarious currents." Benjamin, "On the Image of Proust," in SW 2, 240.

[41] Benjamin, AP, 460 [N2,2].

[42] Benjamin, *Das Passagen-Werk*, in GS V, 587–88 [N7a,1].

[43] This reading may help explain another enigmatic fragment from Convolute N: "What are phenomena rescued from? Not only, and not in the main, from the discredit and neglect into which they have fallen, but from the catastrophe represented very often by a certain strain in their dissemination, their 'enshrinement as heritage.'–They are saved through the exhibition of the fissure within them.– There is a tradition that is catastrophe." Benjamin, AP, 473 [N9,4].

[44] Benjamin, AP, 471 [N7a,7].

[45] Rebecca Comay, "Benjamin's Endgame," in *Walter Benjamin's Philosophy: Destruction and Experience*, eds. Andrew Benjamin and Peter Osborne (London and New York: Routledge, 1994), 247.

[46] Benjamin, "The Task of the Translator" in SW 1, 254.

[47] Benjamin, "One-Way Street," in SW 1, 463.

[48] In the "Theological-Political Fragment," we find this index actualized: "Only the Messiah himself completes all history, in the sense that he alone redeems, completes, creates its relation to the messianic. For this reason, nothing that is historical can relate itself, from its own ground, to anything messianic. Therefore, the Kingdom of God is not the telos of the historical dynamic; it cannot be established as a goal. From the standpoint of history, it is not the goal but the terminus [*Ende*]. Therefore, the secular order cannot be built on the idea of the Divine Kingdom, and theocracy has no political but only a religious meaning. [...] The secular order should be erected on the idea of happiness. The relation of this order to the messianic is one of the essential teachings of the philosophy of history." SW 3, 305.

[49] Benjamin, "On the Concept of History," in SW 4, 389.

[50] Ibid., 390.

[51] Ibid., 397.

[52] "We have seen that past, present, and future were not at all three parts of a single temporality, but that they rather formed two readings of time, each one of which

is complete and excludes the other: on one hand, the always limited present, which measures the action of bodies as causes and the state of their mixtures in depth (Chronos); on the other, the essentially unlimited past and future, which gather incorporeal events, at the surface, as effects (Aion). [...] Thus the time of the present is always a limited but infinite time; infinite because cyclical, animating a physical eternal return as the return of the Same, and a moral eternal wisdom as the wisdom of the Cause. *Sometimes, on the other hand,* it will be said that only the past and future subsist, that they subdivide each present, ad infinitum, however small it may be, stretching it out over their empty line." Gilles Deleuze, *The Logic of Sense,* (London: Athlone Press, 1990), 61–62.

53 See Jacques Derrida, "On a Newly Arisen Apocalyptic Tone In Philosophy" in *Raising the Tone of Philosophy,* ed. Peter Fenves, (Baltimore: Johns Hopkins University Press, 1999); Jacques Derrida, *Acts of Religion,* ed. Gil Anidjar (New York: Routledge, 2002); Henry Sussman, "The Afterlife of Judaism: From the Book of Splendor to Benjamin's Shooting Stars" in this volume.

54 For Deleuze's quotation of Nietzsche, see *The Logic of Sense,* 61. For a reference to Benjamin about the theological meaning of Blanqui's eternal return in relation to Nietzsche, see his letter to Horkheimer, January 6, 1938, in Corr., 549.

55 I lean heavily here on Gilles Deleuze's analysis in *Foucault* (Paris: Les Editions de Minuit, 1986). See also Agamben, "Absolute Immanence" in *Potentialities.*

56 Catherine Waldby, *The Visible Human Project: Informatic Bodies and Posthuman Medicine* (London: Routledge, 2000). See especially the chapter "Iatrogenesis, Digital Eden and the Reproduction of Life."

57 "An abstract machine in itself is not physical or corporeal, any more than it is semiotic [...]. It operates by matter, not by substance; by function, not by form." Gilles Deleuze and Félix Guattari, *A Thousand Plateaus: Capitalism and Schizophrenia,* (London: Athlone Press, 1992), 141.

58 Deleuze, *Foucault,* 42, 44, 45. My translation.

59 Benjamin Lewin, *Genes V* (Oxford: Oxford University Press, 1994), 633.

60 Cathryn Vasseleu, "Parent Pending: Laws of Invention, Animal Life Forms and Bodies as Ideas," in *Thinking Through the Body of the Law,* ed. P. Cheah et al. (Sydney: Allen and Unwin, 1996), 115. Quoted in Waldby, *The Visible Human Project,* 133.

61 Benjamin's more explicit revolutionary hopes and expectations for photography must be said to have been overstated, not least when he mused: "it would not be surprising if the photographic methods which today, for the first time, are harking back to the preindustrial heyday of photography had an underground connection with the crisis of capitalist industry." Benjamin, "Little History of Photography," in SW 2, 507.

75

[62] See Howard H. Pattee, "Instabilities and Information in Biological Self-Organization," in *Self-Organizing Systems: The Emergence of Order*, ed. F. Eugene Yates (New York: Plenum Press, 1987); Stuart Kaufmann, *The Origins of Order: Self-Organization and Selection in Evolution* (Oxford: Oxford University Press, 1993). Philosophically this distinction is perhaps most clearly formulated by Deleuze in his book on Foucault as a relation between the diagrams of power and the archives of knowledge: "Knowledge concerns formed matters (substances) and formalized functions, divided up segment by segment according to the two great formal conditions of seeing and speaking, light and language: it is therefore stratified, archivized, and endowed with a relatively rigid segmentarity. Power, on the other hand, is diagrammatic: it mobilizes non-stratified matter and functions, and unfolds with a very flexible segmentarity." Gilles Deleuze, *Foucault* (London: Athlone Press, 1988), 73.

[63] For a relevant critique of hylomorphism in digital technology, quite different from the one forwarded here, see Adrian MacKenzie, *Transductions: Bodies and Machines at Speed* (London: Continuum, 2002), especially 29–56.

[64] In fact, Derrida did say so at a conference on *Glas* in Denmark 2001. See the publication from the seminar, *Glossing Glas*, eds. Roy Sellars and Per Krogh Hansen, forthcoming from University of Nebraska Press.

[65] Lewin, *Genes V*, 164.

[66] Gilles Deleuze, *The Logic of Sense*, 72–73.

[67] Deleuze, *Foucault*, 130.

[68] See Manuel DeLanda, *A Thousand Years of Nonlinear History* (New York: Zone Books, 2000), 131.

[69] Deleuze and Guattari, *A Thousand Plateaus*, 351–423.

[70] Manuel DeLanda, *Intensive Science and Virtual Philosophy* (Continuum: New York, 2002), 97.

The Aura in Photography and the Task of the Historian

Catherine D. Dhavernas

In his discussion of the early stages of photography, Walter Benjamin identifies a time, difficult to imagine today, when "photography had not yet become a journalistic tool" and thus was not a given of everyday life.[1] He draws our attention to an epoch for which the photograph remained something foreign—a time quite distinct from the image-based reality of today, where images can at times be said to be livelier than people. Given this, it would seem that a reversal in the traditionally derivative relation between reality and image has occurred, such that life, no longer the fundamental premise of reality, has rather become merely a gradated quality of reality. If such is indeed the case, what then should we understand to be the status of the reality of images which, as many have claimed, determine our contemporary world? What then should we understand to be our relation to these images?

Turning to Benjamin, the present investigation will seek to account for the genesis of our current image-world through his discussion of the progressive disappearance of the aura in the context of the photographic image. It will also approach the aura in relation to a broader realm, namely that pertaining to the task of the historian. In this latter case, turning to the work of Marguerite Duras, we will explore how the aura of the past, demanding to be acknowledged in the present, emerges as a compulsion to write, as a potential which, while perhaps unattainable, compels us, as Benjamin has suggested, to find "the inconspicuous spot where in the immediacy of that long-forgotten moment the future nests so eloquently that we, looking back, may rediscover it."[2]

The Early Stages of Portrait Photography

In addressing what Benjamin meant by aura in relation to photography, we must first consider that past where reality and photography had not yet become indissociably linked, when our experience of reality was not yet predetermined by the world of images.[3] At the time, photography was not part of common everyday experience; images were not in full mass circulation. Certainly, the first individuals to be photographed, Benjamin writes, "entered the visual space of photography with their innocence intact—or rather, without inscription. Newspapers," he notes, "were still a luxury item, which people seldom bought, preferring to consult them in the coffeehouse."[4] Being photographed or even seeing a photograph, was an experience limited to a small minority, something exceptional rather than commonplace. "In short," Benjamin summarizes, "the portraiture of this period owes its effect to the absence of contact between contemporary relevance and portraiture."[5]

At the time of which he speaks, photography was seen to present a magical phenomenon, "a great secret experience" quite different from the micro-version of death seen by many to characterize much of portrait photography today. Whereas present-day photographers are all too aware of the death in which, as Roland Barthes notes in *Camera Lucida*, their gesture will embalm the sitter,[6] Benjamin takes us back to a time when the photographer is said to have shied away from the people he photographed, believing that "the little tiny faces in the picture could see [him]."[7] Thus, for the early photographer, photography's potential far exceeded his own as technician. It was not, as often today, associated with death but rather seen to offer a means for the mysterious capture of life.

Early Photography and the Aura

What then, might we ask, could have prompted this radical inversion? Focusing on the early stages of portrait photography, Benjamin outlines how, in its initial phase, because of the nature of the early apparatus and technique (something eradicated through later 'advances' in technology), the closely intertwined and interdependent elements of time and space in effect conveyed an aura upon its very process. Here photography involved a fragile process of craft which depended on the photographer's punctual adjustments to uncontrollable, yet determinant, conditions of light. Benjamin explains how "the low light-sensitivity of the early plates made prolonged exposure outdoors a necessity."[8] This meant that the model had to remain still for extended lengths of time while the photographer simultaneously worked to fine-tune the image-to-be. Benjamin, drawn by perceptible evidence of early photography's tentative and delicate procedure, notes how, in the work of David Octavius Hill, "light struggles its way out of darkness."[9]

It is as a result of these conditions, which have radically changed, that the very process of early portrait photography can be said to have had an auratic quality which has since disappeared. Let us reiterate Benjamin's now widespread and well-known description of "what is aura:"

> What is aura, actually? A strange weave of space and time: the unique appearance or semblance of a distance, no matter how close it may be. While at rest on a summer's noon, to trace a range of mountains on the horizon, or a branch that throws its shadow on the observer, until the moment or the hour become part of their appearance–this is what it means to breathe the aura of those mountains, that branch.[10]

The photographic image, resulting from the process of long exposure, can be seen to involve a 'coparticipation' of disparate entities parallel to that found in Benjamin's description above, in which each entity speaks to the specific configuration of a precise moment, that is, of its aura. In other words, the process of early photography was oriented toward a progressively circumscribed moment in time and space, in which photographer, model, light and setting each played an integral part. "Everything about these early pictures was built to last," Benjamin stresses, "the very creases in people's garments have an air of permanence. Just consider Schelling's coat. It will surely pass into immortality along with him: the shape it has borrowed from its wearer is not unworthy of the creases in his face."[11] Furthermore, "the procedure itself," he writes, "caused the subject to *focus his life in the moment* rather than hurrying past it; during the considerable period of the exposure, the subject (as it were) grew into the picture."[12] "The aura," he specifies, "was by no means the mere product of a primitive camera. Rather, in this early period, subject and technique were as exactly congruent as they became incongruent in the period of decline that immediately followed."[13] Hence, the aura at that early stage stemmed from the simultaneous coexistence and co-penetration of those separate entities which came to be momentarily and reciprocally entwined as they entered that punctual realm of a specific "here and now" captured by the stilled image.

Photography's Decline

Having touched on the auratic which Benjamin attributes to the actual process of early photography, I would at this point like to turn to its subsequent period of decline. My objective will be to identify changes that emerged in later portraiture and to discuss their impact on the photographic aura.

In outlining the conditions of early portraiture in which photographer, sitter, light and setting were intimately interconnected, Benjamin draws particular attention to the fact that the sitter, commonly propped up to facilitate the long duration of the pose, seems to belong within the photograph's setting. As a means of illustrating this, Benjamin poetically refers to a series of portraits by the photographer Hill taken at the Edinburgh cemetery of Greyfriars, taking particular notice of "the way his subjects were at home there."[14]

This characterization in which models were seen to belong in their surroundings is brought into dramatic contrast in Benjamin's discussion of later portraiture. Indeed in this latter period, transposed into the staged and hostile environment of the photographer's studio, with its "draperies and palm trees, their tapestries and easels," the sitter suddenly appears utterly estranged:

[T]he boy stands, perhaps six years old, dressed up in a humiliating tight child's suit overloaded with trimming, in a sort of greenhouse landscape. The background is thick with palm fronds. And as if to make these upholstered tropics even stuffier and more oppressive, the subject holds in his left hand an inordinately large broad-brimmed hat, such as Spaniards wear.[15]

The boy described is a young Franz Kafka, seen here by Benjamin to testify to the emergence not only of a new era within photography's history, but of a new world: a world which, as I argue below, like photography, speaks of transience and artifice.

For Benjamin, in the early phase of photography, the sitter was naturally integrated into the image's setting, a setting which, he specifies, assumed the configuration of the interior of a home:

The cemetery itself [...] looks like an interior, a separate closed-off space where the gravestones propped against gable walls rise up from the grass, [...] with inscriptions inside instead of flames.[16]

Whether indoors or out, the sitter felt 'at home' as a result of the natural outcome of the long exposure required by the photographic process at the time. "But this setting could never have been so effective," Benjamin confirms, "if it had not been chosen on technical grounds." Indeed the model needed to be taken "to some out-of-the-way spot where there was no obstacle to quiet concentration."[17] Whereas the photographer was initially the one to adapt to the conditions in which the sitter came to feel 'at home,' in later portrait photography it would be up to the sitter to adjust to the artificial conditions of the studio which now furnished the setting of portraiture. Here, simulated backdrops and alien objects emerged, thus exposing the sitter to a constructed world of props. Again it is in the portrait of Kafka that this is most evident for Benjamin:

He [Kafka] would surely be lost in this setting were it not for his immensely sad eyes, which dominate this landscape predestined for them.[18]

81

Benjamin's reading of this portrait reveals two worlds at odds, forced to collide with each other through such staging. As has aptly been pointed out by Eduardo Cadava, there are revealing parallels between Benjamin's description of Kafka and aspects of his own childhood experience.[19] Of particular interest for us however is Benjamin's insight in pointing to a broader realm which extends well beyond the personal significance of the photograph. Indeed the nostalgia signaled by the boy's "immensely sad eyes" emerges both as a specific marker of subjective experience while also signaling a more generalized historical phenomenon: namely that suggested earlier of the transition to the image world.

If this portrait is said to testify to "infinite sadness," it is because the boy has been transplanted into a world having no common measure with his own. Thus what can retrospectively be seen is the symptomatic, isolated impact of a phenomenon that was to bring about a determining shift in human experience. Indeed, as we shall see, the initial impact perceived in the portrait of Kafka would eventually come to subside as the conventions of photography would be integrated into the so-called normal course of everyday life and, perhaps more importantly, as estrangement would become the normal condition of modern life.

It is necessarily difficult for us today to grasp how the routine and apparently benign conditions of photography could be, or have been, the symptomatic site of a profoundly determinant shift in our perspective on the world. Benjamin's efforts to restore the conditions of early photography in relation to their auratic quality are therefore essential in this regard.

As suggested, the Kafka portrait is seen to capture a privileged moment which speaks to the impact of the historical development of photography on human experience, that of the loss of aura. In order to try to understand the specific impact revealed by this portrait, I would like to return to photography's early period to gain a better understanding of what it might have meant to be 'at home' in one's surroundings, then, and what being at home has come to signify today.

The Subject and the World of Objects

In *Mythologies*, Roland Barthes recalls how ordinary objects such as toys, which nowadays "die very quickly," were once made to last, to live with the child so to speak.[20] Thus, unlike the transient objects of today, they were made of durable substances such as wood and, through wear and handling, over time came to bear the mark of cohabitation with their owner. As such, objects played a role in determining one's private space. Furthermore, the particular configuration of one's private space can be said to have dictated one's understanding of and relationship to the world. Indeed, inhabiting a space in the past entailed developing a singular relationship with the world of objects over time. Proceeding from the durability of objects, this relationship fostered an empirical understanding of the world as a stable and enduring entity.

Attesting to the singular complicity between individuals and objects, Angela Cozea, in her *La Fidélité aux Choses: pour une perspective benjaminienne*, explores the significance of objects "as fragments of truth," as material traces of the "passage of time," through which one may retrospectively encounter, and for the first time experience, unexperienced moments of one's own past. As such, she argues, objects also have the potential to speak of individuals in their absence.[21]

If objects speak of those who have lived in close proximity to them, it is from having loyally accompanied them on their trajectory through time. As such, familiar objects which have been invested with one's daily existence have the reassuring effect of an enduring kinship, while also attesting to the fact of the dependability and stability of the elements constituting one's world. We are reminded here of Benjamin's description of garments whose folds parallel those of the wearer's face. Relating to this, Benjamin, referring to a portrait of Schopenhauer seen receding into the depths of an armchair, points out how Schopenhauer belonged to a "generation that was not obsessed with going down to posterity in photographs," and which rather shyly drew back "into their private space in the face of such proceedings."[22] More than an arbitrary or interchangeable prop, the object here serves to ensure the permanence of the

83

sitter's private living space through its reassuring presence. Despite the intrusion of the photographic procedure, the familiar armchair thus functions as a refuge, allowing the sitter to maintain an enduring relation with his own world; something to which we are witness today still, since, as Benjamin points out, unlike nowadays, people then "allowed that space, the space in which they lived, to get onto the plate with them."[23]

The situation described here is quite different from that witnessed in the portrait of Kafka in which the presence of familiar objects has been altogether denied. Unlike Schopenhauer, who is able to withdraw into known surroundings, the boy as Benjamin describes him is seen transposed into a simulated world, dissociated from any prior form of living space. There is no potential for refuge, that is, no evidence of the familiar, reliable and reassuring quality of things. Props, clothing, pose and backdrop are artificially imposed to produce a temporary setting whose sole function is that of staging the photograph.

As outlined earlier, our objective in alluding to this portrait is to discuss its significance beyond the punctual experience of the young boy as symptom of a broader social phenomenon. In keeping with this goal, let us return to Benjamin: in early photographs "people did not yet look out at the world in so excluded and godforsaken a manner as this boy."[24] Set in contrast to that of "people" of an earlier generation, Kafka's experience of photography here stands to exemplify the generation to follow. In this way, the specific "here" of the portrait (the hostile environment of the studio) speaks for the general by taking on the proportions of the "world" of daily existence. While signaling the disorienting impact of the new conventions of photography within the circumscribed space of the portrait studio, the portrait can be seen to prefigure an epistemological shift in our perspective on the world which Benjamin addresses in "The Storyteller:"

> Every glance at a newspaper shows [...] that our image not only of the external world but also of the moral world has undergone changes overnight, changes which were previously thought impossible.[25]

Further probing the consequences of technology for modern-day existence, Benjamin, in "On Some Motifs in Baudelaire," notably points out how man suddenly found himself increasingly unable to assimilate the data of the world around him by way of experience, thereby closely echoing his description of a young Kafka overwhelmed by his surroundings.[26] The impact initially signaled in the context of photography is hence seen to extend to the more generalized sphere of modern-day experience, and is perhaps best illustrated in the following example, also from "The Storyteller," in which Benjamin notes the troubling case of soldiers who participated in the First World War:

> A generation that had gone to school on horse-drawn streetcars now stood under the open sky in a landscape where nothing remained unchanged but the clouds and, beneath those clouds, in a force field of destructive torrents and explosions, the tiny, fragile human body.[27]

It is not surprising that Benjamin should further point out that these soldiers returned from battle with no stories to tell. In a parallel way to Kafka's encounter with the photographic studio, though in admittedly rather more extreme circumstances, these men found themselves transplanted into a world which was incommensurable with their own, and were hence utterly disoriented and muted by shock. As a result of this, the events of the war remained inassimilable to them, which is to say, beyond the reach of experience.

Shock and the Modern World

Whereas the example of war may present an exceptional case, Benjamin considers the impact of shock to have progressively established itself as the norm of modern-day existence. "Beginning with the First World War," he explains, "a process became apparent which continues to this day."[28] Indeed, in "On Some Motifs in Baudelaire," Benjamin, elaborating on his diagnosis, situates shock at the basis of modern-day experience and identifies "the emancipation from isolated experiences"[29] as its consequence. Seeking to shed light on this phenomenon, Benjamin turns to

Marcel Proust's "attempt to produce experience [...] in a synthetic way."[30] Drawing from Proust's *Remembrance of Things Past*,[31] Benjamin thus works to outline the difference between voluntary and involuntary memory, explaining how voluntary memory is able to recall information about the past at will without however retaining any trace of it. Involuntary memory, on the other hand, which, unlike voluntary memory, does not respond to efforts of the intellect to conjure up the past, is that through which traces of the past do in fact have the potential to emerge. Whereas voluntary memory can be called upon at will, involuntary memory is triggered by chance encounters with an object through which a sensation associated with it is activated. As a means of addressing the modern experience of shock, Benjamin establishes a parallel between Proust and Sigmund Freud who saw "'becoming conscious and leaving behind a memory trace [to be] incompatible processes with each other within one and the same system.'"[32] According to Freud, the traumatic moment or event has a more profound and lasting impact because traces of the event never reached consciousness at the time of its initial occurrence.[33] Putting things back into Proustian terms, Benjamin specifies "that only what has not been experienced explicitly and consciously, what has not happened to the subject as an experience, can become a component of the *mémoire involontaire*."[34]

Following from this, if we go back to our original context, the 'event' as shock encounter which, in both the case of Kafka and that of soldiers returning from war, is precluded from being assimilated, would thus have the potential to become a component of involuntary memory. However, whether or not it is to be experienced rests on chance, for, as Benjamin citing Proust explains, it dwells "'somewhere beyond the reach of the intellect and its field of operations, in some material object..., though we have no idea which one it is.'"[35] We therefore have no way of knowing if we will ever encounter it. And it is here, at what he considers to be the heart of modern experience, that Baudelaire's poetic enterprise can be said to intervene:

Baudelaire [...] speaks of a duel in which the artist, just before being beaten, screams in fright. This duel is the creative process itself. Thus, Baudelaire placed shock experience [*Chockerfahrung*] at the very center of his art.[36]

Baudelaire's poetry is hence seen to root itself in that which punctually and repeatedly determines the paradoxical fate of modern experience as deferment of experience or, as the above passage suggests, as that which, through efforts of the intellect to cope with shock, might at best be turned into a moment lived as fright. In either case, the event is neither assimilated nor experienced directly. Through Baudelaire's *correspondances* it is brought into association with an unattainable and perished realm. "The important thing," Benjamin explains, "is that *correspondances* encompass a concept of experience which includes ritual elements. Only by appropriating these elements was Baudelaire able to fathom the full meaning of the breakdown which he, as a modern man, was witnessing."[37] Furthermore, as Benjamin tells us, "*Correspondances* are the data of recollection—*not historical data, but data of prehistory.* [...] *There are no simultaneous correspondences* [...]. What is past murmurs in the correspondences, and the canonical experience of them has its place *in a previous life.*"[38] In other words, it is not a component of contemporary experience. It is perhaps worth noting a potential parallel between the dynamic at work in Baudelaire's *correspondances* and the Kafka portrait. The modern poet, in similar fashion to the young boy, attests to the breakdown of experience through the disintegration of the past, a past lost and long-forgotten whose disappearance corresponds with the disappearance of the aura. To go back to our prior discussion, while in the past objects progressively became intimately entwined in individual experience, later, as mechanically reproduced and reproducible, they acquired a different status. Indeed, as a result of the technological progress of industrialization, objects could be manufactured in vast quantities at an unprecedented rate of production and, as a result, they became increasingly disposable. Rather than enduring and maintaining a link with the past, objects now fulfilled an entirely different function: that of perpetuating the ever-changing new, a demand possibly best exemplified by the concept of fashion. As a result of this, the singular complicity

87

between individuals and objects eventually gave way to a relationship predicated on estrangement rather than familiarity, one whose impact seems, following Benjamin's account, to have left its mark in the Kafka portrait.

Let us in fact here return to the portrait. If the boy appears lost, it is, as noted, an outcome of his unfamiliar surroundings. Since alien objects in the studio function as props intended to prescribe a projected identity, the intent is for Kafka to make the setting his; to appropriate the incongruously "large hat" set in his hand as his own. Stated differently, Kafka, as we will see later, is asked to adapt to the modern imperative of shock. Yet, we are told, he is unable to do so. What then are we to understand of the boy's inability to comply with the demands of the modern world of his time? Here, what Benjamin perceived as our responsibility to the past would seem to be called into play. To reiterate, it is, according to Benjamin, our task to find and dwell on "the inconspicuous spot where in the immediacy of that long-forgotten moment the future nests so eloquently that we, looking back, may rediscover it."[39] That spot being, as Benjamin suggests, inscribed in the boy's gaze, might perhaps be said to speak to a sensibility or intuition which has no place in the present—one perhaps belonging, as in the case of Baudelaire, to a perished realm of remembrance or prehistory. Kafka would thus appear caught between two incompatible and incommensurable worlds: the first pertaining to the staged, material, phenomenological space of the studio in which he finds himself; and the second, to a forsaken and unattainable realm to which he is somehow nevertheless intuitively compelled, through a poetic sensibility akin to that of which Benjamin speaks in reference to Proust's *Remembrance of Things Past*[40]—a sensibility upon which Kafka's experience of the modern world seems to have been predicated and which, giving rise to a sense of incongruity, permeated his writings throughout his life.

Identity and Image in Marguerite Duras

Whereas early photographers, working to wrestle an image out of the dark, adjusted to the auratic conditions of the living, as will be shown, later portrait photography sought to stage life. As a result, the sitter's identity in this later phase assumes the temporary and staged conditions of the studio. Of interest again for us here are the ways in which the mechanisms within contemporary portraiture may be seen to exemplify the general conditions of the everyday. And if photography can be said to stage identity as image, I would now like to explore the implications of this shift in terms of the staging of image as identity, and more generally, as life by introducing Marguerite Duras into our discussion. Specifically, I would like to consider a number of images described in her auto-biographical novel *L'Amant*. The first image I wish to address pertains to a photograph that was never taken:

> I think it was during this journey that the image might have detached itself, that it might have been removed from all the rest. It could have existed, a photograph could have been taken, just like any other, elsewhere, in other circumstances. But it wasn't. The subject was too slight. Who could have thought of taking it? It could only have been taken if someone could have known of the importance it was to have in my life, that event, that crossing of the river. But while it was taking place, no one even knew of its existence. Except God. And that's why—it couldn't have been otherwise—the image doesn't exist. It was omitted. Forgotten. It was never detached or removed from all the rest. And it's to this, to this failure to have been created, that the image owes its virtue: the virtue of representing, of being the creator, of an absolute.[41]

Working to reactivate the punctual locus of shock (trigger of the "forgotten" image), Duras' writing may be seen to parallel Baudelaire's *correspondances* while also revealing affinities with Proust. We are reminded here of the workings of the unconscious in relation to the experience of shock. The "crossing of the river" which emerges as the shock event takes the form of a "forgotten" or "omitted" image, one which cannot "exist" as a photograph since it has not been experienced explicitly and consciously ("the image does not exist," whereas photographs do).

For the purpose of demonstrating the unconventional pursuit of her writing, Duras' text works to establish an opposition between photography and cinema, on the one hand, and image and literature, on the other. It should however be noted that Duras does not for that matter dismiss the potential of photography or cinema. Rather, the opposition, which has a punctual and strategic function in this case, allows Duras to formulate a certain insight regarding her own endeavour as a writer, namely that of opposing what she deemed to be the limited nature of the most common and widespread forms of representation. Since my objective here is to show how Duras' quest through writing closely parallels Benjamin's historical enterprise in relation to photography, and since Benjamin's references are to actual photographs, it is worth clarifying the nature of Duras' relationship to photography and cinema. When Duras speaks of images (photographic or cinematic) in opposition to writing, she is referring to a certain type of image consumption and production which, for her, has its match within a certain genre of literature of which she is equally dismissive.[42] Thus Duras does not altogether dispute the potential of images but rather the ways in which they are nowadays most conventionally approached, produced and consumed. The fact that Duras herself turned to cinema and published photographs from her personal collection certainly works to confirm this. It is however as an alternative and indeed in opposition to widespread practices of image-making and writing that her own work asserts itself; that is, through the vigilant pursuit of writing, on the one hand, aware of and working to nuance the ideological trappings inherent to language and, on the other, in the case of her films, revealing the prevalent deceptive claims of images. Here is Duras on cinema: "What I show in my films is this very paradox: that nothing can be shown. In other words what I show is this impossibility to show. That's what interests me."[43] Thus, according to Duras, key and determinant events cannot be grasped or represented at will and, if they emerge, it is, just as for Benjamin, rather a matter of chance or accident. Within Duras' opposition between photograph and image, photographs appear to share in the workings of voluntary memory, while the image, virtual yet lost to experience, could be seen to become a possible component of the *mémoire involontaire*. And while the image's distinction stems from never being actualized, it is that toward which Duras' writing will strive. For it is in remaining virtual that the image retains its full potential. In her words, "it's to this [...] failure to have been created, that the image owes its virtue: the virtue of representing, of being the creator, of an absolute."[44]

The implication here that life's key events (or what Proust calls 'true' or 'real' life) remain beyond the horizon of the photograph follows from the posited association between voluntary memory and photography; one also inferred by Benjamin, who notes how photography and *mémoire volontaire* work in close correlation to bring about the destruction of aura:

> Proust, complaining of the barrenness and lack of depth in the images of Venice that his *mémoire volontaire* presented to him, notes that the very word "Venice" made those images seem to him as vapid as an exhibition of photographs. If the distinctive feature of the images arising from *mémoire involontaire* is *seen* in their aura, then photography is decisively implicated in the phenomenon of a "decline of the aura."[45]

I would like to highlight Benjamin's suggestion here that the aura, although not actualized, is said to be perceptible as a virtual potential within the domain of the *mémoire involontaire*.

Photography and the Self as Other

Returning to Duras, the next passage, in which the narrator from *L'Amant* recalls her mother going to the photographer's to have her portrait taken in Indochina, shows the destruction of aura as an intended outcome of the photographic process:

> When she was old [...] she went to the photographer's, alone, and had her photograph taken in her best dark-red dress and her two bits of jewelry [...]. The better-off natives used to go to the photographer's too, just once

in their lives, when they saw death was near. Their photos were large, all the same size, hung in handsome gilt frames near the altars to their ancestors. All *these photographs of different people* [...] *gave* practically *identical results, the resemblance was stunning.* It wasn't just because all old people look alike, but because the portraits themselves were invariably touched up in such a way that any facial peculiarities [...] were minimized. [...] *This was what people wanted.* This general resemblance [sic].[46]

This passage, which hyperbolizes a process intended to efface singularity on the one hand and promote the self as a predetermined type on the other, proves particularly disturbing for the narrator as she discovers her mother embodied as another. "They all had that same expression," she recalls, one "which today still I would recognize anywhere. And my mother's expression in that portrait of the red dress is *theirs.*"[47] Although the ritual described in this case refers to a particular tradition, the photograph, which here has the role of defining and legitimating the self, nevertheless exemplifies traits common to contemporary portraiture and the social realm beyond it. Wedding, graduation, family and professional portraits can for instance be said to function in very much the same way as symptoms of ready-made concepts on which life is seen to model itself. There indeed seems to be a compulsion nowadays to photograph: to turn experience itself into a way of seeing. It is as though to become legitimate, to be actualized, having an experience meant, taking a photograph of it. In a different passage, Duras makes a similar point by recalling the exaggerated significance of portraits in her mother's life:

Every so often my mother declares, Tomorrow we'll go to the photographer's. She complains about the price but still goes to the expense of family photos. [...] My mother only has photos taken of her children. Never anything else. I don't have any photographs of Vinh Long, not one, of the garden, the river, [...] the house, [...] not a single image of those incredible places.[48]

In the case of the above examples, photographs do not serve to record memories of lived experience but rather stand in for experience. They are means through which the narrator's mother achieves a dignity precluded by the harsh reality of her day-to-day existence. Accordingly, on her occasional trips to France to visit family, photographs, projecting a norm denied by circumstance, literally take the place of her living children:

> For some mysterious reason my mother used to show her children's photographs to her family when she went home on leave. We didn't want to go and see them. *My brothers never met them.* At first she used to take me [...]. Then later on I stopped going, because *my aunts didn't want* their daughters *to see me* any more on account of my shocking behaviour. *So my mother has only* the *photographs* left *to show,* so she shows them, naturally, reasonably.[49]

In taking the place of lived life, photographs in *L'Amant* relegate the living to a forgotten realm, a process which, through habit, has been normalized, as is suggested by Duras' above use of the terms "naturally" and "reasonably." Within the framework of this dynamic, the potential for aura fully disappears. Duras' narrator, bearing witness to her mother's "mysterious" compulsion, is however neither duped nor lured by photography's deceptive powers. She is, rather, bewildered by her mother's concerted efforts to submit to a conceptual norm, to uphold an image of her life which is utterly at odds with the reality of her destitute existence and her children's unruly behavior. Consequently, Duras sets herself a task which will run in direct opposition to the course taken by her narrator's mother. Her work, like Proust's, like Baudelaire's, and significantly for us here, like Benjamin's, will be to evaluate the loss of that which remains concealed through the ordinary course of the day-to-day. "The story of my life doesn't exist," she tells us. "There are great spaces where one is led to believe that there was someone, but it's not true, there was no one."[50] Hereby underscoring the autobiographical dimension of *L'Amant*, the narrator, who early on comes to understand that she is predestined to write, will thus seek to shed light on these aporia and, as such, to acknowledge the virtual realm of deferred experience. "The story of one small part of my youth I've already written, more or less—I mean, enough to give a glimpse of it. [...] Now I'm talking about the hidden stretches of that same youth, of certain facts, feelings, events that I buried."[51]

We have at this point, in a sense, come full circle, as that reality initially evoked in which images were claimed to be livelier than people has woven its way back into our account of portraiture. Indeed the above examples bear witness to certain symptomatic changes through which the photograph, initially at the service of life, can be said to have become the privileged and sole legitimating medium of existence; that through which life comes to be acknowledged and to exist. Or, to state things differently, as these examples have served to illustrate, one does not experience an event as event but as a photograph, as something always already predetermined as an image.

If, for the narrator's mother, the photograph is the model of existence, and if one, to exist, must be transformed into a photograph, then one is faced with the very imperative confronting the young boy in the Kafka portrait: that of becoming other. Within this dynamic, the expulsion of the moment from the reach of experience coincides with the assertion of the projected entity of the photograph. In short, the photographic image world, or the world as image, is founded on a double gesture: the deferral of aura as that potential to 'grow into' a particular moment, countered by the assertion of the self as other. As such, the image works hand in hand with the experience of shock, with the latter expropriating the event/ self from the reach of consciousness in the form of a forgotten image. Thus what remains is that which reaches consciousness and which, akin to actualized photographic images, determines our everyday. Following from this, the experience of the everyday can be described as both the experience of perpetual shock and consequent denial of self or, translated into Proustian terms, the perpetual deferral of 'true life.' Indeed, for Duras, as for Proust, the photographic norm is no longer seen to pertain to that secret and magical procedure through which the early photographer set about mysteriously to capture life. It is rather deemed to rid things of their 'reality;' that which art and literature, in partnership with the *mémoire involontaire*, have the privileged role of acknowledging–that which is seen to be sacrificed through the course of daily existence. "*Real life*," Proust tells us, is "life at last bare and illuminated." Therefore, life "which can be said to be really lived is literature." And while "life thus defined is in a sense all the time immanent in ordinary man no less than in the artist," most men, he continues, "do not see it because they do not seek to shed light upon it."[52] Accordingly, Duras, having evoked the fact of a virtual image which was never actualized into a photograph, will set out to pinpoint the latter's original context by accounting for it in her writing: "it was during this journey that the image became detached, removed from all the rest."[53] Thus, as a means of countering the recuperative trend of the predetermined image-reality she so vehemently challenged, Duras, like Benjamin in his approach to select photographs, will seek to isolate the decisive moment pertaining to a particular event. Moreover, as we have seen, in the case of the narrator of *L'Amant*, the 'event' is the crossing of the river, evoked in our initial passage, of which no photograph was ever taken.

Benjamin's Historian

In what follows, I would like to draw a parallel between the task of writing in Duras and the task of the historian as Benjamin conceived of it. In "The Task of the Translator," Benjamin evokes the possibility of "an unforgettable life or moment" which has nevertheless been forgotten by all men. "If the nature of such a life or moment required that it be unforgotten, that predicate would imply not a falsehood," he argues, "but merely a claim unfulfilled by men."[54] The task of the historian is thus in a sense to inform the present of the virtual possibility of such a moment, something achieved by way of Benjamin's dialectical image. "Historical materialism," Benjamin explains, "wishes to hold fast that image of the past which unexpectedly appears to the historical subject in a moment of danger."[55] I would like to suggest evidence of a similar dynamic in Duras' description of an event or moment that might have been recorded as a photograph, but was not, and was thus "forgotten."

95

The fact of highlighting such a possibility implies that the event's omission does not however preclude its having taken place. The event, as forgotten image, is hence seen to retain its full potential in a state of virtuality, that is, within a realm which has proved to be forgotten by humankind and which is therefore inaccessible to experience. As for Benjamin's historian, writing's task is therefore to awaken that which, precluded from becoming manifest, patiently awaits the opportunity to be acknowledged.

If I have chosen to approach the complex interweaving of memory and image, writing and the past, through Duras, it is because her writing seems aptly to echo much of Benjamin's thought in terms of the disappearance of aura and the task confronting the historian today. Before proceeding further with Duras, however, I would like to quote a passage from Benjamin's "A Berlin Chronicle" which will serve to orient what follows. Here, then, is Benjamin:

> Anyone can observe that the length of time during which we are exposed to impressions has no bearing on their fate in memory. [...] It is not, therefore, due to insufficient exposure time if no image appears on the plate of remembrance. More frequent, perhaps, are the cases when the half-light of habit denies the plate the necessary light for years, until *one day from an alien source it flashes* as if from burning magnesium powder, and now a snapshot transfixes the room's image on the plate. It is we ourselves, however, who are always standing at the center of these rare images. Nor is this very mysterious, since such moments of sudden illumination are at the same time moments when we are separated from ourselves, and *while our waking, habitual, everyday self is involved actively or passively* in what is happening, *our deeper self rests in another place and is touched by the shock* [...]. *It is to this immolation of our deepest self in shock that our memory owes its most indelible images.*[56]

It is in light of this passage that I would now like to return to Duras.

At the very beginning of *L'Amant*, the narrator tells of how the writing of her story was prompted by an accidental encounter with a stranger:

96

One day, I was already old, in the entrance of a public place a man came up to me. He introduced himself and said, "I've known you for years. Everyone says you were beautiful when you were young, but [...] I think you're more beautiful now than then. [...] I prefer your face as it is now. Ravaged."[57]

This unexpected encounter incites Duras to reflect on the stranger's comment. In doing so, she is confronted with an image of herself which arises from the past, one which does not exist as such, but which, in a similar way to Benjamin's 'snapshot'[58] above, emerges as a memory: "I often think of the image only I can see now, and of which I've never spoken."[59] Here I would suggest that the image in question, that evoked initially with regards to the river crossing, can be said to pertain to the initial shock event to which the narrator's face owes its remarkable demarcation, something which progressively comes to light through the process of her writing. "Very early in my life it was too late," she tells us. "Between eighteen and twenty-five my face took off in a new direction. I grew old at eighteen. [...] And I've kept it ever since, the new face I had then. It has been my face."[60] Writing thus becomes the means for the narrator to dwell on these traces and to allow the virtual image of the past to find its place in the present. In Benjamin's words, "the historical index of the images not only says that they belong to a particular time; it says, above all, that they attain to legibility only at a particular time."[61]

Art, Writing and the Past

In her attempt to recover the past, the narrator proceeds to approach things in a way which runs counter to that of empirical habit. In this way, her quest runs parallel to Proust's, who, in *Remembrance of Things Past*, describes the task of art in the following terms:

> This work of the artist, this struggle to discern beneath experience, beneath words, something that is different from them, is a process *exactly the reverse* of that which, in those everyday lives which we live with our gaze averted from our self, is at every moment being accompanied by vanity and passion

and the intellect, and habit too, when they smother our *true impressions*, so as to entirely conceal them from us, beneath a whole heap of verbal concepts and practical goals which we falsely call life.[62]

"My aging was very sudden," the narrator tells us. "I saw it spread over my features one by one, changing the relationship between them [...]. But *instead of being dismayed*," she further confides, "*I watched* this process *with* the same sort of *interest* I might have taken in the reading of a book."[63] Assuming both the task of the artist and that of the historian, the narrator of *L'Amant* hence demonstrates a receptiveness to that reproachable facet of existence which her mother sought so desperately to efface. As mentioned, her challenge will be to retain the potential of that which was expelled from experience by summoning it in the present through her writing. In Benjamin's words, writing as such is "that wherein what has been comes together in a flash with the now to form a constellation."[64]

As a means of exploring this further, I would now like to turn to Duras' description of that moment evoked earlier which failed to become a photograph:

> The shoes aren't what make the girl's attire *unexpected, extraordinary* on that particular day. No, it's the fact that the young girl is wearing a man's flat-brimmed hat, a brownish-pink fedora with a broad black ribbon.
> The *crucial ambiguity* of the image lies in the hat.
> How I came by it I've forgotten. [...] I think my mother bought it for me upon my request. The one thing certain is that it was another markdown, another final reduction. But why was it bought? No woman, no girl wore a man's fedora in the colony back then. [...] What must have happened is this. I tried on the hat, just for fun, and then, looking at myself in the mirror, I saw: beneath the man's fedora, the *incongruously* thin shape, the *inadequacy* of childhood, transformed into something else. It ceased to be the brutal, fatal, given of nature. It became, quite the opposite, a provoking choice, a choice of the mind. It had all of a sudden become deliberate. Suddenly I see *myself as another*, as another might be seen, out there, available to all, available for all to see, in circulation for cities, journeys, desire. I take the hat, [...] the hat which alone wholly defines me, and never take it off.[65]

"The historical power of shock," claims Eduardo Cadava, quoting Cathy Caruth, "'is not just that the experience is repeated after its forgetting, but that it is only in and through its inherent forgetting that it is first experienced at all.'"[66] "If history is to be history of this 'posthumous shock,'" Cadava continues, "it can only be referential to the extent that, in its occurrence, it is neither perceived nor experienced directly."[67] Accordingly, the narrator of *L'Amant*, who in trying to apprehend the posthumous image of shock is seen struggling with the vagueness of her impressions, must allow that which dialectically coincides with her present self to surface and reveal itself as such. "The shoes aren't what makes the girl's attire unexpected," she at first hesitates. "No, it's the fact that [she] is wearing a man's flat-brimmed hat." Dwelling, in as much as she can, on that ephemeral image of her past, or, rather, proceeding to call forth and elucidate that instant, it is through the act of writing that certain elements, owing to their revealed significance, progressively come to be identified as definitive. "It is not what is experienced that 'plays the main role'," states Cadava in reference to Proust, "'but rather the weaving of [...] remembrance'."[68] Indeed, whereas initially evoking her image in the third person, the 'I' of the narrator will in the end assert itself through the appropriation of that which, "touched by shock" and pertaining to her deeper self, was cast into "another place." In other words, the above passage shows how the writing 'I' works to prepare the ground for that ephemeral instant of shock to find its significance; where for the very first time the deeper self, denied by shock, is brought to its point of recognizability. In this fragile instant in which the double-faceted 'I' emerges, passivity and agency paradoxically come to determine the very same event. The "brutal, fatal, given of nature" simultaneously becomes "quite the opposite, a provoking choice of the mind,"[69] as a new means of apprehending the unexpected image reflected in the mirror.

Let us return momentarily to the portrait of Kafka to compare the two images. Both can be seen to point to a parallel experience. Indeed, in each case, the intrusive presence of a foreign object (the hat) works as a catalyst to a shock experience. Whereas in the case of Kafka, the initial impact of shock translates into the helpless resistance perceived in the boy's gaze, in the case of Duras's narrator it is said to translate into a "deliberate choice." "I see myself as another," she tells us, "as another might be seen, [...]. I take the hat, [...] the hat which alone wholly defines me, and never take it off." By contrast, Kafka, who, we are told, "would surely vanish" were it not for his "immensely sad eyes," attests to the uncompromising resistance of childhood to the *modus operandi* of the studio through which the actualization of self as other is effected. By appropriating the image revealed in the mirror—in other words, by willing the transformation of her own image into that of another—Duras' narrator, unlike Kafka, overcomes the "brutal, fatal given of nature" through what might perhaps best be called a cultural choice—one opposing 'mind' and 'nature,' one informed by a world wherein the self is always already *a priori* other, a world culturally predetermined by images. As we have seen, life for the narrator's mother exists and is legitimated through the norm of photographs. The potential of an underlying reality has neither meaning nor bearing for her. Indeed, within the realm of the narrator's family, that which stands in opposition to the reality of photographs is actively denied. In short, it does not exist. As an example, the narrator recalls the self-imposed silence shared with her siblings, through which, owing to their humiliating circumstances, daily life was, as a rule, forbidden from being acknowledged. "Never any need to talk," she recounts. "Everything always silent, muted, kept at a remote distance. It's a family of stone, petrified so deeply it's impenetrable. Every day we try to kill one another, to kill. Not only do we not talk to one another, we don't even look at one another. [...] The word conversation is banished. I think that's what best conveys the shame and the pride. [...] We are united in a fundamental shame at having to live."[70]

Although actively silenced within the realm of her family's daily existence, the deferred potential of experience surfaces through the tortuous process of acknowledgement in Duras' writing. As suggested, prompted to writing by the image of her ravaged face accidentally summoned during her encounter with a stranger, the narrator of *L'Amant* proceeds to apprehend her past. In this way, she is led to another image, that of the crossing of the river through which she rediscovers herself as a child wearing a man's flat-brimmed hat. And it is here that evidence of a double-faceted self eventually comes to light. As the narrator attempts to recall the experience through which she acquired the hat or, rather, to pinpoint that singularly self-defining image, something akin to what Benjamin has called a "deeper self," suddenly emerges from the depths of her past. Suddenly the "inadequacy of childhood," which initially stands in blatant contradiction to the man's hat, is revealed in the mirror before making way for the staged yet equally visible image of adulthood implied here by the term 'desire.' Writing here thus allows a latent potential to emerge into the present, one akin to the uncompromising sense of loss noted earlier in the young boy's gaze. In the case of Duras, the symptomatic evidence of a natural disposition of childhood which emerges as an image and comes to light through the act of writing would thus parallel that irreducible reality in certain photographs of which Benjamin spoke and which today still refuses to be silenced. Here is Benjamin:

> [I]n Hill's Newhaven fishwife, her eyes cast down in such indolent, seductive modesty, there remains something that goes beyond testimony to the photographer's art, *something that cannot be silenced, that fills you with an unruly desire to know what her name was, the woman who was alive there, who even now is still real and will never consent to be wholly absorbed in "art."* [...] No matter how artful the photographer, no matter how carefully posed his subject, the beholder feels an irresistible urge to search such a picture for the tiny spark of contingency, of the here and now, with which reality has (so to speak) seared the subject.[71]

If history can be seen to remain virtual in a realm forgotten by men, so too, perhaps, might that tiny spark of accident, that incongruity of childhood, denied by the shock of modern experience potentially awaiting to be acknowledged in a future moment to come. As the narrator's encounter with the stranger reveals, the dismissal of nature under the impact of shock does not preclude its effect.

Indeed, the process through which the "fatal, given of nature" is seen to be transformed into a deliberate choice proves heavy with consequences, one through which the narrator's childhood is prematurely sacrificed. "What must have happened is this," the narrator tells us as she attempts to reconstitute the conditions under which the impact might have occurred. "I tried on the hat, just for fun, and then, looking at myself in the mirror, I saw [...]." Yet, at that very moment, she both sees and does not see. Or, rather, within that ephemeral instant summoned by writing, two potential and, in this case, incompatible facets (nature and culture) momentarily coexist in a flash, as one comes to eclipse the other. This crucial moment, suggesting the sudden and premature transformation of childhood, still in the course of its progression, into adulthood, can thus retrospectively be seen to prefigure the narrator's future encounter with the stranger. Indeed, the unexpected encounter works to confirm the initial impact of shock—the sacrifice of childhood—and its effect over time, in the singular demarcation of the narrator's worn, elderly face.

In *L'Amant*, then, the impact of the splitting of self experienced as shock is approached like "the reading of a book" with the narrator retrospectively recalling the details of her illicit relationship with an older Chinese man, thus allowing that which had previously been silenced to assume its particular significance in her life:

> Now I see that when I was very young, [...] I already had a face that foretold the one I acquired through drink in middle age. Drink accomplished what God did not. [...] I acquired that drinker's face before I drank. Drink only confirmed it. The space for it existed in me. [...] Just as the space existed in me for desire. [...] I had the face of pleasure, and yet I had no knowledge of pleasure. [...] That was how everything started for me—with that flagrant, exhausted face, those rings around the eyes, in advance of time and experience.[72]

Whereas Duras might claim the medium of photography to be impervious to that other historical reality which it is seen deceptively to silence, the aura whose potential is described by Benjamin as that "tiny spark of accident," that symptomatic "here and now" which continues to burn through photographs, can thus be seen to surface through her writing as that which has been lost to experience.[73] Our task, then, would therefore be to allow for the possibility of that "inconspicuous spot where in the immediacy of that long-forgotten moment the future nests so eloquently that we, looking back, may rediscover it."[74]

Notes

[1] Walter Benjamin, "Little History of Photography," in SW 2, 512.

[2] Ibid., 510.

[3] Benjamin addresses a brief period, between the 1840s and 1850s, before photographic portraiture became commercialized and conventionalized into a system.

[4] Benjamin, "Little History of photography," in SW 2, 512.

[5] Ibid.

[6] Roland Barthes, *Camera Lucida* (New York: Hill and Wang, 1996), 14.

[7] Benjamin, "Little History," in SW 2, 512.

[8] Ibid., 514.

[9] Ibid., 517.

[10] Ibid., 518f.

[11] Ibid., 514.

[12] Ibid., 514.

[13] Ibid., 517.

[14] Ibid., 512.

[15] Ibid., 515.

[16] Ibid., 512ff.

[17] Ibid., 514.

[18] Ibid., 515.

[19] Eduardo Cadava, *Words of Light: Theses on the Philosophy of History* (Princeton: Princeton University Press, 1997), 106-115.

[20] Roland Barthes, *Mythologies* (London: Paladin Grafton Books, 1989), 61.

[21] Angela Cozea, *La Fidélité aux Choses: pour une perspective benjaminienne* (Montréal: Balzac, 1996), 127. (Translation by author.)

[22] Benjamin, "Little History of Photography," in SW 2, 519.

23 Ibid., 519.
24 Ibid., 515.
25 Benjamin, "The Storyteller," in SW 3, 143.
26 Benjamin, "Little History of Photography," in SW 2, 515.
27 Benjamin, "The Storyteller," in SW 3, 144.
28 Ibid., 143.
29 Benjamin, "On Some Motifs in Baudelaire," in SW 4, 318
30 Ibid., 315.
31 Marcel Proust, *Remembrance of Things Past* (London: Chatto and Windus, 1981).
32 Benjamin, "On Some Motifs," in SW 4, 317.
33 Sigmund Freud, *Beyond the Pleasure Principle* (New York: W.W. Norton, 1989), 27.
34 Benjamin, "On Some Motifs," in SW 4, 317.
35 Ibid., 315.
36 Ibid., 319.
37 Ibid., 333.
38 Ibid., 333f. Emphases added.
39 Benjamin, "Little History of Photography," in SW 2, 510.
40 Benjamin, "On Some Motifs," in SW 4, 315.
41 Marguerite Duras, *The Lover* (New York: Pantheon Books, 1998), 10. (Translation modified.)
42 "I think that what I blame books for, in general, is that they are not free. One can see it in the writing: they are fabricated, organized, regulated; one could say they conform. […] At that moment, the writer becomes his own cop. By being concerned with good form, in other words the most banal form, the clearest and most inoffensive." Marguerite Duras, *Writing* (Cambridge: Lumen, 1998), 18.
43 Marguerite Duras, *Duras Filme*, dir. Jean Mascolo and Jérôme Beaujour, 1991.
44 Duras, *Writing*, 10.
45 Benjamin, "On Some Motifs," in SW 4, 338. Emphasis added.
46 Duras, *The Lover*, 97. (Emphasis added.)
47 Duras, *L'Amant* (Paris: Minuit, 1984), 119. (Emphasis added, translation by author.)
48 Duras, *The Lover*, 95.
49 Ibid., 95. (Emphasis added.)
50 Duras, *L'Amant*, 14. (Translation by author.)
51 Duras, *The Lover*, 8.
52 Proust, *Remembrance of Things Past*, 931. (Emphasis added.)
53 Duras, *The Lover*, 10.
54 Benjamin, "The Task of the Translator," in SW 1, 254.
55 Benjamin, "On the Concept of History," in SW 4, 391.
56 Benjamin, "A Berlin Chronicle," in SW 2, 633. (Emphasis added.)

57 Duras, *The Lover*, 3.

58 I recognize that there are important distinctions to be made between snapshots and photographic portraits. However, such is not my purpose here.

59 Duras, *The Lover*, 3.

60 Ibid., 4.

61 Benjamin, AP, 462 [N3,1].

62 Proust, *Remembrance of Things Past*, 932. (Emphasis added.)

63 Duras, *The Lover*, 4. (Emphasis added.)

64 Benjamin, AP, 462 [N2a,3].

65 Duras, *The Lover*, 13. (Emphasis added, translation modified.)

66 Cadava, *Words of Light*, 103.

67 Ibid., 104.

68 Ibid.

69 Duras, *The Lover*, 13.

70 Ibid., 55. (Translation slightly modified.)

71 SW 2, 510 (emphasis added). Benjamin, "Little History," 510, emphasis mine.

72 Duras, *The Lover*, 9.

73 I wish here to point out that while those on the basis of whose work I have selected to explore Benjamin's notions of aura and the task of the historian are all writers, writing here, as for Proust, is seen to pertain to the general realm of art. The present analysis is not intended to preclude attempts to approach Benjamin through the visual field.

74 Benjamin, "Little History of Photography," in SW 2, 510.

Ruinous Aura

From Sunset Boulevard to Mulholland Drive

Claus Krogholm Sand

It is usually the decline of the aura that is focused upon when discussing
the concept of aura. However, the question is if the appearance of film is
not also the origin of a new concept of aura. This new concept would
have to do with the nature of film. As Benjamin notes in the "Work of
Art" essay, what is shown on the screen is not (or rarely) a representation
of what was present before the camera when shooting the film. A film
consists of edited pro-filmic material. The editor can choose from several
different shots of a scene, which may have been shot in a different order;
or two chronological scenes may have been shot days apart in reverse
order, etc. The film is created in the editing. So what is present on the
screen has no referent outside the film itself. What is represented is not
what was present when shooting the film. What is present on the screen
was absent when shooting. In a way, film is the presence of absence.
Further: the film is not a segment of a complete whole that has been
edited. There never was anything but fragments in the first place. The
film is created from editing scenes shot in different order, on different
locations or from several different versions or fragments of the same
scene. It is the nature of film to be ruinous.

> The illusory nature of film is of the second degree; it is the result of
> editing. That is to say: *In the film studio the apparatus has penetrated so deeply
> into reality that a pure view of that reality, free of the foreign body of equipment, is the
> result of a special procedure, namely, the shooting by the specially adjusted photographic
> device and the assembly of that shot with others of the same kind.* The equipment-
> free aspect of reality has here become the height of artifice, and the vision
> of immediate reality the Blue Flower in the land of technology.[1]

106

The presence of an absence seems to be the definition of aura. Further, if the nature of film is its state of ruin, then we could talk of a ruinous aura.

In her reading of the "Work of Art," Miriam Hansen proposes that "the cinema becomes an object—as well as a medium—of 'redemptive criticism'" and that "Benjamin actually tries to redeem an auratic mode of experience for a historical and materialist practice."[2] The decline of aura is a historical process linked to changes in human perception. This means that a change in perception may lead to a change in the nature of aura. Here the concept 'dialectical image' is relevant. It is a concept that seems to be closely related to aura. In the dialectical image "what has been comes together in a flash with the now to form a constellation."[3] To the extent that the dialectical images are expressing the aura, the distance in the aura is not so much of a spatial nature, but is temporal. One thing that Benjamin wants to achieve with the *Arcades Project* emerges from the following statement: "Overcoming the concept of 'progress' and overcoming the concept of 'period of decline' are two sides of one and the same thing."[4] "The first stage in this undertaking will be to carry over the principle of montage into history."[5] The goal is to wrest the true images, the repressed wish-images, free from the chronological, but empty, linear history as it is written by historicism.

> Historicism contents itself with establishing a causal nexus among various moments in history. But no state of affairs having causal significance is for that very reason historical. It became historical posthumously, as it were, through events that may be separated from it by thousands of years. The historian who proceeds from this consideration ceases to tell the sequence of events like the beads of a rosary. He grasps the constellation into which his own era has entered, along with a specific earlier one. Thus, he establishes a conception of the present as now-time shot through with splinters of messianic time.[6]

What is obvious here is that Benjamin sees film—or at least a special mode of film characterized by the principles of montage—as an important tool. The "optical unconscious"[7] —the ability in film and photography to make phenomena visible that were invisible to the human eye—is relevant for history too. The montage of historical events reveals the true content of the wish-images of the past—the repressed and unconscious of the past's dreaming-collective. This return of the repressed through montage might also be the return of aura. The moment when the past momentarily steps into constellation with the present is an auratic moment. But it is a ruinous aura. "Yet only in the process of disintegration can the aura be recognized, can it be registered as a qualitative component of (past) experience."[8]

This resurrected, ruinous aura might be something that is particularly of interest in film. In another recent article Miriam Hansen further argues that "classical Hollywood cinema could be imagined as a cultural practice on par with the experience of modernity, as an industrially-produced, mass-based, vernacular modernism."[9] Although it is common to talk of 'classical Hollywood cinema' (i.e. the mainstream commercial film), classical in this context does not mean 'as opposed to modern.' The film as medium and art form is from the outset both modern and reflective of the experience of modernity:

> The juncture of classical cinema and modernity reminds us, finally, that the cinema was not only part and symptom of modernity's experience and perception of crisis and upheaval; it was also, most importantly, the single most inclusive cultural horizon in which the traumatic effects of modernity were reflected, rejected or disavowed, transmuted or negotiated.[10]

What is new or non-classical even in classical film is, according to Miriam Hansen, the development and production of a new sensory culture. This has to do with the optical unconscious. Film opens up "unperceived modes of sensory perception and experience."[11] It is capable of fulfilling the task that Benjamin formulated this way: "*For the tasks which face the human apparatus of perception at historical turning points cannot be performed solely by optical means—that is, by way of contemplation. They are mastered gradually—taking their cue from tactile reception—through habit.*"[12] This tactile appropriation

108

becomes habit in the distracted absorption of the artwork: this might be architecture or it might be film. And it would rather be the classical film than the avant-garde or modernist film.

> Once we begin looking at Hollywood films as both a provincial response to modernization and a vernacular for different, diverse, yet also comparable experiences, we may find that genres such as the musical, horror, or melo-drama may offer just as much reflexive potential as slapstick comedy, with appeals specific to those genres and specific resonances in different con-texts of reception [...] the reflexive dimension of these films may consist precisely in the ways in which they allow their viewers to confront the constitutive ambivalence of modernity. The reflexive dimension of Holly-wood films in relation to modernity may take cognitive, discursive, and narrativized forms, but it is crucially anchored in sensory experience and sensational affect, in processes of mimetic identification that are more often than not partial and excessive in relation to narrative comprehension.[13]

The Time-Image

In his great works *Cinema 1* and *Cinema 2*, Gilles Deleuze operates with two main types of images: movement-image and time-image. The movement-image characterizes the classical, narrative type of film. The time-image comes about around 1940—with Orson Welles' *Citizen Kane* (1941) as the first important film with time-images. The time-image is not concerned with the forward thrust of the narrative drive. The time-image examines the image in depth in order to make time itself visible. An example in *Citizen Kane* is where we see the young Charles Foster Kane playing in the snow. We see him in the background, through the window, from inside the house. In the house his mother is making ar-rangements with a lawyer concerning Kane's future. In one image is a constellation of past, present and future at once. The innocence of childhood—Kane playing in the snow—is already a past memory, almost obscured by the falling snow and framed like a screen within a screen by the window. Inside is the present meeting with the lawyer, a decisive turning-point in Kane's life, since it regulates and arranges the conditions for his future.

In the time-image past, present, and future come together in one image. The movement-image will deal with time in narrative sequences: past events have caused the present situation and lead to actions that will affect the future. The movement-image is concerned with action. The time-image on the other hand is concerned with observation and contemplation. There is in the time-image something of Benjamin's dialectical image or the image as dialectics at a standstill. The time-image is very well described by Benjamin in "On the Concept of History" as "blast[ing] a specific era out of the homogeneous course of history—blast[ing] a specific life out of the era, a specific work out of the lifework."[14] The chain of events has been brought to a standstill, creating a constellation that will come as a shock.

The time-image becomes particularly interesting when considered as a recollection in the form of a dialectical image. Deleuze, however, does not relate to Benjamin, but to Bergson. There are two types of recollection, according to Bergson. There is pure recollection that is all virtuality, and there are recollection-images, that are the actual recollection. This has to do with the nature of time and what Deleuze labels the 'crystal-image':

> What constitutes the crystal-image is the most fundamental operation of time: since the past is constituted not after the present that it was but at the same time, time has to split itself in two at each moment as present and past, which differ from each other in nature, or, what amounts to the same thing, it has to split the present in two heterogeneous directions, one of which is launched towards the future while the other falls into the past. Time has to split at the same time as it sets itself out or unrolls itself: it splits in two dissymmetrical jets, one of which makes the present pass on, while the other preserves all the past. Time consists of this split, and it is this, it is time, we *see in the crystal*. The crystal-image was not time, but we see time in the crystal.[15]

The past is preserved in time as pure recollection. This recollection is virtual: "it exists outside of consciousness, in time, and we should have no more difficulty in admitting the virtual insistence of pure recollection in time than we do for the actual existence of non-perceived objects in space."[16] What happens when we remember is that the virtual recollection becomes an actual recollection-image. This can be triggered by an arbitrary incident, like the *mémoire involontaire* where images from a prehistoric past—the pure recollection—are evoked and can indeed be triggered by shock experience. But—according to Benjamin—Bergson is blind to this historical dimension to experience:

> It was the alienating, blinding experience of the age of large-scale industrialism. In shutting out this experience, the eye perceives a complementary experience—in the form of its spontaneous afterimage, as it were. Bergson's philosophy represents an attempt to specify this afterimage and fix it as a permanent record.[17]

This complementary experience, this afterimage is a dialectical image. It is a constellation of past and present—of absence and presence. The complementary experience remains an apparition—an afterimage it takes a Marcel Proust to develop in its full potential. In Proust the apparition becomes the *mémoire involontaire*. Experience takes on its historical dimension when recollection is no longer under the control of free will. Memories that never were conscious, and therefore never were experience in the proper sense, make themselves conscious by way of repetition (the Freudian repetition compulsion). What never was experienced becomes experience by way of repetition as *mémoire involontaire*. This complementary experience is the unique apparition of its own conditional distance, and its breakdown. It is the ruinous aura of the crystal-image.

Such a crystal-image is the famous 'Rosebud' in *Citizen Kane*. Rosebud is Kane's dying word, and the film's plot is a reporter's quest for the meaning of Rosebud. He interviews people who knew Kane; in other words he explores different layers of the past, but never finds the meaning of Rosebud. However, we know the secret as we see that Rosebud was the name of the sleigh Kane played with as a child. But as nobody in the film remembers this, the image of Rosebud remains a pure recollection. Rosebud is not actualized as a recollection-image. What is left is the

111

ruinous aura of Rosebud—the absence that is present as the narrative drive.

Aura and the *Mémoire involontaire*
I will now turn to an example of a Hollywood film and a scene from that film which in a different sense can be labeled ruinously auratic. It is a scene that has become famous, a veritable emblem of the classical, yet modern thriller and horror-film: a scene known by most people even though they may not have seen the film, a scene that is living a life of its own outside the narrative context. The film is Alfred Hitchcock's *Psycho* (1960), a Hollywood film just on the edge of the classical paradigm (which according to film theorist David Bordwell ends in 1960), and of course the (in)famous shower scene.

The scene can be seen as a staging of the experience of modernity. The desolate motel functions as a symbol of the homelessness in modern subjectivity. The naked woman in the shower is a fragile subject exposed to random violence. The killing thus represents the experience of modernity and the contingency of modern life. It is both literally and symbolically a shock-experience that happens without any warning or narrative motivations, as a complete break with the narrative up to this point.

This is not all. What is under attack is the film or the cinematic apparatus as such. The knife cuts into the naked body, but it also cuts the film. The editing of the scene is synchronous with the stabbing. It is the film itself that is mutilated. The "equipment-free aspect of reality" which is "the height of artifice" is killed or cut open. Benjamin compares the painter to the magician and the cinematographer to the surgeon: "The images obtained by each differ enormously. The painter's is a total image, whereas that of the cinematographer is piecemeal, its manifold parts being assembled according to a new law."[18] The screen—the shower curtain—is pulled down, leaving us with the dismantled narrative of what we believed to be a classical Hollywood film. The linear, continuous and causal narrative is cut to pieces leaving us with the empty gaze of a dead star. Another quality of the aura is that it allows the object to return the gaze. Here it is the pseudo-aura of the star that is disclosed. The star is not a subject but an object in the hands of the cinematic apparatus.[19] It is the apparatus that returns the gaze. It is the presence of what is absent in film—what is supposed to be behind the screen, out of the audience's sight. It is the piecemeal film that obtains the ruinous aura.

Finally, there is the ruinously auratic figure of the killer. Who is the knife-stabbing murderer? It is neither Norman Bates nor the mother. It is at one and the same time neither of them and both. Physically it is Norman Bates dressed up as the mother. That is the presence of the killer—a presence in space. But psychologically, as is explained towards the end of the film, it is the dead mother who has possessed the good son. The dead and thereby absent mother is the killer—an absence in time. The absent in what is present is the ruinous aura.

In many ways *Psycho* is the origin of the modern horror-movie and to some extent the origin of the modern Hollywood film. What I find particularly interesting here is that it is a horror-film, which stresses another observation made by Miriam Hansen: the relationship between Benjamin's concept of aura and Freud's notion of *das Unheimliche* (the uncanny). In "On Some Motifs in Baudelaire," Benjamin writes on the object's ability to return our gaze: "Experience of the aura thus arises from the fact that a response common of human relationships is transposed to the relationship between humans and inanimate or natural objects. [...] To experience the aura of an object we look at means to invest it with the ability to look back at us. This ability corresponds to the data of the *mémoire involontaire*."[20] To this Miriam Hansen remarks:

> The gaze that nature appears to be returning, however, does not mirror the subject in its present, conscious identity, but confronts us with another self, never before seen in a waking state. Undeniable, this kind of vision is not wholly unrelated to the sphere of the daemonic, in particular Freud's notion of the "uncanny" [...] The Freudian connotation, like the reference to the *mémoire involontaire* and Benjamin's glossing of Proust as an expert in matters of the aura, suggests what commentators have pointed out: that the "unique appearance of a distance" which manifests itself in

113

the perception of spatially present objects is of a *temporal* dimension, marking the fleeting moment in which the trace of an unconscious, "prehistoric" past is actualized in a cognitive image.[21]

At stake here is Benjamin's reading of Baudelaire's poem "*Correspondances*": "*L'homme y passe à travers des forêts de symboles / Qui l'observent avec des regards familiers*" ("Man wends his way through forests of symbols / Which look at him with their familiar glances").[22] The *regard familier* of the returned gaze is the uncanny in Baudelaire. The uncanny is not what is strange or unknown to us, but something that once was well known and familiar. This once-familiar now appears as uncanny and strange because of distortion through the process of repression. In other words, what is uncanny is something (temporally) distant in the present or presence before us. Such an uncanny figure is the *Doppelgänger*. This pertains to the *mémoire involontaire*. The *mémoire involontaire* evokes images from a prehistoric past, images in which we recognize our past selves, though immediately, straight through the temporal distance, and doubled as a different self for the self that remembers. We recognize ourselves in images—indeed afterimages—never seen before, yet familiar. Thus the moment or ruinous aura becomes uncanny. We should pay attention to the word *Erscheinung* when Benjamin defines aura as the "*einmalige Erscheinung einer Ferne, so nah sie sein mag.*"[23] *Erscheinung* does not alone mean appearance—that is, "the unique appearance [...] of distance, no matter how close it may be."[24] *Erscheinung* can be translated as 'apparition,' 'ghost' or 'specter' as well. There is a ghostly quality to the aura. In this conjunction of aura, *mémoire involontaire* and the uncanny, the spectral quality is attached to repetition. In *Specters of Marx* Jacques Derrida relates this to characteristics of the ghost: the *revenant* (that which comes back). "A question of repetition: a specter is always a *revenant*. One cannot control its comings and goings because it *begins by coming back*."[25]

The Silent Aura
The question of repetition takes on a special dimension when we talk of "movies about the movies"[26], films that have Hollywood's collective

114

memory as subject matter. Such a film is Billy Wilder's *Sunset Boulevard* (1950). It is a film about the decline of the aura in a certain ruinous sense. The film depicts two transitional periods in Hollywood: first the transition from silent to sound film in the portrayal of the former silent star Norma Desmond; and second, in a subtler way, the transition from the star system to a Hollywood ruled by the producers and capital interests. This is portrayed through the other protagonist—and the narrator of the film—Joe Gillis: a screenwriter who has failed in Hollywood. He has now become disillusioned by the new Hollywood, thanks to too many experiences with screenplays with artistic aspiration that have ended up as yet another mass production aiming at the lowest common denominator. Consequently he takes on the task of editing Norma Desmond's manuscript for her big come-back—"Salomé."

Trying to escape his creditors, Joe Gillis accidentally ends up in the driveway of an old Hollywood mansion on Sunset Blvd. The mansion is in a state of decay, the shades are pulled, the pool—a symbol of Hollywood success—is empty, and a gloomy atmosphere surrounds the whole place. It turns out to be the residence of the former star Norma Desmond. Her career ended with the silent film. She now lives in splendid isolation; her only company is the butler Max and her memories of past glory. She is, however, preparing her come-back, certain that one day Cecil B. De Mille will call her and ask her to return to the silver screen. She has written a manuscript for her come-back role as Salomé. Joe Gillis—who is desperate for a job—accepts to move in and edit the script, although he is too cynical to believe Norma Desmond will ever be in the movies again.

Norma Desmond is a star whose aura has faded. In her house she is surrounded by images of herself from her glory days. She refuses, however, to recognize that she is no longer a star. "I remember you. You used to be big," Joe Gillis says when they first meet. "I am big. It is the pictures that got small," Norma replies. It is not her aura, but the film industry that has changed. In the film, Norma Desmond is played by Gloria Swanson— herself one of the biggest stars of the silent film—whose career faded

115

away with the transition to sound. All the pictures in Norma Desmond's house are actual publicity photographs of Gloria Swanson. It is this doubling of the faded star that gives the film a certain aura. The faded aura of Norma Desmond is supported by the presence of Gloria Swanson–herself a presence of the past. In a way she is a star who died with the silent film, but whose light can still reach us in *Sunset Boulevard*. Her aura still radiates from the screen. In a key scene, Norma and Joe are watching an old Norma Desmond movie in her private theater. The screen within the screen doubles Norma Desmond: the elder Norma whose bodily presence wears the marks of time, and the young Norma immortalized by the film. The irony is, however, that the film they are watching is itself marked by time. It is a silent film that nobody is watching any more; it has become a thing of the past. The light of the immortal star will reach us long after she herself has faded away.

There is a further irony. The film Norma and Joe is watching is actually *Queen Kelly* (1929), a film starring Gloria Swanson but never finished, partly due to director Erich von Stroheim's legendary habit of going over budget. As this happened just as the transition to sound was taking place, the producers feared the film would never make enough money and withdrew support when only a third of the film was completed. So what we are watching on the screen within the screen is light radiating from a film never seen before. The light reaches us 21 years after the film itself died. Further irony is added by the fact that the director of *Queen Kelly*–Erich von Stroheim–plays the role of the butler Max in *Sunset Boulevard.* So what we are witnessing is "'the unique apparition of a distance,'"[27] however near it may be. The screen within the screen becomes a crystal-image where we see time itself in the doubling of the aging Norma Desmond of the present day and the immortal star Norma Desmond who in a way has become pure recollection. It is the ruinous aura of a past that is present to us only as the fragment of a film that was never complete.

Norma Desmond represents a return of the repressed. Her aura stems from the silent age, an era only a few years back. But the temporal distance is far greater. The silent age has become prehistorical. Now Norma Desmond resides like an undead in her uncanny Hollywood mansion. She has become a vampire-like character, who needs the life-blood of a young writer to stay alive in the movies, i.e. she needs the words and dialogue provided by a screenwriter. She is the return of the repressed to Joe Gillis, because she represents an era when dialogue was not needed: "We didn't need dialogue. We had faces!"[28] And on the other hand Joe is threatened by the new Hollywood, where producers will take his precious artistic endeavors as a screenwriter and turn them into mediocre mass productions.

Norma Desmond is living on as a ghost that haunts the present Hollywood. She is an afterimage of Hollywood's radiant past. The star has died, leaving the bodily remains to live on. But she refuses to acknowledge the fact that—as far as Hollywood is concerned—she is dead. She still awaits her return to the screen and to Hollywood. But what will return is a ghost. She will return as an apparition—appear as she did on the screen in a silent film that died before anybody actually saw it.

Hollywood Aura–Ruinous Aura

David Lynch's *Mulholland Drive* (2001) alludes to *Sunset Boulevard* by its title. The latter is known as the home of the Hollywood stars, the former for the view over Los Angeles—a view most people will know from Hollywood films. David Lynch has described *Mulholland Drive* as a love story in the city of dreams. The film is structured like a dream—or perhaps rather like a nightmare. As with *Lost Highway* (1997), the film consists of two narratives that seem to be connected, but where the connecting joint is missing. One narrative could be embedded as a dream in the other, but it is uncertain which one is the dream and which is reality. Further, there are several subplots that are simply left unresolved and never find their way back to the main story line again. The two protagonists completely change character towards the end of the film. The amnesiac, bewildered Rita becomes the self-conscious Camilla Rhodes, and the naïvely, optimistic Betty Elmes becomes the depressed and suicidal Diane Selwyn. In their

117

pursuit of Rita's lost identity, Betty and Rita are searching for Diane Selwyn only to find her rotting corpse. Later they discover a mysterious blue box. When the box is opened they apparently are absorbed by it and the screen turns black. When the image returns Betty has been transformed to Diane and Rita to Camilla, who used to be Diane's lover but now has left her for the film director Adam Kesher. In the end jealousy and de-pression drive Diane to suicide. It is her partly decomposed body that Betty and Rita find later–or earlier–on. So the mystery of the identity of the dead body is solved. But how Betty becomes Diane, and how she can find her own corpse, remain a mystery.[29] There are several possible explanations, but none is completely satisfying. Furthermore, the film– and David Lynch–is obviously not making any attempt at creating a coherent narrative. As in a dream, characters can change completely and still be consistent with the inner logic of the narrative.

Mulholland Drive has a certain atmosphere that is particular to a David Lynch film. The whole film seems to be under the influence of a narrative black hole whose gravitational force distorts and twists the plot until you end up on the flip side of the narrative. As with *Lost Highway*, the Möbius strip could be the topological structure of *Mulholland Drive*. Much has been made of the fact that *Mulholland Drive* was originally intended as a TV series, but was abandoned by ABC because the executives found the pilot too mysterious. The many unresolved sub-plots would eventually have been taken up in the following episodes. The abandoned TV series was turned into a feature film when the French *Studio Canal* brought in money that enabled Lynch to shoot additional material. However, Lynch has chosen to keep the unresolved sub-plots in the film. Although the film differs from the original TV pilot, it still remains fragmented and ruinous. It is still an unfinished torso with vital, narrative limbs missing. But it is intended to be so. There is no attempt to cover up the fragmented character of the film. It constantly refers to the absence of a complete whole, of which the film we see is a mere fragment. There is no whole, only fragments. The artificiality of "the equipment-free aspect of reality" is laid bare.

A key scene takes place in the 'Club Silencio' that Betty and Rita visit late one night, just before they find the blue box and everything is changed. The scenery is a David Lynch trademark: the stage. Except for the Master of Ceremonies, the stage is empty. In a mixture of Spanish and English, he points out the illusionary character of what we witness: "There is no band, and yet we hear a band." There is a discrepancy between the senses, between the visual and the audible, and—perhaps even more crucial—between existence and perception, between ontology and aesthetics. There is no band, yet we hear a band. We tend to forget this just a little later when Rebekah Del Rio sings Roy Orbison's "Crying" in Spanish. Here, what we see seems to be congruent with what we hear. Suddenly she collapses on the stage, but the song continues.[30] What seemed to be present—a voice embodied in the woman we see on stage—suddenly becomes the presence of an absence or the *acousmêtre*—the disembodied voice.[31] This confusion of knowing what sense to trust is mirroring the confusion between which narrative is embedded in the other. The sensory perplexity makes the viewer aware of his or her bodily presence as the locus of perception. On several occasions in *Mulholland Drive* the image goes either very dark or is blurred and out of focus. The spectator's reaction is either to try to adjust to the darkness or to try to focus. The perception is not purely intellectual, but becomes bodily or tactile. The spectator will try to bring his or her bodily presence in agreement with the filmic presence. But there will remain a hiatus. No matter how hard you try to focus, the image will stay blurred. The bodily presence will be experienced as absent in the image and the presence of the image will be absent to the sensory-motor perception. What is perceived is the aura of being present to the past. This is what Deleuze has labeled the crystal-image:

> What we see in the crystal is therefore a dividing in two that the crystal itself constantly causes to turn on itself, that it prevents from reaching completion, because it is a perpetual *self-distinguishing*, a distinction in the process of being produced; which always resumes the distinct terms in itself, in order constantly to relaunch them.[32]

119

This is an expression of the ruinous aura. It is the strange weave of a bodily presence in space and the image of an absent past, of time itself. The crystal image is a formation of an image with two sides, the actual and the virtual, that are indiscernible and interchangeable. This seems to be the case of the two narratives in *Mulholland Drive*. In the first two-thirds of the film the narrative of Betty and Rita is the actual one and the narrative of Diane and Camilla the virtual. But at certain points the virtual is actualized and scenes belonging to a different layer interchange with the first narrative. There are two narratives—the actual and the virtual—that are indiscernible.

> In fact the crystal constantly exchanges the two distinct images which constitute it, the actual image of the present which passes and the virtual image of the past which is preserved: distinct and yet indiscernible, and all the more indiscernible because distinct, because we do not know which is one and which is the other.[33]

There is always an absent or virtual image as the reverse of the present or actual image. When the image is momentarily out of focus, it is as if there is an exchange between present and past, actual and virtual, phenomenon and being. The spectator's sensory motor response is an attempt to gain control over the present, to force the actual back into focus. This is an attempt to gain control of the present in space and to avoid the return of the repressed. That is, the ontological is momentarily making a return as a phenomenon perceptible to the senses. It is this hiatus, where phenomenon and being are interchangeable, that— ironically—constitutes the ruinous aura. What is really at stake here is time: "Time is not the interior in us, but just the opposite, the interiority in which we are, in which we move, live and change. [...] Subjectivity is never ours, it is time, that is, the soul or the spirit, the virtual."[34] This is evidently true in Proust and the *mémoire involontaire*. And this is what is essential to the Freudian notion of the uncanny. The uncanny is the temporal distance in the presence before us; or "the 'unique appearance of a *distance*,' which manifests itself in the perception of spatially present objects, is of a *temporal* dimension, marking the fleeting moment in which the trace of an unconscious 'prehistoric' past is actualized in a cognitive image."[35] The moment when Betty finds the corpse of Diane Selwyn—her own double, or herself from another layer of time—is the moment of the *mémoire involontaire*: the ruin of the auratic mode of experience and the experience of the ruinous aura. Benjamin said it most clearly:

> Concerning the *mémoire involontaire*: not only do its images not come when we try to call them up; rather, they are images which we have never seen before we remember them. This is most clearly the case in those images in which—like in some dreams—we see ourselves. We stand in front of ourselves, the way we might have stood somewhere in a prehistoric past, but never before our waking gaze. Yet these images, developed in the darkroom of the lived moment, are the most important we will ever see.[36]

Notes

1 Walter Benjamin, "The Work of Art in the Age of Its Technological Reproducibility (Third Version)," in SW 4, 263.
2 Miriam Hansen, "Benjamin, Cinema and Experience: 'The Blue Flower in the Land of Technology'," in *New German Critique*, vol. 14: 40 (1987), 182 and 186.
3 Benjamin, AP, 463 [N3, 1].
4 Ibid., 460 [N2, 5].
5 Ibid., 461 [N2, 6].
6 Benjamin, "On the Concept of History," in SW 4, 397.
7 Benjamin, "The Work of Art," in SW 4, 266.
8 Hansen, "Benjamin, Cinema and Experience," 189.
9 Miriam Hansen, "The Mass Production of the Senses: Classical Cinema as Vernacular Modernism," in *Modernism/Modernity*, vol. 6: 2 (1999), 65.
10 Ibid., 69.
11 Ibid., 72.
12 Benjamin, "The Work of Art," in SW 4, 268.
13 Hansen, "The Mass Production of the Senses," 71.
14 Benjamin, "On the Concept of History," in SW 4, 396.
15 Gilles Deleuze, *Cinema 2: The Time-Image* (Minneapolis: University of Minnesota Press, 1989), 81.

16 Ibid., 80.
17 Benjamin, "On Some Motifs in Baudelaire," in SW 4, 314.
18 Benjamin, "The Work of Art," in SW 4, 263–64.
19 This resembles how the subject in modernity becomes objectified in the hands of capitalism. Gilles Deleuze remarks that money is the reverse or dark side of cinema: "This conspiracy is that of money; what defines industrial art is not mechanical reproduction but the internalized relation with money. The only rejoinder to the harsh law of cinema—a minute of image which costs a day of collective work—is Fellini's: 'When there is no more money left, the film will be finished.'" *Cinema 2*, 77.
20 Benjamin, "On Some Motifs," in SW 4, 338.
21 Hansen, "Benjamin, Cinema and Experience," 188.
22 Benjamin, "On Some Motifs," in SW 4, 333.
23 Benjamin, "Kleine Geschichte der Photographie," in GS II, 378.
24 Benjamin, "Little History of Photography," in SW 2, 518.
25 Jacques Derrida, *Specters of Marx: The State of the Debt, the Work of Mourning and the New International* (New York: Routledge, 1994), 11.
26 Christopher Ames, *Movies About the Movies: Hollywood Reflected* (Lexington: The University Press of Kentucky, 1997).
27 Benjamin, "On Some Motifs," in SW 4, 338.
28 This remark recalls Roland Barthes's "The Face of Garbo." The aura of the star emanates from the face. "Garbo still belongs to that moment in cinema when capturing the human face still plunged audiences into the deepest ecstasy, when one literally lost oneself in a human image as one would in a philter, when the face represented a kind of absolute state of the flesh, which would be neither reached nor renounced." Barthes, *Mythologies* (London: Paladin, 1973), 62.
29 This motif is one of the allusions to *Sunset Boulevard*, a film whose narrator is found dead, floating in a swimming pool at the beginning of the film.
30 This scene is an allusion to David Lynch's *Blue Velvet* (1986), where Ben (Dean Stockwell) is miming Roy Orbison's "In Dreams." Here too the illusion is broken when he stops miming and the song continues.
31 See Michel Chion, *Audio-Vision: Sound on Screen* (New York: Columbia University Press, 1994).
32 Deleuze, *Cinema 2*, 81–82.
33 Ibid., 81.
34 Ibid., 82–83.
35 Hansen, "Benjamin, Cinema and Experience," 188.
36 Benjamin, "*Aus einer kleinen Rede über Proust, an meinem vierzigsten Geburtstag gehalten*," in GS II, 1064. English translation in Hansen, ibid., 179.

The Inactuality of Aura

Figural Relations in Walter Benjamin's "On Some Motifs in Baudelaire"

David Kelman

At the very moment that his *Habilitation* is being aborted by the university, he anticipates a much worse fate—namely, the day when it will be *re*habilitated. Not merely will such belated restoration to academic favor come at a moment when the original scandal has receded far enough into the past to have become, in its turn, a historicist fairy tale that happened once upon a time. Worse yet, later rehabilitation, as Benjamin visualizes it, hardly marks any improvement on the original verdict. It seems merely to be a new, improved version of the old treatment—a friendly historicism in lieu of a hostile one, resentment that is still more self-effacing. (Irving Wohlfarth)[1]

What would it mean to read Walter Benjamin now, to re-actualize writings that were hardly read immediately after their inception? Granted, this question is rather untimely, given that Benjamin's re-actualization has already begun. Not only has criticism of his work taken on a curious momentum over the last thirty years; there have also been warnings against the incorporation—even if by means of careful explanation—of Benjamin's (often initially rejected) writings into academic discourse. As Irving Wohlfarth remarks in the above epigraph, these warnings can carry high stakes. Referring to Benjamin's rejected *Habilitation*-thesis *The Origin of German Tragic Drama* (*Ursprung des deutschen Trauerspiels*), Wohlfarth implies that the recuperation and monumentalization of Benjamin's writings in academia today might signal an even worse catastrophe than the one suffered during his lifetime.

Wohlfarth's polemical statement points to a problem that strikes any close reader of Benjamin: while his writings certainly speak to many issues in contemporary academic literary criticism, any attempt to make Benjamin's thought relevant to the present seems misplaced. At the very least, such an attempt ignores Benjamin's own warning against such a procedure, when, in the "Epistemo-Critical Prologue" to *The Origin of German Tragic Drama*, he uses the figure of delirium to describe the desire to take up "past or distant spiritual worlds" and "unfeelingly incorporate them into [the present's] own self-absorbed fantasizing."[2] Any critic asking about the actuality of Benjamin's 'aura' must therefore confront a difficult question: not only, what is aura, but more essentially, what does it mean to talk about its actuality? What kind of temporality is this figure of actuality suggesting, and what notion of relation does it propose? Rather than investigate Benjamin's definition of aura, on the one hand, and actuality on the other, this study will focus on a particular figuration of the actuality of aura in his reading of Charles Baudelaire. In fact, the 1939 essay "On Some Motifs in Baudelaire" (*Über einige Motive bei Baudelaire*) stages the problem of actuality precisely as a problem of relation. Actuality figures in that essay as something that happens only in moments of non-relation, in those moments when the aura is said to be decayed or disintegrated. Strangely, the phrase 'actuality of aura' seems impossible in "On Some Motifs"—one can say 'the inactuality of aura' or 'the actuality of the disintegration of the aura,' but never 'the actuality of aura.' Whence this impossibility of speaking about the actuality of aura?

One of the key moments in Benjamin's figuration of both actuality and aura happens at the end of "On Some Motifs." Paradoxically, Benjamin states that aura exists in Baudelaire's poetry only insofar as it is there as a disintegrated or decayed aura:[3] "[Baudelaire] named the price for which the sensation of modernity could be had: the disintegration of the aura in immediate shock experience [*Chockerlebnis*]. He paid dearly for consenting to this disintegration—but it is the law of his poetry. This poetry appears in the sky of the Second Empire as 'a star without atmosphere.'"[4] Although Baudelaire still stands in his historical context, he relates to this context in a strange structure of non-relation. As a star without atmosphere, Baudelaire's poetry seems disconnected from the context in which it is embedded. It is as if the figure of Baudelaire had been strangled, deprived of the air or vaporous cloud that surrounds it. The problem of actuality, then, is not only our problem (as present-day readers), but is already the problem that constitutes Baudelaire's poetry in the first place. It seems that Baudelaire never had any kind of actuality: his poetry is a ruin, its aura already decaying from the start. Benjamin suggests, therefore, that Baudelaire's poetry is constituted by a certain inactuality or untimeliness, a non-relation not only between the literary text and its future readers but already between the literary text and the historical context. How to speak, then, of an aura that is inactual from its very beginnings?

In order to pursue this question, it might help to turn to the way Benjamin's essay is itself the performance of a non-relational relation. In fact, one of Benjamin's closest readers, Theodor Adorno, was concerned precisely with Benjamin's method of forming relations. The story of the debate between these two figures is well-known, but deserves to be repeated if only to highlight the way Adorno marks a certain structure of non-relation in Benjamin's text. The story is this: after reading an earlier version of Benjamin's work on Baudelaire—"The Paris of the Second Empire in Baudelaire"—Adorno was alarmed not only by the structural gaps that marked Benjamin's argument, but also by the way his theoretical armature seemed to lack mediation. Adorno focused on the fact that Benjamin enumerated motifs without a Marxist "mediation by means of the total social process," and that the "[m]otifs are assembled but not developed."[5] There is, in other words, a lack of theory that would adequately mediate between the literary (Baudelaire's poetry) and the historical (Paris of the Second Empire).

In response to Adorno's criticism of his work, Benjamin wrote his now-canonized "On Some Motifs," which was immediately published in the *Zeitschrift für Sozialforschung* in 1939. Instead of adequately responding to Adorno's call for more theory to mediate the apparent "positivism" of

125

"The Paris of the Second Empire in Baudelaire," Benjamin again gathered motifs together in the shorter essay "On Some Motifs." This time there was no attempt, in the title at least, to relate these motifs in an intentional way to the Paris of the Second Empire. As Timothy Bahti notes, Benjamin never sought a "solution" to the problems Adorno posed.[6] The new essay again described a host of motifs without recourse to Marxist mediation. As we shall see, however, Benjamin did indeed write a 'solution,' in the sense of a loosening of relations (from *solvere*, to loosen, to release, to free). "On Some Motifs" is thus important, among other reasons, for its status as the presentation—and not the exposition or explanation—of a theoretical response to Adorno's criticism.[7]

Far from simply being a scathing judgment of Benjamin's methodology, Adorno's remarks indicate a resistance to some of the most radical insights of Benjamin's *The Origin of German Tragic Drama*. This is not to say that Adorno rejected the earlier study out of hand; his own 1933 *Habilitation*-thesis on Kierkegaard quotes approvingly from Benjamin's theory of allegory.[8] What Adorno objected to was the notion of relation Benjamin outlined in his earlier work. Addressing his remarks to Benjamin, Adorno stated that, without theory, "you almost superstitiously ascribe to the enumeration of materials a power of illumination."[9] By asserting that Benjamin superstitiously enumerated materials, hoping that something rather than nothing would happen, Adorno is actually paraphrasing a crucial passage from *The Origin of German Tragic Drama*: "For it is common practice in the literature of the baroque to pile up fragments ceaselessly, without any strict idea of a goal, and, in the unremitting expectation [*Erwartung*] of a miracle [*ein Wunder*], to take the repetition of stereotypes for a process of intensification [*Steigerung*]."[10] The enumeration of individual fragments or ruins (we are of course in the "Ruins" section) is also the assemblage of stereotypes or repeatable figures. There is no goal to this exercise—the baroque artist does not expect a Hegelian result or concept to arise from the enumeration. Rather, the only permitted expectation—and it is more patient waiting (*Erwartung*) than an expectation of something already known in advance—is that *something* might happen rather than nothing. The exact nature of that something is unknown—the intensification (*Steigerung*) is a surprising miracle (*ein Wunder*).

Adorno's objection focused precisely on this notion of an intensification or miracle. He derided the suggestion that "illumination" occurs from the enumeration of fragments, or, in the case of the first version of the Baudelaire study, from the enumeration of motifs. Adorno referred to Benjamin's notion of relation as the "wide-eyed presentation of the bare facts,"[11] although he recognized that this notion of relation might have worked in earlier texts such as *The Origin of German Tragic Drama* and his essay on Proust. Adorno objected to the lack of a more proper (i.e., an orthodox Marxist) mediation between the motifs themselves and, more generally, between the literary and the historical. Benjamin's response—the essay "On Some Motifs"—indeed *solved* the problem of mediation, though not in the way Adorno had in mind. Rather, the new essay proposed a general loosening of relations by showing that the motifs in Baudelaire's poetry made the possibility of *any relation* questionable.

This impossibility does not mean that there is no relation between Baudelaire's poetry and nineteenth-century Paris. In fact, it is precisely this impossibility of relation that makes "On Some Motifs" far more successful than its predecessor, in that it shows how Baudelaire is "embedded in the nineteenth century."[12] This image, which Benjamin uses in a letter to Gershom Scholem and then later, more explicitly in a letter to Max Horkheimer, suggests that Baudelaire and nineteenth-century Paris relate as do a stone and the earth in which the stone is embedded. The relation between the two leaves an "impression" that "must emerge as clearly untouched as that of a stone that one day is rolled away from the spot on which it has rested for decades."[13] In order to read this impression (to read what lies under the rock), Benjamin must indicate the disconnection between Baudelaire and his epoch; he must show that Baudelaire had absolutely no connection with his time. By doing so, Benjamin is then able to read the impression that this stone has left in the surface of the nineteenth century.

Stars Without Atmosphere

The problem of relation, and specifically the relation between Baude-laire and nineteenth-century Paris, explicitly appears in the conclusion of "On Some Motifs." It is an enigmatic conclusion, not because its articulation is obscure, but rather the opposite: it seems to wrap up the enumerated motifs too conclusively. To cite Benjamin again: "the dis-integration of the aura in immediate shock experience [*Chockerlebnis*] is the law of his poetry. This poetry appears in the sky of the Second Em-pire as 'a star without atmosphere' [*ein Gestirn ohne Atmosphäre*]."[14] In an essay that insists that Baudelaire fully exhausts lyric poetry, this con-clusion, and its closing image, should not be surprising. Benjamin seems to suggest that the exhaustion of lyric poetry in Baudelaire is not accidental; rather, it has to do with a change in the structure of experi-ence.[15] To be able to sense the way in which the structure of modern experience has changed, to be able to bear witness to the Paris of the nineteenth century, Baudelaire must be loyal to this change in the structure of experience. His poetry must repeat the experience of the decay of the aura; he must make his own poetry aura-less. The phrase 'a star without atmosphere' seems to provide an image that expresses Baudelaire's aura-less poetry quite adequately. It is as if this image were able to provide access to what remains, in Benjamin, a very difficult thing to grasp: not only what Benjamin means by aura, but also what it might mean to talk about the aura's decay.

The alarming ease with which contemporary criticism reads Benjamin's images coincides with the larger problem concerning Benjamin's actualization in the academy today and the way in which critics have read the complex relation between the image and terms like aura. More than just another image, these terms seem to carry a conceptual weight. However, the question remains: is the image in Benjamin a medium through which we may gain knowledge of a term such as aura? Or does the image disrupt knowledge, producing instead a discontinuous rela-tion between the image and the term aura? However, if the image in Benjamin does not give access to his ideas, how can we ever hope to actualize such terms as aura? The burden of the present essay, at the very least, is to show the unknowability of Benjamin's images and of the image of Benjamin. One is tempted to repeat publisher Peter Suhrkamp's comments after the commercial failure of *Berlin Kindheit* in 1950: Benjamin's image "will likely remain undigested for a long time."[16] To say that Benjamin's image produces 'indigestion' does not mean that his image can never be actualized. However it does suggest that its actualization may not depend on knowledge, that the actualization of Benjamin's image may be more on the order of a non-cognitive act.

The problem with the 'star without atmosphere' image is precisely the way readers have attempted to digest it and put it to work as a concept. In fact, the image seems so in keeping with Benjamin's theory of the decay of the aura that one almost forgets to notice that this image, 'a star without atmosphere,' is in quotes. These quotes are even harder to see in the first English translation of Benjamin's essay in *Illuminations*, since Harry Zohn's version does not include the source footnotes provided in the German original.[17] In the last footnote to "On Some Motifs," in reference to the phrase 'a star without atmosphere,' Benjamin refers to Friedrich Nietzsche's *Unzeitgemäße Betrachtungen* (*Untimely Meditations*). The essay to which Benjamin refers is perhaps the most widely-read essay of Nietzsche's early book: "*Vom Nutzen und Nachteil der Historie für das Leben*" ("On the Uses and Disadvantages of History for Life"). Nietzsche's argument entails something of a warning against a certain kind of unrestrained historicism. He uses the example of some Hegelian perspectives on Christianity in order to derive a more generalized diagnosis of an exaggerated historical sense:

> What one can learn in the case of Christianity—that under the influence of a historical treatment it has become denaturized, until a completely historical, that is to say just treatment resolves [*auflösen*] it into pure knowledge about Christianity and thereby destroys [*vernichtet*] it—can be studied in everything else that possesses life: that it ceases to live when it is dissected completely, and lives a painful and morbid life when one begins to practise historical dissection upon it.[18]

The kind of historiography Nietzsche here attacks is the one that dissolves (*auflösen*) a phenomenon's connections to life, that is, a historiography that dissects and destroys (*vernichtet*) the life of phenomena. This unrestrained historical sense negates life, but gains knowledge through this negation.

It is already possible to sense some of the reasons why this particular essay by Nietzsche might have interested Benjamin, even if we have not yet reached the passage he quotes. As Benjamin insists, Baudelaire's poetry is a highly conscious poetry. For the sake of awareness, it detaches itself from unconscious experience (*Erfahrung*) so that it may have shock experience (*Chockerlebnis*) as its basis.[19] Benjamin insists that Baudelaire designated (*hat bezeichnet*) the price for this sensation as "the disintegration of the aura in immediate shock experience."[20] By naming this change in the structure of experience, and by forming his poetry on the basis of this designation, Baudelaire thereby became a dead star in the sky of the Second Empire, a stellar figure with no atmosphere of its own. For this reason, Benjamin alludes to "On the Uses and Disadvantages of History for Life," where, in the name of an ambiguous "life," Nietzsche denounces precisely the kind of ironic historical sense that feeds on the life of phenomena for the sake of knowledge: "All living things require an atmosphere around them, a mysterious misty vapour [*geheimnisvollen Dunstkreis*]; if they are deprived of this envelope [*Hülle*], if a religion, an art, a genius is condemned to revolve [*kreisen*] as a star without atmosphere, we should no longer be surprised if they quickly wither and grow hard and unfruitful."[21] Thus there is an opposition between life, which is characterized by a mysterious vapor-circle (*geheimnisvollen Dunstkreis*), and a star without atmosphere, which is unproductive and circles (*kreisen*) endlessly. Without its aura or envelope (*Hülle*), the autonomous and singular circle becomes an unproductive thing that circles repeatedly.[22] What is strange about this opposition is that the terms are not quite symmetrical. For Nietzsche, the opposite of a present and living thing is not an absent and dead thing, as one would expect if the relationship were symmetrical. Rather, Nietzsche talks about something more haunting, an object that is both present and dead. This ghostly presence is due to the repetitive nature of the dead thing, as if the dead never really passed away. You can never quite get rid of this dead thing: it keeps repeating, circling back. In this way, the very presence of historical phenomena is redefined as that which is continually coming back, revolving, *kreisen*, going in circles: a never-ending death that repeats itself. Like the ghosts in the *Trauerspiel*, these stars without atmosphere are condemned to return, but in death.

For Nietzsche, this repetition in death is a process; it happens as the result of an unrestrained historicism. In Benjamin's citation, however, this temporal dimension seems to vanish. Nothing comes along and happens to Baudelaire's poetry from the outside. Rather, his poetry is dead from the very beginning, circling eternally as a star without atmosphere. At the very moment of conception, it is already in a kind of afterlife. For Benjamin, then, Baudelaire's poetry is essentially untimely. Out of joint with its own time, his poetry does not appropriately fit within its age or *Zeit*: it is *unzeitgemäß* or *inactuel* (as in the French translation of *Unzeitgemäße Betrachtungen: Considérations inactuelles*). Yet according to Benjamin this does not mean that Baudelaire is some kind of absolute singularity whose genius transcends the age in which he lives. Instead Benjamin paradoxically insists that Baudelaire relates to his age by virtue of his very non-relation. A more literal translation of the passage in question would note that Baudelaire's poetry just stands there in the picture of its age: it "stands [*steht*] in the sky of the Second Empire" like a star without atmosphere.[23] Baudelaire relates to his age by just standing there, sticking out like a sore thumb, in an afterlife that Nietzsche describes as "painful and diseased" (*schmerzlich und krankhaft*): a denatured or unnatural (*unnatürlich*) life.[24] To the extent his poetry relates to his age in its non-relation, Baudelaire thus has a very strange temporality: he belongs to a no-time, the un-time of eternal circling. Surprisingly, however, Baudelaire's historical significance or survival is due precisely to this un-timely nature.

The instant in which Baudelaire's poetry appears is therefore a unique event while at the same time always happening somewhere else in its repetition. In fact, Benjamin finds this very predicament thematized in Baudelaire's poetry as the motif of the non-present or untimely instant. In Baudelaire's poem "*À une passante*," this untimely instant is figured by a passing woman. Her passing is precisely what makes her into what Benjamin calls the figure of shock or catastrophe (*"die Figur des Chocks, ja die Figur einer Katastrophe"*).[25] Yet this formulation seems paradoxical: a shock, and especially one equated with a catastrophe, is something that is, by definition, unrepeatable and unpredictable. How then to figure an event that, according to its own logic, cannot be figured? After all, figuration would entail a certain repeatability of the event, as if it could be substituted for something else, as if it were now taking the place of something else.

The problem of figuration in Benjamin leads directly to the strange temporality we have noted in Benjamin's reading of Baudelaire's place in the context of the Second Empire. We must follow him, then, when he insists that the woman passing by is a figure of shock and catastrophe. In Baudelaire's poem, the crowd brings this woman to the poet, but just as quickly takes her away. The poet's delight, Benjamin notes, resides precisely in the fact that he is seeing the woman for the last time. For this reason, Benjamin can say that this instant of appearing and disappearing "is an eternal farewell [*ein Abschied für ewig*] which coincides in the poem with the instant of enchantment [*mit dem Augenblick der Berückung*]."[26] The instant or *Augenblick* of the passerby's appearance is in fact a parting-from (*Abschied*), a separating-from (*scheiden*, to separate), that happens eternally (*für ewig*). The instant is an eternal parting and for that reason this instant is the moment of enchantment. However, this enchantment is not a psychological response to the passerby's disappearance; rather, the eternal parting of the instant means the instant's eternal repetition. The *Berückung* is not so much an enchantment as it is a haunting: *Rück*, of course, is one of the ways the German language allows repetition to be compounded with other words; it is like the 're' in return (in German, *Rückkehr*) or in reflection (*Rückschau*). To talk about the "instant of *Berückung*" is to refer to the happening of an event which—at that very instant—repeats itself like a haunting. In the poem *"À une passante,"* the passerby fascinates precisely because the instant of her appearance and disappearance is continually happening: it is the happening of repetition itself.

The passerby thus designates the repeatability of shock and for that reason can be called the figure of shock. What she shocks, however, is not the poet, but rather the instant, the *Augenblick*.[27] For this reason she is similar to the photographic apparatus, which Benjamin says gives the *Augenblick* or instant a "posthumous shock."[28] To be able to appreciate the significance of this phrase, it is important to remember that *Augenblick* is made up of two words: 'eye' and 'glance' or 'gaze.' In German, the instant is an eye-glance, an anthropological metaphor that emphasizes the way the instant takes place in a moment of relation: it is the precise moment when an eye corresponds or reciprocates with the world. As Benjamin notes, looking at someone is "an experience [*Erfahrung*] of the aura in all its fullness," because "inherent in the gaze [...] is the expectation that it will be returned by that on which it is bestowed."[29] We can therefore follow Benjamin in thinking about the instant or *Augenblick* in terms of the aura. If something has happened to the aura, then something similar must be going on with the instant. In fact, Benjamin notes that Baudelaire describes eyes that "have lost their ability to look," where "the expectation roused by the look of the human eye is not fulfilled."[30] For Benjamin, the fact that Baudelaire's figures of eyes do not share glances means that the instant itself is affected. Rather than a fully corresponding *Augenblick*, we get only *Augen*; rather than relation, non-relation. If the poem *"Correspondances"* evokes "something irretrievably lost," as Benjamin remarks earlier in the essay, what is lost is the corresponding gaze, or more precisely, the word 'gaze': every time Benjamin writes *Augenblick*, the *Blick* should be crossed out, leaving only *Augen-*.[31] The Benjaminian instant or *Augen-* is not the connecting moment between past and present, nor does it refer to a moment that can be simply related to other moments. The instant is rather the untimely itself—that which leaps out of time.

One must then ask: if the instant in Benjamin resists relation, how does relation happen at all? How does he relate, for instance, the motifs he insists thread their way through Baudelaire's text? After all, relation indeed happens in Benjamin's writings; "On Some Motifs" itself is not so much an essay on Baudelaire as it is a way of relating Baudelaire, Henri Bergson, Marcel Proust, Sigmund Freud, Edgar Allan Poe, and Friedrich Engels, among others. How does relation happen in Benjamin's own presentation of Baudelaire?

As much as Baudelaire's poetry may be about the instant, it should also be clear that Baudelaire is himself, as a figure, an instant. As a star without atmosphere, Baudelaire is the image of an eye without a gaze (an *Augen-*). How does Baudelaire, as an instant or *Augen-*, relate to other figures or instants? An answer might be possible if one realizes that the phrase 'a star without atmosphere,' as it appears at the end of Benjamin's essay, is also an instant. It no longer relates to its context (Nietzsche's "On the Uses and Disadvantages of History for Life") but rather sits awkwardly in this new text (Benjamin's "On Some Motifs"). As a citation, bounded by quotation marks, "a star without atmosphere" stands out in its non-relation to what surrounds it. This means that at any moment a configuration might form in which this instant ('a star without atmosphere') will relate to other contexts in its afterlife. These other contexts even include its original context, as long as it is now understood that there is no natural relation between the phrase and the original context.

In fact, as Benjamin knew, this citation is a repetition from the very beginning. *Untimely Meditations* is not the first time that the phrase 'a star without atmosphere' appeared in Nietzsche's writings. In a short note in the Baudelaire section of *The Arcades Project*, Benjamin writes: "Nietzsche calls Heraclitus 'a star devoid of atmosphere.' Cited in Löwith [...]."[32] Benjamin had been reading Karl Löwith's *Nietzsche's Philosophy of the Eternal Recurrence of the Same*, while working on what he, in a letter to Adorno, called the "third part of Baudelaire."[33] This third part of his Baudelaire work, as he explained in a letter to Horkheimer, dealt "with the historical configuration, where the *Flowers of Evil* joins Blanqui's *Éternité par les astres* and Nietzsche's *Will to Power* (the eternal return) by virtue of the *idée fixe* of the new and the immutable."[34] In his attempt to present a configuration of these three figures Benjamin must have run across a passage from Nietzsche's early, unfinished essay "Philosophy in the Tragic Age of the Greeks" in Löwith's commentary on the eternal return. The development of Nietzsche's argument is not as important here as the specific citation that attracted Benjamin's attention. In a section on Heraclitus, Nietzsche writes:

> Such men [as Heraclitus] live inside their own solar system; only there can we look for them. [...] [Heraclitus] is a star devoid of atmosphere [*ein Gestirn ohne Atmosphäre*]. His eye [*Sein Auge*], flaming toward its inward center, looks [*blickt*] outward dead and icy, with but the semblance of sight [*wie zum Scheine nur*].[35]

Whereas in the later *Untimely Meditations*, Nietzsche uses the phrase 'a star without atmosphere' to designate the result of a particular kind of historicism, here he uses the same phrase to talk about a figure's non-relation to a determinable context. Unlike the historicized object, nothing comes along and happens to Heraclitus: he is lifeless and inhuman right from the beginning. As Nietzsche remarks, "[p]erhaps in some remote sanctum, among idols, surrounded by a cold serene sublime architecture, such a creature [Heraclitus] may seem more comprehensible. Among human beings, Heraclitus as a human being was unbelievable."[36] Essentially inhuman, Heraclitus is but an eye that only appears to see; his eye (*[s]ein Auge*), gazes in pretense (*blickt* [...] *wie zum Scheine nur*), thus bearing no relation with or correspondence to the outside world.

These are, of course, the inhuman eyes Benjamin also finds in Baudelaire's poetry. In Benjamin's Baudelaire, however, these inhuman eyes belong not to the figure of the poet, but to the object of the poet's gaze; it is the passerby whose eyes have only the semblance of sight. The poet, on the other hand, "has decayed or lapsed [*verfallen*] into the gaze-less eyes [*blicklosen Augen*] and has surrendered without illusions to their realm of power [*Machtbereich*]."[37] Benjamin's essay puts both of Nietzsche's texts

135

into play. On the one hand, here he emphasizes the way something befalls or happens to the poet, just as a certain historicism engages the object of historical inquiry from the position of power and kills it off. In effect, the poet decays before the specter of the *Augen-*, that is, before the gazeless eyes that also signal a decayed instant. On the other hand, Benjamin also suggests that Baudelaire is dead from the start, auraless; as we have seen, his poetry is itself constituted as a star without atmosphere right from the outset. The phrase 'a star without atmosphere' presents this relation between two possible readings of the decay of aura in Baudelaire. The phrase does not establish this relation explicitly, however. It performs this presentation by the very quoting of a phrase that is itself a star without atmosphere, always shifting out of context.

The phrase 'a star without atmosphere' is therefore itself a repeating instant, an instant without life repeated in multiple contexts. The instant presents itself as completely inactual, that is, the very opposite of what may be called 'the present instant' (as the word *Aktualität* is sometimes translated). Yet, although the instant is not fully present, it nevertheless happens: the phrases's inactuality is also what allows a certain connection (or actualization) to take place. By citing this phrase then, Benjamin seems to be suggesting another way of thinking about how figures such as Baudelaire relate, or how they are actualized. The kind of relation that takes place has less the structure of a connection based on similarity than one based on repetition. Relation happens insofar as the instant repeats itself in its very death or decay—in its very inactuality.

It might seem that the kind of relation Benjamin addresses has the structure of a motif, as the title of his essay indicates. A motif, traditionally defined as a recurring figure, is only a motif when a given figure is revealed to conceal an enumeration of figures throughout the text. A motif includes within it, as it were, all the other instances of that figure. The singularity of the motif (the fact that you can say, "here's a motif") depends on the precise repetition of a certain linguistic element. A motif is thus a motif when a figure is revealed to exist outside of itself—not, that is, in some metaphysical elsewhere, but rather dispersed within a text or texts.

Once a motif is identified as such other instances do not have to be located and linked in a fixed way. Rather, relation happens regardless of whether the other instances are found. After all, the *potentially* endless enumeration of figures is precisely what makes it a motif in the first place.

We could therefore say that the kind of inactual relation Benjamin performs in his essay deals precisely with the structure of motifs. Yet Benjamin insists that one of the most important motifs in Baudelaire's poetry is never put forward as such. In Benjamin's argument the crowd becomes the hidden figure that runs throughout Baudelaire's poetry. How can one talk about a motif that is never there in the first place? For it is one thing to say that a motif, because of its constitutive repetition, is always outside of itself and therefore never present in itself. It is quite another thing, however, to say that the motif, as a discrete linguistic element, never even appears on the page as such. What then is a hidden figure? What kind of relation does it suggest, and how might the hidden figure evince an untimely actuality?

Constellations

In his discussion of Baudelaire's *"Le soleil,"* Benjamin notes the strange way the figure of the crowd appears in Baudelaire's poetry. He writes: "This crowd, whose existence Baudelaire never forgets [*nie vergißt*], has not served as the model for any of his works; but it is imprinted on his creativity [*Schaffen*] as a hidden figure [*verborgene Figur*], just as it constitutes the hidden figure in the fragment quoted above."[38] What does it mean to talk about a *verborgene Figur*, a figure that is in some way concealed or invisible? Its invisibility perhaps comes from the way the crowd, as an exemplary hidden figure, is imprinted on the creativity of the poet. It is not that the crowd makes an impression on Baudelaire's consciousness; rather, it makes its mark on the poet's creative activity (*Schaffen*), which is what makes him a poet in the first place. Anything that emerges from the creative faculty must then bear the mark of the crowd; it can never be forgotten (*nie vergißt*). As a result, all of Baudelaire's poetry can be said to originate from this matrix. For Benjamin it is as if Baudelaire's poetry had only one *idée fixe*; but this idea, while firmly placed at its origin, is never presented as such in his poetry. The crowd would therefore seem to be doubly invisible: not only because it seems to be placed out of sight, but also because the crowd is the blind spot from which everything originates.

However, as many commentators have noted, the crowd indeed shows up as an explicit figure in much of Baudelaire's work.[39] For instance, in the prose poem "Lost Halo," the poet loses his halo because he is attacked by a "churning chaos in which death comes galloping at you from all sides at once."[40] The crowd, personifying death itself, jostles the poet thereby destroying his aura. It seems as if this prose poem tells an origin story, that is, the origin of how the poet came to be 'a star without atmosphere.' At the center of this origin story the image of the crowd seems to shine forth. Like every origin story, however, "Lost Halo" is an allegory. Whereas the crowd is supposed to have originated the poet in the first place, this prose poem figures the crowd as something that happens to him from the outside: a fully constituted poet walks across the street and is attacked by the crowd. The prose poem therefore paradoxically refers to an event that constituted the possibility of writing "Lost Halo" in the first place. The crowd here thus cannot be a *verborgene Figur* or hidden figure: there is nothing hidden about it. The "churning chaos" of the boulevard is clearly a figuration of the crowd. A process of substitution takes place in which the figures in the poem stand in for the unnamed crowd. A hidden figure, however, cannot take part in this kind of substitution. To Benjamin the word 'hidden' suggests rather an absolute anteriority that cannot be figured as such: it is the originating figure behind all the figures in Baudelaire's poetry. While "Lost Halo" is certainly an allegory of the experience of poetic origination, it cannot contain, as it were, the hidden figure.

Again, what then is a hidden figure? What would it mean to talk about a figure that could not be figured? It helps to notice that Benjamin speaks of the crowd not only as a hidden figure, but also as a secret constellation or *geheime Konstellation*.[41] Both terms ('hidden figure' and

138

'secret constellation') appear in his discussion of Baudelaire's "*Le soleil.*"
This poem is a strange point of reference to talk about the crowd in
Baudelaire if only because, as Benjamin notes, the *faubourgs* described in
the poem are deserted. Nevertheless, Benjamin insists that "*Le soleil*" is a
secret constellation or hidden figure which he names 'the crowd.' More
precisely he remarks that this constellation should probably be taken as
"a phantom crowd [*Geistermenge*]: the words, the fragments, the beginnings
of lines, from which the poet, in the deserted streets, wrests poetic booty."[42]
Rather than speaking of a phenomenal crowd, Benjamin here conjures
up the image of a *Geistermenge* or spirit (phantom) crowd. He therefore
reads these word-fragments as a figure for the crowd. If "Lost Halo" is
an allegory of the poet's origination, "*Le soleil*" is an allegory of the poet's
Schaffen, his creative activity at work. Reading this new allegory, Benjamin now notes the linguistic nature of the crowd. It is true that Benjamin
also describes the crowd as "nothing but the amorphous crowd of pass-
ers-by, the people in the street."[43] The crowd is certainly this mass of
individuals on the everyday streets of Paris. However, as a *verborgene
Figur* or hidden figure, that is, as the constitutive matrix of Baudelaire's
poetry, the crowd is linguistic in nature. The crowd is a secret constellation
of linguistic instants that somehow relate to form a figure.

These allegories of the hidden figure continue throughout Benjamin's
essay, without offering knowledge of the nature of this relationship. While
his essay might perform this relationship by constructing a series of
allegories of the hidden figure, it rather rigorously refrains from providing a theoretical explanation of its presentational procedure. The closest
Benjamin comes to a definition can be found in his analogy of the sailboat:
"In the sonnet '*À une passante*' the crowd is nowhere named in either
word or phrase. Yet all the action hinges on it, just as the progress of a
sailboat depends on the wind."[44] Elissa Marder cogently analyzes this
analogy and notes that Benjamin resorts to an almost Nietzschean play
of forces when reading the crowd in Baudelaire's poetry:

Through this analogy, Benjamin implies that the action depicted in the poem, like the progress of the ship to which he compares it, is primarily a medium for rendering visible an ineffable force that motivates it. [...] For Benjamin, the action of the poem, like the sailboat's 'progress', is read in its resistance to the force of the crowd through which the passing figure passes. Instead of focusing on the figure of the passing woman, he looks at the force (the mass of the crowd) through which her passage can be marked.[45]

We might wonder, however, if it is precise to emphasize a process of rendering visible in relation to Benjamin's term hidden figure. Perhaps we should ask, what would a hidden figure actually look like? Would it indeed look like anything? Is the hidden figure not precisely something that cannot be rendered visible, even if "read through a series of relayed looks"?[46] What if the analogy of the sailboat, insofar as it is an image itself, does not permit any kind of knowledge of how the hidden figure could appear? To what extent is the image of the hidden figure—and the images that seek to figure it—resistant to theoretical articulation?

If it seems difficult to read Benjamin's images, perhaps it might be possible to read the invisible relations he sets up. By using the terms 'hidden figure' and 'secret constellation,' Benjamin insists we read "On Some Motifs" in relation to those texts in which he employs a similar language. In his 1923 translation of Baudelaire's *Tableaux parisiens* Benjamin included his famous meditation "The Task of the Translator." In this essay Benjamin suggests that translation is like other relational concepts or *Relationsbegriffe*, in the way that the human is not the measure of their actualization.[47] In fact, translation is all about relation for Benjamin—not so much the relation between the original and the copy, but rather between languages. These relations are not the consequence of human intentions, however, but are rather an effect of the inner structure of language. Benjamin writes: "Translation thus ultimately serves the purpose of expressing the inner relationship between languages. It cannot possibly reveal or establish this hidden relationship [*dieses verborgene Verhältnis*] itself; but it can present [*darstellen*] it by realizing it in embryonic or intensive form."[48] The actualization of this hidden relationship is therefore not something a translator can plan on or account for. Rather, a translation can present this relationship–a relationship he will soon call 'pure language'–through *Darstellung* or presentation. The presentation of this relationship is hidden in the sense that the relationship is never explicitly put forward. To prepare the way for the relation characteristic of pure language, a translator must carry over the syntax from one language to another by means of a certain literalness or *Wörtlichkeit*. The translator should therefore focus on the word (*das Wort*); such a syntactical translation necessarily interrupts the sense of the original sentence as it gets posited in the translator's language.[49] The *verborgene Verhältnis* or hidden relation between languages (pure language) is therefore presented in this accumulation of word-fragments, but not represented or intentionally displayed. Strangely, the word-fragments are taken out of context not by an intentional swerve away from sense, but rather by an attempt to be as loyal as possible to each word. By faithfully reproducing the syntax of the original language, pure language faithlessly leaps out and presents the relationship between languages.

At this point it must be admitted, however, that it is still far from clear how relations come about to form a secret constellation. How might a star without atmosphere, for example, relate to a constellation? The figure of the stars in Benjamin's image of Baudelaire perhaps enables us to notice another text where this stellar rhetoric appears. In the "Epistemo-Critical Prologue" to *The Origin of German Tragic Drama*, Benjamin most explicitly develops his notion of presentation or *Darstellung*.[50] Although the presentational procedure of his *Habilitation*-thesis is very similar to that of "On Some Motifs"–to the extent that Benjamin could have called the former "On Some Motifs in the German *Trauerspiel*"–it is nevertheless different from the essay on Baudelaire if only because *The Origin of German Tragic Drama* contains a theoretical introduction that fully explains (if obscurely) his notion of presentation. As the title suggests, Benjamin sought to describe the origin of the German *Trauerspiel*, that is, the origin of the idea '*Trauerspiel*' (the German baroque drama). However, Benjamin expressly does not seek to represent this idea; he simply enumerates

141

motifs, a procedure that makes for quite difficult reading. The problem Adorno correctly identified in Benjamin's first Baudelaire study is also seen here: an exaggerated philological method produces a spell that precludes any view of the whole or of an overall thesis. Motifs such as 'melancholy,' 'mourning,' 'intrigue,' 'allegory,' 'death's head,' and so on, follow one after another without any mediation. How then does Benjamin relate these disparate motifs to something he calls the idea of the *Trauerspiel*? And for that matter, what is an idea?

In his "Epistemo-Critical Prologue" Benjamin asks, how do phenomena enter into true relations? Furthermore, what is the role of the critic in making these relations? Do these relations emerge from an intentional and timely act, or do they happen when one least expects it? Benjamin seeks to answer these questions by noting that the goal of his study is not to present the concept of the *Trauerspiel*, but rather its idea. He writes: "*Trauerspiel*, as a concept, could, without the slightest problem, be added to the list of aesthetic classifications. But not as an idea, for it defines no class and does not contain that generality on which the respective conceptual levels in the system of classification depend: the average."[51] Rather than seek to subsume a set of characteristics into a literary-historical concept, Benjamin seeks a different way to present the phenomena of the *Trauerspiel*. He calls this other mode of presentation 'the idea.'

Once again we are faced with a relation of non-relation, now between phenomena and ideas. For, Benjamin writes, "phenomena are not incorporated in ideas. They are not contained in them."[52] Ideas are rather the presentation (*Darstellung*) of phenomena, which means that phenomena do not relate to ideas in a simple manner. In effect, the aura of phenomena must be destroyed before they can take part in the realm of ideas. Benjamin explains:

> Phenomena do not [...] enter into the realm of ideas [*das Reich der Ideen*] whole, in their crude empirical state, adulterated by appearances [*Schein*], but only in their basic elements, redeemed. They are divested of their false unity so that, thus divided [*aufgeteilt*], they might take part [*teilzuhaben*]

in the genuine unity of truth. In this their division [*Aufteilung*], phenomena are subordinate to concepts [*Begriffen*], for it is the latter which effect the loosening of things [*Dingen*] into their constituent elements.[53]

Maintaining this difference between the idea and the concept insofar as each relates to phenomena, Benjamin suggests that the concept is an analytical tool that grasps the parts that it has broken up (Benjamin is of course alluding to the way the German noun *Begriff* etymologically suggests the act of grasping). Under the violent grasp of the concept, phenomena become mere things loosened up (*Lösung*) into discrete parts. The concept therefore divides phenomena into parts (*aufteilen*) by divesting mere appearance or *Schein* of its false unity. By means of this process, the concept prepares phenomena for a certain kind of *participation*, a taking part (*teilhaben*) in what Benjamin is here calling truth.

There are therefore two complex relations in play: between the idea and phenomena and between the concept and the idea. By focusing on the latter relation, Benjamin elucidates the link between ideas and phenomena. On the one hand he distinguishes carefully between concept and idea, noting that the idea has nothing to do with the differentiating and dividing power of the concept. However, Benjamin also notes that the two are connected in an essential manner. As he explains, without the conceptual grasp, phenomena could not be prepared for entry into the realm of ideas, *das Reich der Ideen*. It is at this point that Benjamin uses an analogy that describes the relation (or non-relation) between ideas and phenomena. He writes: "A comparison may present the significance [of this relation]. Ideas are to things as constellations are to stars. [*Ein Vergleich mag deren Bedeutung darstellen. Die Ideen verhalten sich zu den Dingen wie die Sternbilder zu den Sternen]*"[54] Benjamin here is already speaking of 'things,' that is, phenomena dissolved into material elements (*dinglicher Elemente*) within the grasp of the concept.[55] Whereas phenomena, in their division into material elements, bear a determining relation to concepts, the same cannot be said about their relation to ideas. Rather, Benjamin describes the relation between ideas and things as a constellation. Just as

143

the constellation or star-image (*Sternbild*) does not refer to any one star (*Stern*), an idea has no direct relation to any single element in the constellation. The idea, then, is something like a frame, but this simile is misleading if it is taken to mean that the frame simply encloses phenomena. Rather, phenomena, in their division into material elements, are the frame itself. Benjamin says that "the idea is described as the forming or framing of the connection (the hanging-together) in which the unique-extreme stands with those that are like it. [*Als Gestaltung des Zusammenhanges, in dem das Einmalig-Extreme mit seinesgleichen steht, ist die Idee umschrieben.*]"⁵⁶ The dissolved phenomena, which Benjamin defines as unique and extreme singularities, hang together with other elements in what he calls an "objective, virtual arrangement" (*objektive virtuelle Anordnung*).⁵⁷ Even though each element is unique-extreme, each one is also *like* other elements (*mit seinesgleichen*) in this virtual arrangement. These singular repetitions hang together in such a way that, at the right moment, they become something other: the stars enter into a constellation or *Sternbild*.

One might wonder, however, when this right moment occurs, and in what way these singular repetitions become something other. Benjamin explains this process by again distinguishing between ideas and concepts, this time on the basis of their respective modes of intention. The difference between the two lies, however, not in degrees of intention, but whether there is intention at all. Benjamin explains: "While the concept emerges from the spontaneity of the intellect [*aus der Spontaneität des Verstandes*], ideas are given for [the purposes of] meditation [*Betrachtung*]."⁵⁸ The concept, for Benjamin, is on the side of intention. The point of the concept is the collecting of phenomena; it collects these phenomena through the force (*Kraft*) of the differentiating intellect (*des unterscheidenden Verstandes*).⁵⁹ Again we see that the concept, for Benjamin, takes phenomena apart by force, subdividing them into parts so that they may be known. The concept is therefore firmly on the side of knowing, intention, and the differentiating intellect.

The idea, however, has no such intention and is certainly not knowledge. Ideas, like constellations, are simply given to be observed or lend themselves to a certain kind of meditation (*Betrachtung*). In fact, Benjamin notes that the idea is given not so much as a primordial language or *Ursprache* as a primordial perception or *Urvernehmen*.[60] If the idea is then something given for meditation or observation, and if it has less to do with a primordial language than a kind of primordial perception, this might suggest that the idea is something like an image, and Benjamin indeed goes in that direction. However, he immediately adds that this primordial perception is a kind of reading "in which words possess their own nobility as names, unimpaired by cognitive meaning."[61] This idea-image is then not something to be seen by the eyes. Benjamin writes:

> here it is not a question of making [ideas] present in an illustrative or vision-based way; but rather, in philosophical contemplation, the idea is released from the heart of reality as the word, reclaiming its name-giving rights. [...] Ideas are given, without intention, in the act of naming, and they have to be renewed by philosophical contemplation.[62]

On the one hand, ideas are images; on the other hand, Benjamin insists that ideas are names, that is non-visual, linguistic things: "The idea is something linguistic" (*Die Idee ist ein Sprachliches*).[63] How to be both at the same time?

We can address this question by focusing on the way in which a concept becomes an idea. If a concept forcefully groups phenomena together into a cohesive whole, an idea on the other hand happens as an unintentional event: the idea is a concept that has suddenly become something else, something other. Rather than a concept, the idea becomes a name. However, the movement from the concept to the idea is discontinuous; the two belong to completely different realms. Benjamin writes: "There is no analogy between the relationship of the individual to the idea and its relationship to the concept: in the latter it falls under the concept and remains what it was—individuality; in the former it stands in the idea and becomes what it was not: a totality."[64] Benjamin calls this event—from concept to idea, from what it is to what it is not—a configuration: "ideas are not presented in themselves, but solely and exclusively in an arrangement of concrete elements in the concept: as the configuration of these elements."[65] Through the accumulation of divided phenomena (or word-fragments, as I called them above), the concept turns and becomes an idea. The idea is then something linguistic in that it happens as a figure: in a tropological turn, the idea is presented in a configuration (*Konfiguration*).[66] While it is true that there is no analogy between the idea and the concept, this very non-relation between the two institutes the configuration. This relationship can be called dialectic only because the configuration is constituted by a movement between concept and idea. However, this configuration is not a Hegelian *Begriff* that may lead to absolute knowing. Instead, a non-cognitive act of naming takes place in this configuration. Like the hidden figure, the configuration is not visible and cannot be taken up and known. It happens rather as an act: the philosophy of art must name a figural relation, not in an act of knowing (as if it were a concept), but rather in an act of contemplation (as an idea). This contemplation re-establishes or renews (*erneuern*) the original perception of words (*das ürspringliche Vernehmen der Worte*).[67] This kind of philosophical contemplation is the repetition—or the reading—of something that paradoxically cannot be repeated or read: the utterance of an original name. Benjamin's notion of presentation is thus a kind of reading that is also the inscription of a non-cognitive event.

Configuration therefore only takes place in a kind of inactual reading, a reading that is never present in itself and that constitutes an instant that is both a repetition and an origin. In "On Some Motifs," Benjamin calls this configuration a hidden figure. The crowd is thus not just one motif among many, but rather the hidden figure that emerges from the enumeration of motifs. The motifs or linguistic phenomena in Benjamin's essay constellate into the *Sternbild* of the crowd. Yet just because we can read this crowd does not mean we can grasp or comprehend it. For Benjamin reading is neither seeing nor knowing. To read means the presentation of a figural relation through the undialectical enumeration—or crowd—of motifs.

Benjamin's essay therefore does not seek to actualize Baudelaire by making his poetry knowable and graspable. Rather, "On Some Motifs in Baudelaire" bears witness to an experience of untimeliness that is called 'the decay of the aura.' It is true that we can always try to know what this decay of the aura means by focusing on the various definitions of aura that traverse Benjamin's essays. However, the last sentence of "On Some Motifs" frustrates the attempt to define the experience of the decay of the aura. Rather than knowledge, all we are left with is an image. The more we try to actualize this image as knowledge, the more de-actualized it gets and the more it presses on the present instant (*Aktualität*) demanding to be read. This is the image of inactuality I have tried to read throughout this essay: it is the star without atmosphere. To read this image would mean the presentation of a non-cognitive configuration: an idea. Benjamin names this idea: Baudelaire.[68]

Notes

[1] Irving Wohlfarth, "Resentment Begins at Home: Nietzsche, Benjamin, and the University," in *On Walter Benjamin: Critical Essays and Recollections*, ed. Gary Smith (Cambridge, Mass.: The MIT Press, 1988), 247.

[2] Walter Benjamin, OGT, 53.

[3] Eduardo Cadava expresses it best when he states, in relation to Benjamin's theory and rhetoric of photography, that "the experience of aura is always also an experience of its disintegration." *Words of Light: Theses on the Photography of History* (Princeton: Princeton University Press, 1997), 120.

[4] Benjamin, "On Some Motifs in Baudelaire," in SW 4, 343.

[5] Benjamin, Corr., 583, 580. The debate between Adorno and Benjamin has already received much critical attention. For example, Tom Cohen seeks to read the possibility of a materialist historiography in this debate between the two; see *Ideology and Inscription: "Cultural Studies" after Benjamin, de Man, and Bakhtin* (Cambridge: Cambridge University Press, 1998). Timothy Bahti's chapter "Benjamin, Baudelaire, and the Allegory of History," on the other hand, attempts to read this debate in terms of the problem of allegory; see *Allegories of History: Literary Historiography after Hegel* (Baltimore: Johns Hopkins University Press, 1992). Giorgio Agamben, in his *Infancy and History* (London: Verso, 1993) reads the debate in

terms of the problem of mediation in Hegel and Marx. Finally, Gerhard Richter reads in the exchange between Adorno and Benjamin a drive not towards an orthodox Marxism, but rather "towards an unorthodox materialist form of negative dialectics;" see "Adorno and the Excessive Politics of Aura," in *Benjamin's Blind Spot: Walter Benjamin and the Premature Death of Aura*, ed. Liss Patt (Topanga, CA.: The Institute of Cultural Inquiry, 2001), 31.

6   Bahti, "Benjamin, Baudelaire, and the Allegory of History," 208.

7   Nägele makes a similar point in "The Poetic Ground Laid Bare": "Benjamin's second essay, '*Über einige Motive bei Baudelaire*,' is both a revision of the first essay and a new text. The revisions take Adorno's critique into account by refuting it in an implicit rephrasing of the question of the ground and the cause." Rainer Nägele, "The Poetic Ground Laid Bare (Benjamin Reading Baudelaire)," in *Walter Benjamin: Theoretical Questions*, ed. David S. Ferris (Stanford: Stanford University Press, 1996), 122.

8   In fact, Adorno's early *Kierkegaard: Construction of the Aesthetic* (Minneapolis: University of Minnesota Press, 1989) remains highly Benjaminian in its presentation, a method that Adorno will not always follow. See Robert Hullot-Kentor's translator's notes for a short discussion of the relation between Benjamin and Adorno.

9   Benjamin, Corr., 583.

10   Benjamin, OGT, 178; GS I, 354.

11   Benjamin, Corr., 582.

12   Ibid., 482, 557.

13   Ibid., 557.

14   Benjamin, "On Some Motifs," in SW 4, 343; GS I, 653.

15   See Benjamin, "On Some Motifs," in SW 4, 314.

16   Quoted by Gary Smith in the editorial note to Adorno's "Introduction to Benjamin's *Schriften*," in *On Walter Benjamin: Critical Essays and Recollections*, ed. Gary Smith (Cambridge, Mass.: The MIT Press, 1988), 2.

17   See Walter Benjamin, "On Some Motifs in Baudelaire," in *Illuminations*, translated by Harry Zohn (New York: Schocken Books, 1968). The new translation of "On Some Motifs" in SW is perhaps even stranger in regard to the last line of the essay. In Harry Zohn's revision of his earlier translation, he again omits Benjamin's source footnote but now adds a footnote of his own. Instead of referencing *Untimely Meditations* (as Benjamin does), Zohn provides a very precise reference to Nietzsche's early, uncompleted work "Philosophy in the Tragic Age of the Greeks." As we will see in the present essay, Zohn's bibliographic remark is correct, even if the choice of including it in the translation seems arbitrary.

18   Friedrich Nietzsche, "On the Uses and Disadvantages of History for Life," in

Untimely Meditations (Cambridge: Cambridge University Press, 1997), 97; "*Vom Nutzen und Nachteil der Historie für das Leben,*" in *Werke in Drei Bänden,* ed. Karl Schlectha (München: Carl Hanser Verlag, 1977), 253.

19 Benjamin, "On Some Motifs," in SW 4, 318; GS I, 614.

20 Ibid, 343; GS I, 653.

21 Nietzsche, "On the Uses," 100, 97; Nietzsche "*Vom Nutzen,*" 254.

22 It is perhaps no accident that Benjamin uses this same word, *Hülle,* to describe the decay of aura in his earlier "Work of Art" essay: "The stripping of the veil [*Hülle*] from the object, the destruction of the aura," see "The Work of Art in the Age of its Technological Reproducibility (Third Version)," in SW 4, 255–6; GS I, 479. In this description the destruction of aura takes place in precisely the same terms Nietzsche used to describe the work of a strong historical sense. In both cases the envelope or veil (*Hülle*) is destroyed.

23 Benjamin, GS I, 653.

24 Nietzsche, "*Vom Nutzen,*" 253.

25 Benjamin, GS I, 623.

26 Benjamin, "On Some Motifs," in SW 4, 324 (translation modified); GS I, 623.

27 See two important studies that treat the instant or *Augenblick*: Samuel Weber's "Mass Mediaauras; or, Art, Aura, and Media in the Work of Walter Benjamin," in *Walter Benjamin: Theoretical Questions,* ed. David S. Ferris (Stanford: Stanford University Press, 1996), 43–44; and Nägele's "The Poetic Ground Laid Bare," 132.

28 Benjamin, "On Some Motifs," in SW 4, 328.

29 Ibid., 338.

30 Ibid., 339.

31 Ibid., 333.

32 Benjamin, AP, 369 [J80a,4].

33 Benjamin, Corr., 577.

34 Ibid., 557.

35 Friedrich Nietzsche, *Philosophy in the Tragic Age of the Greeks* (Chicago: Henry Regnery Company, 1962), 65–67; "*Die Philosophie im tragischen Zeitalter der Griechen,*" in *Nachgelassene Schriften: 1870–873,* eds. Giorigio Colli and Mazzino Montinari (Berlin: Walter de Gruyter, 1973), 328.

36 Nietzsche, *Philosophy in the Tragic Age,* 67.

37 Benjamin, GS I, 649.

38 Benjamin, "On Some Motifs," in SW 4, 321 (translation modified); GS I, 618.

39 For instance, Margaret Cohen disagrees with "Benjamin's argument for Baudelaire's elision of the crowd," as "it does not quite characterize Baudelaire's relation to the crowd, which, while undeniably problematic, is by no means suppressed. Far from 'hidden' or 'a part of Baudelaire's interior,' the crowd fills Baudelaire's

writings." *Profane Illumination: Walter Benjamin and the Paris of Surrealist Revolution* (Berkeley: University of California Press, 1993), 209. Cohen goes on to chide Benjamin for wavering between a psychoanalytic and a Marxist explanation of the hidden figure (211). I would argue, however, that Benjamin uses the term 'hidden figure' to talk about a structure of language that is also a mode of presentation. The crowd, for Benjamin, would therefore not be located at those moments when the word 'crowd' appears, but rather when a certain structure of language goes into presentation or actualization. As we will see, Benjamin calls this structure a 'constellation.' I thank Elissa Marder for informing me of Cohen's argument.

[40] Baudelaire, quoted in Benjamin's "On Some Motifs," in SW 4, 342.

[41] Benjamin, GS I, 618.

[42] Benjamin, "On Some Motifs," in SW 4, 321; GS I, 618.

[43] Benjamin, "On Some Motifs," in SW 4, 321.

[44] Ibid., 323.

[45] Elissa Marder, *Dead Time: Temporal Disorders in the Wake of Modernity (Baudelaire and Flaubert)* (Stanford: Stanford University Press, 2001), 70.

[46] Ibid., 68.

[47] Christopher Fynsk develops a reading of Benjamin's *Relationsbegriffe* in "The Claim to History," published in his *Language and Relation ... that there is language* (Stanford: Stanford University Press, 1996). For a reading of Benjamin's insistence on taking translation outside the realm of the human, see Paul de Man's "'Conclusions': Walter Benjamin's 'The Task of the Translator'," in *Resistance to Theory* (Minneapolis: University of Minnesota Press, 1986).

[48] Benjamin, "The Task of the Translator," in SW 1, 255 (translation modified); GS IV, 12.

[49] Ibid., SW 1, 255; GS IV, 18.

[50] For two important discussions of 'presentation' in Benjamin, see Hans-Jost Frey, "On Presentation in Benjamin," in *Walter Benjamin: Theoretical Questions*, ed. David S. Ferris (Stanford: Stanford University Press, 1996) and Christopher Fynsk, *Language and Relation.* For some insightful discussions of the motif of the star in Benjamin, see Cadava *Words of Light.* There Cadava suggests that "[t]he star is always a kind of ruin," a formulation that has certainly played a part in my reading of the phrase 'a star without atmosphere.' See Cadava, *Words of Light*, 30.

[51] Benjamin, OGT, 38.

[52] Ibid., 34.

[53] Ibid., 33; GS I, 213.

[54] Benjamin, GS I, 214. As Frey notes, the comparison in Benjamin can be called something like the presentation of presentation. He notes that "comparison is not, as it may first appear, an illustration or elucidation of presentation, but rather

is the presentation of presentation. In other words, [Benjamin's] comparison of the treatise with the mosaic [in the "Epistemo-critical Prologue"] has itself the character of the treatise. [...] Many of Benjamin's comparisons are presentations in the strict sense. They arise not out of metaphorical similarities, but out of the mystery of affinity. In them, what is compared comes together unforeseeably" Frey, "On Presentation," 149.

55 Benjamin, GS I, 215. The translation of "*dinglicher Elemente*" as "material elements" comes from Carol Jacobs' discussion of Benjamin's work in her *In the Language of Walter Benjamin* (Baltimore: Johns Hopkins University Press, 1999), 4.

56 Benjamin, GS I, 215.

57 Ibid., 214.

58 Ibid., 210.

59 Ibid., 215.

60 Ibid., 216.

61 Benjamin, OGT, 36.

62 Ibid., 37 (translation modified).

63 Ibid., 36; GS I, 216.

64 Benjamin, *Ursprung des deutschen Trauerspiels*, translated by Timothy Bahti in *Allegories of History*, 258. Bahti notes, in his chapter "End and Origin: Benjamin's *Ursprung des deutschen Trauerspiels*," that this operation–from what it is to what it is not–already suggests the structure of allegory.

65 Benjamin, OGT, 34 (translation modified).

66 Benjamin, GS I, 214.

67 Ibid., 217.

68 I thank Thomas Cerbu, Elissa Marder, and Jennifer Ballengee for their careful reading of earlier versions of this essay.

Is There an Answer to the Aestheticization of the Political?

Some Remarks on a Passage in Benjamin's "Work of Art" Essay

Peter Fenves

I offer the following remarks with one reservation: a sense that, at a certain point, this reflection on a passage in Walter Benjamin's "The Work of Art in the Age of Its Technical Reproducibility" succumbs to a temptation that has no place in either commentary or critique, as Benjamin understands these terms—a temptation of literary and cultural scholarship that is called, in German, *Rechthaberei*, which is to say, wanting to be right by showing where someone else went wrong. There are few texts in which commentators have more thoroughly indulged in this temptation than the "Work of Art" essay, as some recent volumes largely devoted to exposing its errors demonstrate with sufficient clarity. And the answer I give to the question posed in my title seems to succumb to the very same temptation. For in response to the question "is there an answer to the aestheticization of the political?" I say 'no.' That this 'no' is not, after all, an instance of *Rechthaberei* is for others to decide. In any case, there is no question that it appears to contradict the famous last words of Benjamin's "Work of Art" essay, which I quote as a preface to the remarks below: "Humanity, which was once a spectacle for the Olympian gods, has become one for itself. Its self-alienation has reached such a level that it can experience its own annihilation as an aesthetic enjoyment of the highest order. Thus it stands with the aestheticization of the political perpetuated by fascism. Communism answers it with the politicization of art."[1]

The closing words of Benjamin's essay, like its first, allude to Marx's famous claim: "Humanity poses for itself only such tasks as it is able to solve."[2] These words appear in the Preface to the *Critique of Political Economy*, at a crucial point where Marx concludes a condensed exposition of historical materialism, in which the development of productive forces—and therefore the course of technological innovation in the widest sense—is identified as the matrix and motor of human history. According to the schema Marx outlines in these preliminary pages, at certain moments charged with revolutionary potential the social relations of production begin to "fetter" the forces of production they have hitherto supported, and these relations can be sustained only by further intensification of class conflict—and in any case (such at least is the supposition or hope) not for long. "The Work of Art in the Age of Its Technical Reproducibility" takes its point of departure from the prolegomena to historical materialism contained in the *Critique of Political Economy*: whereas the latter concerns itself primarily with the base or foundation, as the term is defined in its preface, the former inquires into that which appears to stand above and alone. And from the perspective of classical German aesthetics, this means above all the work of art. The critical passages of Benjamin's essay are therefore those that address the question: upon what, after all, is the work of art founded? The answer to this question is bound up with the earlier question: under what condition—if any—can humanity solve its tasks.

Marx's confident claim that "Humanity poses for itself only such tasks as it is able to solve" is also an allusion, for it self-consciously retrieves and rescinds the opening pronouncement of the only previous critical project comparable to his own: "Human reason has the peculiar fate that in one species of knowledge it is burdened by questions it cannot dismiss, for they are given as tasks by the nature of reason itself, which, however, cannot be answered, for they overstep all power of human reason."[3] Thus writes Kant at the opening of the Preface to the first edition of the first *Critique*. That "species of knowledge" is metaphysics, and the inability of human reason to answer questions it inevitably poses generates what Kant calls "transcendental semblance" (*transzendentaler Schein*). Semblance of this kind cannot be simply demystified, for it belongs to the very structure of finite rationality and is, as such, inseparable from the means and ends of demystification. Properly understood as both unsolvable and unavoidable, the questions of metaphysics turn into infinite tasks—precisely what Marx denies. In the case of Benjamin's essay, such reflections would mean something like this: any definitive answer to the aestheticization of the political misconstrues the task in question for a problem that can be definitively resolved; together, the two answers— here called "aestheticization of politics" and "politicization of art"—would constitute an antinomy, which, following the same shadow of an argument, derive from a common misconception: that the world can somehow be grasped independently of the manner and mode in which it is perceived—or, to use Benjamin's lexicon, independently of "the human perceptual apparatus" (GS VII, 381). Comprehending this misconception yields the infinite task of gradually adapting to, and therefore entering into, this very condition: the absence of a world above and beyond the apparatus in which it becomes perceivable.[4]

That Benjamin's essay moves in a similar direction gives some indication that the previous remarks are not entirely removed from the field of its argumentation, even if they are quite remote from the desperate circumstances of its composition. From the perspective of these circumstances the phrase "aestheticization of the political" can be readily understood in the following manner: certain regimes conceive themselves as works of art, the primary materials of which—namely human beings—are nothing more than inert matter at the disposal of form-giving political artists, who, in making their *Gesamtkunstwerke*, need worry about the fate of their material as little as Wagner need concern himself with the sentiments of his singers. There are doubtless those who have accurately deployed the phrase "aestheticization of the political" in this manner: as a description of those regimes that purge politics of legal and moral standards by more or less explicitly proffering aesthetic ones in their stead.

Not only does Benjamin not pose the question in this manner, he could not do so given his point of departure, for—and this is nowhere presented more succinctly than in the Preface to Marx's *Critique of Political Economy*—political categories cannot be collapsed into legal or moral ones. This is a premise of historical materialism, which is usually expressed by saying that legal functions are as much a part of the superstructure as moral codes and mythological creatures. Even if the final section of Benjamin's essay parenthetically proposes that the aestheticization of the political corresponds to a time in which the "masses" are deprived of their rights and are given the opportunity for "expression" instead, the rights in question cannot be identified either with the positive rights guaranteed by a particular regime or the natural rights that, according to some legal theorists, are the source of its legitimacy and under certain conditions the rationale for revolt. They consist, rather, in the right to alter "the relations of ownership" (GS VII, 382), which is to say, the right to something other than rights, as they are generally formulated. By making use of the questionable term 'right' in this context, Benjamin aligns himself with—and at the same time subtly distances his line of argument from—those who develop the phrase "aestheticization of the political" in order to answer the lingering question of how it is possible for certain social relations, in particular those of advanced capitalism, to sustain themselves when, because of wide-scale economic crises, they hinder the further development of productive forces. "The right to alter the relations of ownership" functions in Benjamin's essay as a *political right*, which, however, is only another way of naming the same problem: a 'right' outside the order of law and yet removed from the sphere of nature as well. The categories and criteria of the political—whatever these may be, and Benjamin for good reason remains silent about them here— enjoy a relative independence from those of legality, and this independence, which betrays itself in exceptional circumstances, makes the question posed by its aestheticization far more difficult, far less open to answers that take the reassuring form: shape political affairs according to legal norms.

The independence of political from legal criteria is, moreover, the source of its proximity to aesthetics, understood as a particular philosophical discipline first created and developed in the context of classical German, that is to say, Leibnizian metaphysics. And here, for better or worse, is a little *Rechthaberei*: the last sentence of the penultimate section of Benjamin's essay (in all but the final version) is wrong—not necessarily in what it says about film but in what it says about aesthetics. It reads: "Thus [film] shows itself from here on out as, for the time being, the most important object of that theory of perception, which, among the Greeks, was called aesthetics" (GS VII, 381). Many commentators have more or less strenuously rejected Benjamin's account of film. I do not take sides in this debate. Instead, I object to his remarks concerning the word 'aesthetics.' Of course, the term derives from the Greek verb *aesthesnesthai* according to the model of word-formation that has given rise to a large number of technical terms, including the word 'technical' itself. It was not, however, among the Greeks that the term developed in this manner but, rather, among certain eighteenth-century Germans, in particular Alexander Baumgarten who invented 'aesthetics' as a technical term for a branch of metaphysics.[5] "The excellent analyst Baumgarten" (A 21; B 35), to cite the first footnote in Kant's own "Transcendental Aesthetic," does not appear among the dozen or so *Deutsche Menschen* [Germans] whose letters Benjamin edits and briefly discusses while working on the "Work of Art" essay. Nor does Benjamin mention Baumgarten in conjunction with his rediscovery of Carl Gustav Jochmann, whose largely forgotten treatise "On the Retreat of Poetry," as Benjamin retrospectively realized, could serve as a prolepsis of his own philosophical-historical reflections. Despite this lacuna it is possible to identify certain affinities between Baumgarten's and Benjamin's inquiries into the "human perceptual apparatus" each conducts under the rubric of aesthetics. From the perspective of the reception of their respective inquiries, the term 'affinity' fails to do justice to this relation; 'identity' is better, for in both cases the aesthetica they proposed has been widely recognized and largely repudiated, often in the very same gesture.

Here is not the place for a broad exploration of the relation between

Baumgarten's massive *Aesthetica* and Benjamin's miniature one–and not only because Benjamin neglects to mention his predecessor. This much can be stated, however: something in Baumgarten's invention of the technical term 'aesthetics' corresponds to Benjamin's attempt to develop entirely new terms for the study of both artwork and the human sensorium at large, and this correspondence is nowhere more apparent than in the place where Benjamin overlooks Baumgarten's innovation. For Benjamin, the theory of perception called 'aesthetics' must henceforth acknowledge the indispensable function of 'distraction,' for Baumgarten, that of 'confusion.' *Zerstreuung* (distraction), as Benjamin presents this term, may even be considered a consolidation and intensification of Baumgartenian *confusio*. Whereas Benjamin makes a case for the aesthetic validity of distraction in 1935, Baumgarten does the same with regard to confusion exactly two hundred years earlier–and thereby invents aesthetics as a double discipline: devoted on the one hand to the critique of taste and on the other to the nature of perception. According to Baumgarten's *Philosophical Meditations Pertaining to Poetry* (1735), poetry–the study of which holds a principal place in the new science of aesthetics–consists in the perfection of distinct yet confused perceptions: distinct, because the object of perception is distinguishable from every other; confused, because the concept under which this object falls eludes its creator and perceivers alike. Distinct yet confused perceptions are particularly apt for the representation of individuals, however, since the objects of such perception can be distinguished from other things but cannot be analyzed into their constituent elements. There always remains, to quote Leibniz, an element of *"je ne sais quoi."*[6] In this sense aesthetics makes room for what the 'higher' science of rational metaphysics scorns: singularities, which appear to be different from everything else, although no one can say either how or why. By granting themselves the joy of confusion, without suffering any loss in the ability to make distinctions–quite the contrary–those whom Baumgarten calls 'aestheticians' enter into an independent sphere of perceptibility: a 'lower' sphere in comparison to that of rational cognition, to be sure, but one that nevertheless enjoys a dignity of its own. This sphere can also be described in light of a term Benjamin deploys for the purpose of avoiding the vast terminology of aesthetics developed in the wake of Baumgarten's innovation: the 'lower' sphere of aesthetics arises, namely, in conjunction with the 'decline' of the aura.

Without entering into a lengthy engagement with the specific terms with which Benjamin elucidates the idea of the auratic decline, this much can be said: the aura consists in the appearance of another spatio-temporal nexus in relation to our own: "What is the aura, properly speaking [*eigentlich*]?" Benjamin asks in a rare use of the rhetorical question: "a peculiar web made of space and time [*ein sonderbares Gespinst aus Raum und Zeit*]: the one-time appearance of a distance, no matter how near it may be" (GS VII, 355).[7] The peculiarity of this ghostly web—*Gespinst* verges on *Gespenst*—consists in its violation of those principles of space and time to which Kant gives canonical expression at the opening of his critical project. According to the "Transcendental Aesthetic," closeness can never be predicated of "a distance"—not even once. This is not to say, however, that singularity is an altogether illegitimate predicate, wholly without "objective validity"; the point is, rather, that the category of singularity is illegitimate only in relation to objects of possible knowledge. Whereas the "Transcendental Aesthetic" of the first *Critique* can be called the metaphysical ratification of auratic decline, the "Critique of Aesthetic Judgment" moves in the opposite direction: toward the disclosure of a sphere in which this, the defining category of the aura—its "one-timeness"— can be delicately retained. Take a palace, for example—or, more exactly, "the palace I see before me" (Ak 5, 204): insofar as the palace alone is the subject of my capacity to judge, without regard to any thoughts I might entertain of its function and purpose, the only possible point of reference for my reflective power of judgment is my own state of mind, which is to say, my feeling of pleasure or displeasure. However far it may be from my—or indeed of Kant's—experience, the example of the palace is not chosen arbitrarily. It is drawn from the first example of beauty Kant mentions in the *Critique of Judgment* and the example through which he

158

elucidates the categorial "quality" of the aesthetic mode of judgment: disinterest, which is to say, disregard for the actual, spatial-temporal existence of the object represented in the entirely singular presentation that serves as the subject of the "power of judgment" (*Urteilskraft*). In light of the vast squander of labor poured into the institution of palaces—or, as Kant, ventriloquizing Rousseau, wrote: in view of "the vanity of the great who waste the sweat of the people on such superfluous things" (Ak 5, 204)—this disregard is no small accomplishment.

That the palace is a politically charged example—especially in the fall of 1790, when the third *Critique* was first published and certain palaces came under siege—goes without saying. If, as Kant famously proposed, one of the principal characteristics of beauty is "purposiveness without purpose" (Ak 5, 236), the palace can also be seen to exemplify its inversion: social non-purposiveness with an unmistakable political purpose, namely demonstrating who is ultimately in charge. The aristocracy may have no valid function—this is a point Kant increasingly stresses as he grows older[8]—but the products it commissions can still be judged to be beautiful; indeed, they are exemplary in their beauty for precisely this reason. Yet Kant never goes beyond such suggestions. Politics for him has no right to claim independent criteria and must instead be made into a matter of purely legal norms. Such is the point of *Toward Perpetual Peace* and the source of his increasingly bitter polemic against "practical politicians." Kant therefore refrains from doing what he suggests: politicize aesthetics. And the form of politicization from which he abstains is discernible in the first example of aesthetic judgment: beauty would be the promise of palaces deprived of power.

The same is not true of Kant's successors, however, many of whom propose, invert, and subvert the following thesis: the domain of aesthetic experience is that of non-domination. Inaugurated as an emancipation of perception from its subjection to the 'higher' cognitive faculties, developed in light of the circular and self-grounding liberality of the 'liberal arts,' aesthetics could claim to be a prolegomena for the project of universal human liberation—indeed, an indispensable propedeutic for

159

anyone who wishes to pursue this project without installing regimes that are even more repressive than the ones they replace. Such a politicization of aesthetics, which turns beauty into the perceptual form of freedom, can be answered by reversing its terms: the domain of aesthetics is a symptom and agent of domination—not an immediate enthrallment to princes and palaces perhaps, but a mediated subjection to those economic and bureaucratic powers that constitutively conceal their modes of mastery. The mediated character of such domination makes it all the more insidious: not only is freedom lacking, but so too is the chance of recognizing its absence. New forms of art can then be charged with the task of making the absence of freedom recognizable by subverting their own aesthetic impulses; in turn an aesthetic theory can develop as a second-order propedeutic for the project of liberation—one that takes its point of departure from those self-conscious semblences of autonomy that uneasily retain the rubric of 'fine art.' This proposal, which still maintains an uneasy place for beauty, can be negated in turn: without freedom and without a valid claim to liberation from the semblance of freedom—this is the desolate domain of aesthetics, if this word remains viable. It is as though the exemplary palace in the third *Critique* were no longer an example of beauty, but instead of a sublimity that, unlike Kant's, whispers "no, no, no": "you cannot take charge; you cannot make good on your impotence; and you cannot hope to rescue this double negation by way of negative dialectics." From Schiller through Adorno to Lyotard, the politicization of aesthetics follows this approximate course.

All of this supposes, however, that one is in command of the term 'politicization.' In light of Benjamin's "Work of Art" essay, its counterpart can be defined in a fairly concise manner: 'aestheticization' consists in the transformation of something into an object that is grasped and evaluated from two incompatible yet reinforcing perspectives: self-interested expression and self-alienated enjoyment. Neither perspective is concerned with artworks per se, only with the interests and emotions of its intended audience. In this sense the first victim of aestheticization is, as Heidegger suggests in a series of contemporaneous lectures, the artwork itself.[9] Benjamin proposes something similar—without supposing, however, that this thesis were the opening bid of a 'grand politics' that would revive the era and aura of great art. And it is in response to this question—what is to come of artwork in the absence of its aura?—that the question of its counterpart, namely 'politicization,' can be effectively posed. What Benjamin offers in this context is the following passage, which contains his definitive renunciation of aesthetic autonomy: "At the very moment in which the criterion of genuineness fails to apply to the production of art, the entire social function of art rolls over. Into the place of its founding in ritual, its founding in another praxis has to step [hat zu tritt]: namely, its founding in politics" (GS VII, 357).

With this underlined but unamplified passage, Benjamin turns to other topics: the distinction between cultic-value and display-value in some versions of the essay, the early days of photography, in others. What remains unexplained and unchanged is the awkwardness of the passage itself, especially in its second version: being founded in politics "has to step in place"[10] (GS VII, 357) of being founded in ritual. That Benjamin struggled with the tense in which to formulate this precarious step cannot be doubted: in the first version of the essay the sentence in question is in the past (GS 1, 442), whereas in the third version it is in the present (GS 1, 482); and in the second, in the imperative. At no other juncture in the essay—and, to my knowledge, at no other place in Benjamin's entire corpus—is he so uncertain as to which verb form should be used: "ist getreten" (has stepped) indicates an event that has been completed; "tritt" (steps) something taking place now or forever; and "hat zu treten" (has to step) a causal connection, a metaphysical axiom, or a principle of practical reason. Aesthetics may declare its autonomy—and in the very person of Adorno, it does so for the purpose of Benjamin's edification—but the work of art cannot stand on its own: it must be grounded in some other practice. And this 'must' must somehow be integral to the very workings of 'the work of art'—so much so that, regardless of what anyone means by the term 'work of art,' it says "grounded in a founding praxis" or, in other words, 'derivative.' The axiom with which Benjamin begins his inquiry, "The work of art has in principle always been reproducible" (GS VII, 351), perhaps even derives from its irreducible derivativeness. That is to say: the predicate by which works or art appear to distinguish themselves from other things—singularity, one-timeness—cannot, properly speaking, belong to them; nor does it belong to the practice upon which all works of art, according to Benjamin, was initially founded, namely ritual. In terms of Benjamin's essay there is only one remaining term: politics, the nature of which cannot be determined in advance of its enactment. If, however, politics, unlike the work of art, can indeed be called singular, for this very reason it cannot unambiguously be said to appear as such.

Insofar as every thematization either presupposes a rule or reflexively suggests one, a practice consisting of unhallowed singularities cannot be thematized—and Benjamin avoids doing so. Instead of using the phenomenological term 'thematization,' however, it would be better to remain within the lexicon of the essay and say: 'politicization,' the formulation of a practice in accordance with a rule or reflexively sugges-ting one. From this perspective it is legitimate to say: whereas the work of art is the first victim of aestheticization, the practice of politics is the primary victim of politicization.

Benjamin never says this and for good reason: politics seems incon-ceivable without politicization. The same cannot be said of its counterpart: an aesthetics without aestheticization is at least conceivable, and Benja-min offers his early study of "Two Poem of Friedrich Hölderlin" as an exercise in what he calls "pure aesthetics" (GS II, 105). By contrast, the inconceivability of politics without politicization—the inconceivability of a pure politics, one might say, or, taking a cue from the title of another early project that Benjamin apparently abandoned, the inconceivability of "true politics" (*die wahre Politik*)[11]—draws politics into a particularly tense relation with aesthetics, as the placeholder for singularity in the era of auratic decline. Under the rubric of aesthetics, singularity appears as sheer 'subjective' presentation—as, for example, the presentation of a palace in eighteenth-century Königsberg, which, despite its royal name, had

162

none. Under the same rubric, an object can acquire the label 'autonomous,' insofar as the criterion for its judgment is supposed to be drawn from no power other than that of judgment itself. If, however, the criterion of the political is indeed irreducible to those of the legal order, as the doctrine of historical materialism maintains; and if, as Benjamin indicates, politics is a *new* founding praxis, irreducible to, and independent of, whatever has hitherto claimed this ancient name, then something similar can be said of politics: its criteria can have no source other than the sheer novelty or, better yet, the total topicality of the founding praxis itself. Each case of political praxis cannot even be considered *a* case of politics but is instead, insofar as the praxis is political, another foundation irreducible to anything else. Herein, at best, lies the elective affinity between politics and aesthetics: neither is entirely free of law, and yet neither is bound to it either. And herein, at worst, lies the danger of politics as a *founding* praxis: it can represent its foundational character in legal terms and therefore present itself as the only genuinely autonomous order to which every other is immediately and ultimately subordinate. For the best and for the worst, in short, the praxis called 'politics' resembles the theory of perception called 'aesthetics' under the condition of auratic decline.

All the techniques of Benjamin's effort—from its concern with technical reproducibility through its reflections on mimesis to its dense theory of compact masses—aim to show that this resemblance is mere semblance. But the resemblance between politics and aesthetics cannot be dispelled by means of a categorical demarcation: this falls under one heading, this another. Benjamin thus supports the Brechtian program of politicizing art, which is imperative in any case. It also forms the task to which this program owes its origin: doing away with the conditions under which politics resembles aesthetics and aesthetics politics. Only by doing away with the last trace of the auratic, in other words, do politics and aesthetics finally fail to resemble each other. Such a task cannot fail to assume the appearance of a certain 'nihilism'—and it cannot afford to be anything other than infinite.

Once again, Benjamin does not speak in this manner. Neither term enters the lexicon of his essay: neither 'nihilism,' with which he enigmatically concludes the so-called "Theologico-Political Fragment," nor 'infinite task,' which was one of the topics Benjamin analyzed in conjunction with his "Program for the Coming Philosophy." Instead, Benjamin offers the following account of the tasks in question: "The tasks that are posed to the human perceptual apparatus at historical turning points simply cannot be solved by way of mere optics, thus by contemplation. Under the guidance of tactile reception, they are gradually mastered by habituation" (GS VII, 381). The quotations from Kant and Marx with which this essay began are pertinent here as well. From Marx: "Humanity poses for itself only such tasks as it is able to solve." From Kant: "[certain questions], which are given as tasks by the nature of reason itself, cannot be answered." For Benjamin, the questions can be answered, the tasks solved—*but not by us*: not by those engaged in contemplation, still less by "human reason," and not even by "humanity" at large. The 'not us' is in this sense the primary subject of reflection; its name, for the purpose of this particular essay, is 'the masses,' which solves the pivotal tasks without having the least idea that it is doing any such thing, without realizing that there are tasks in the first place, still less pivotal ones, and above all, solves them without recognizing itself as such: as 'the' masses. The masses do not enjoy—or suffer from—the unity of consciousness, which is to say: the masses are constitutively distracted. The same feature can be expressed in another manner: not in terms of discrete numbers but in terms of their categorial character, the masses are infinite; they are—or it is—'not one.' This 'no one' can gain the semblance of unity under two closely related condition: when its elements, despite their diversity, are in spatial proximity to one another, and space is understood as a homogeneous and empty reciprocal that these elements are there to fill. The masses are then, in Benjamin's term, "compact." Non-compact masses, by contrast, do not appear to be so: they—or it— do(es) not appear to be the masses at all. Only a non-compact mass, however, can be, strictly speaking, *zerstreut* (dispersed). And for the same reason, only non-compact, dispersed, or 'diasporic' masses are in reality the masses: constitutively inconsistent pluralities, the elements of which cannot be grasped as 'one.' The tasks of the non-compact masses are infinite in turn—once again, not because they take an infinite amount of time but because only a distracted-dispersed 'no one' can accomplish them.

The model of a task that can be solved only by those who are no longer of what they are doing is one of the earliest undertaking human beings are asked to perform on their own: learning how to walk. Only insofar as I can walk while distracted, without knowing my way around, can I be said to have definitively mastered the art of walking. In the language of the "Work of Art" essay, the foundational praxis of politics appears in precisely this manner: as the act of taking a step. To cite once again a passage I discussed above: "At the very moment in which the criterion of genuineness fails to apply to the production of art, the entire social function of art rolls over. Into the place of its founding in ritual, its founding in another praxis has to step: namely, its founding in politics." Beyond being a "founding"—emphasized by the threefold repetition of the term *Fundierung* in a single, short sentence—the praxis of politics takes a step: not a step forward, which would amount to 'progress,' but a step 'in place', which runs counter to progress and regress alike. The act of taking a step is generally thought to be based on something; indeed, of all practices, none is perhaps more dependent upon a ground that it cannot provide for itself. According to this passage, however, a certain founding takes a step, namely the new founding of art in "politics." In the tradition to which Benjamin alludes when he mistakenly attributes the term 'aesthetics' to the Greeks, a similar idea appears under a very different name: that of a highest being, whose own immobility generates all movement. Political theology has perhaps never had a more subtle formulation.

No wonder Benjamin could not settle on the exact formulation for the step in question; no wonder he minimized the role of optical reception, for this singular step, like our first, is vertiginous. A glimpse of the awkward situation Benjamin describes in an uncharacteristically awkward way, still more the contemplation of its abyssal dimensions, would doubtless make even the most agile pedestrians think twice—or once: there is neither a way nor a place to go. (This situation is more like walking on ice than on water; in Benjamin's account of Moscow this is every newcomer's first task, so much so that in winter the city transforms them into children: "walking wants to be learned anew on the thick, smooth ice of these streets" (GS IV, 318). It may be for this reason—rather than for reasons of 'politics' as the term is generally understood—that the October Revolution in Russia functions as an exemplary space-time of revolutionary praxis.) Politicization, then, could then be understood as the process by which the awkwardness of the critical step is rectified, given guardrails, and turned into a recognizable program, which connects starting points and final destinations, premises and conclusions. Benjamin's attraction to Parisian passages follows in turn: these elaborate arcades, which draw the exterior into the interior and project the inside onto the outside, betray the process of politicization in a particularly powerful manner. Instead of providing exercise and training for a step unlike any other, a work of art—in this case, a certain form of urban architecture—offers pedestrians the appealing spectacle of planned perplexity. Or, in Baumgarten's words: the passages offer confusing yet distinct perceptions. Or in still other words: they aestheticize what might otherwise be a 'political' step. In this regard, politicizing and aestheticizing go hand in hand.

That the awkward step Benjamin proposes is not a step anyone could accomplish on his or her own is clear—and hardly surprising, since, if it were possible for one to take this step on one's own, it would no longer be a matter of politics; instead, it would be some other kind of concern: an aesthetic, ethical, or religious one, let us say, comparable to a torturous yet unremarkable 'leap of faith' (if I may be allowed to draw on Kierkegaard's questionable enumeration of 'spheres,' which Adorno's *Kierkegaard: Construction of the Aesthetic*, may have impressed again on Benjamin's thought). That this step cannot be formulated as a program for common action is also clear and equally unsurprising: the concept of politics as a "founding" (*Fundierung*) that steps in place of another has as little to do with programs as it does with progress. Least of all does the step consist in a plan behind which a consistent group can form as it falls in line. Perhaps this is ultimately why Benjamin makes the much-disputed pronouncement that the concepts he introduces into the discourse of art are "completely unusable for the purposes of fascism" (GS VII, 350). Still, certain questions remain unanswered, among which the following may be the most insistent, inasmuch as it gives an indication of the manner in which many others might be addressed: When does this all happen? When does the founding of art in the praxis of politics take its step? Only on the basis of an answer to this question could Habermas' famous objection be answered, namely that Benjamin gives no explanation for the "de-ritualization of art."[12] That Benjamin worried about this question—not, however, about Habermas'—is evident from the tense change in the formulation of the passage under consideration: whereas the first version indicates 'earlier,' the third version implies 'now or forever,' and the second says 'perhaps never—but necessarily nevertheless.' This remarkable diffidence does not mean, however, that, in view of Benjamin's essay, there is no definitive answer to the question; on the contrary, the preceding sentence, which remains unaltered throughout all the extent variations, contains one: "At the very moment in which the criterion of genuineness fails to apply to the production of art, the entire social function of art rolls over. Into the place of its founding in ritual, its founding in another praxis has to step: namely, its founding in politics."

The answer to 'when' is therefore: "*in dem Augenblick*," "at the very moment," more literally "in an eye-glimpse," more colloquially "in the blink of an eye"—which, upon reflection, is a surprising turn of speech, especially since the essay everywhere else emphasizes the very qualities to which the Kierkegaardian term *Øieblik* is opposed: gradualness, adjustment, habituation, and tactile receptivity. The social function of art rolls over; the founding of art in politics has stepped, steps, or has to step in the place of its founding in ritual. Despite the temporal uncertainty of this event, one thing is certain: the change from one "founding" to another takes place in the blink of an eye, without any transitional steps.

This *Augenblick* ironically attracts the very attribute that vanishes for the work of art at this very moment: singularity, one-timeness. For the moment is like no other–and for this reason uncertain with respect to its place in any temporal continuum. 'Before' and 'after' the moment, the work of art is founded; at the moment, by contrast, it is not. This 'not' should not, however, be understood to mean that works of art are somehow autonomous for a brief shining moment; rather, artwork as a whole rests on the movement-in-place of its foundation. In light of this singular moment, "for the time being, the most important object of that theory of perception, which, among the Greeks, was called aesthetics" (GS VII, 381), namely film, can be seen to consist in a massive groping in the dark, which corresponds to a task that is at once tactile and tactical: learn how to move without relying on any synopsis of the whole. Nevertheless, for better or worse, the infinitude of the uncompacted 'no one' that adapts itself to the absence of a world independent of its "perceptual apparatus" means that there is no answer to the aestheticization of the political–only an infinite task.

Notes

1 Walter Benjamin, GS VII: 584; hereafter, in parentheses in the text. Unless otherwise indicated, I cite the version published in the seventh volume of the *Gesammelte Schriften*. All translations are my own.
2 Karl Marx, *Zur Kritik der politischen Ökonomie*, in Karl Marx and Friedrich Engels, *Werke*, ed. Institut für Marxismus-Leninismus beim ZK der SED (Dietz: Berlin, 1971), 13: 9.
3 Immanuel Kant, *Gesammelte Schriften*, ed. Königlich Preußische [later Deutsche] Akademie der Wissenschaften (Berlin: Reimer; later, De Gruyter, 1900-), A vii; all further references to Kant in this volume are in parentheses ("Ak"), except for the *Critique of Pure Reason*, as in this case, which refers to the 1781 edition ("A"). For an analysis of the Kantian direction of Benjamin's essay–which is differently oriented than this one–see Rodolphe Gasché, "Objective Diversions: On Some Kantian Themes in Benjamin's 'The Work of Art in the Age of Mechanical

Reproduction," in *Walter Benjamin's Philosophy: Destruction and Experience*, eds. Andrew Benjamin and Peter Osborne (London: Routledge, 1994), 183–204.

4 The passages of the *Critique of Pure Reason* to which the above comments refer are especially A 293–309; B 249–366.

5 The first instance of the technical term 'aesthetics' can be found in the penultimate paragraph of Alexander Baumgarten's treatise, *Meditationes philosophicae de nonnullis ad poema pertinentibus* (Halle, 1735), § 116; *Reflections on Poetry*, (Berkeley: University of California Press, 1954), 78.

6 G.W. Leibniz, *Nouveaux essays sur l'entendement humain*, Book 2, chapter 29.

7 For a nuanced reading of this passage, see Samuel Weber, "Art, Aura and Media in the Work of Walter Benjamin," in *Mass Mediauras: Form, Technics, Media*, ed. Alan Cholodenko (Stanford: Stanford University Press, 1996), 76–107.

8 See, for example, Kant's utter rejection of the nobility in the *Metaphysics of Morals*, Ak 6, 329.

9 See, for example, Martin Heidegger, *Nietzsche* (Pfullingen: Neske, 1961), 1: 91–109.

10 Emphasis added.

11 See in particular Benjamin's letter to Gershom Scholem of in January 1920, reprinted in *Gesammelte Briefe*, eds. Christoph Gödde and Henri Lonitz (Frankfurt am Main: Suhrkamp, 1995-), 2: 109.

12 See Jürgen Habermas, "Bewußtmachende oder rettende Kritik–Die Aktualität Walter Benjamins," in *Kultur und Kritik* (Frankfurt am Main: Suhrkamp, 1977), esp. 316.

In the Midst of the Monad

Reflections on Auratic Alignments of the Everyday in Leibniz and Benjamin

Mikkel Bruun Zangenberg

Clov: It's easy going (Pause). When I fall I'll weep for happiness.
(Samuel Beckett[1])

The monad is auratic and the aura is tightly interwoven with the monad. This conjunction is not, as some might at first glance suspect, a facile and pseudo-elegant antithesis, but the overt statement of a profound, political alignment between Gottfried Wilhelm Leibniz's monadology and Walter Benjamin's attention to the everyday. In this article I argue that an essential affinity exists between Leibniz's monadology and Benjamin's ontology of film, and that the conjunction of these two dimensions in a single terrain—that of everyday miraculousness, as explained below—terminates in a strange, awkward appeal to the moral ideal and political telos of a boring and banal happiness. In his "Theological-Political Fragment" (date uncertain),[2] Benjamin explicitly wrote on the notion of happiness: "The secular order should be erected on the idea of happiness." He added that although the secular order itself is distinct from the messianic order, it "is a decisive category of its most unobtrusive approach." This unobtrusive approach makes itself most vehemently felt in a state of boredom. I glean this from a brief, convoluted sentence in *The Arcades Project*: "We are bored when we don't know what we are waiting for. That we do know, or think we know, is nearly always the expression of our superficiality or inattention. Boredom is the threshold to great deeds.—Now, it would be important to know: What is

170

the dialectical antithesis to boredom?"[3] The conception of boredom mobilized in this statement is congruent–all other differences aside–with Martin Heidegger's portrayal of the state of boredom as a sign of inauthenticity, but in Benjamin's case this is contrasted with the idea of 'great deeds,' bespeaking a revolutionary potential, the utopian possibility of suddenly cracking open the shell of homogeneous time. My claim is that the dialectical antithesis to futile boredom is and ought to be something else altogether, i.e., positive boredom–boredom as the virtual elimination of exceptional events. Exceptional events, or 'great deeds' for that matter, are nearly always catastrophic, or at the very least destructive: war, earthquakes, political revolutions. Certain great deeds tend to destroy the everyday, unsettle the lives of little people, violently reorganize the routines and ways of everyday living. In the course of contemplating the possibility of unleashing the full force of dialectical materialism on pernicious forms of historicism, Benjamin states: "It is more difficult to honor the memory of the anonymous than it is to honor the memory of the famous, the celebrated [...]. The historical construction [rather than the epic form of historicism,] is dedicated to the memory of the anonymous."[4] It is this sense of obligation towards those who never performed great deeds but perhaps suffered their consequences that animates my interest in boredom. For the key to re-conceiving everyday boredom as the site of the miraculous lies in acknowledging positive boredom as the true, dialectical antithesis to boredom. In addition, this would allow us to witness the dissolution of dialectics in infinite, unexceptional everydayness, in essence dialectics come to an unremarkable standstill. I shall suggest that Leibniz's monadology provides vital assistance to such an endeavor. This in turn demands we rethink the precise nature and function of Benjamin's idea of aura.

As is well known, Walter Benjamin defined aura as the character of manufactured singularity embedded in a homogeneous tradition, as opposed to the loss of aura which characterizes the infinite, technical reproducibility of, for example, photographic prints.[5] In "The Work of Art in the Age of Its Technological Reproducibility" (1935–36) Benjamin mentions Abel Gance's enthusiastic appraisal of film as media in 1927 and adds, "he was inviting the reader, no doubt unawares, to witness a comprehensive liquidation."[6] Likewise, Benjamin in the same essay writes of "a decay of the aura,"[7] as well as "[t]he stripping of the veil from the object, the destruction of the aura."[8] Tradition and handcraft are left behind as obsolete, the *hic et nunc* of authentic aura disintegrates and the world is abandoned to a desolate wasteland, an interminable reproduction of indifferent objects and correlative states of mind. The everyday is thus bereft of immanent value and all we are left with is a pale, horrified and indistinct messianism. In *The Origin of German Tragic Drama* Benjamin at one (famous) point recounts the dominant romantic conception of the symbol as opposed to allegory and artfully paraphrases the romantic idea of an allegoric landscape, a paraphrase that is not entirely foreign to the almost sad tonality in his later essay: "in allegory the observer is confronted with the *facies hippocratica* of history as a petrified, primordial landscape."[9] Although Benjamin regards the loss of aura as the precondition for the opening up of revolutionary possibilities,[10] the exact terms in which he describes this dissolution are redolent with sadness.

On its face this melancholy scenario rhymes badly with Leibniz's jubilant and robust rationalism founded on and expressed in the *Monadology*. Leibniz's late philosophy discreetly celebrated the inherent and infinite plenum of the world, the miracle of a manufactured world. One might argue that Leibniz conceived the world as a single gigantic object adumbrated by the divine aura emanating from God's creative act. In Leibniz, aura–thus reconfigured–is ineliminable. By extension we may infer that technical reproducibility merely redistributes the specific logistics and calculus with which objects or parts of objects are turned into aggregates, i.e., complex combinations of objects or substances, such as a painting or a film, a robot or an automobile. From a Leibnizian perspective utmost technicality, complete segregation of hand and machine, are nothing but new folds in the texture of the world,[11] the premise being that the distinction between nature and technology is blurred or merely becomes irrelevant when seen from a monadological perspective.

172

A monad is, of course, the smallest, indivisible extant component and each monad is made in advance by God: "Accordingly, God alone is the primary unity or the original simple substance, of which all the created or derivative monads are products."[12] Furthermore, God has ensured that all monads coexist in harmonious constellations: "These principles have given me a way to explain naturally the union, or rather the conformity of the soul and the organic body. The soul follows its own laws and the body likewise follows its own; and they agree by virtue of the pre-established harmony among all substances, because they are all representations of one selfsame universe."[13] This implies that the world is an uninterrupted and uninterruptible continuum. The continuum is miraculous, i.e., unsupported by any rational reasons we might attempt to establish or deduce.[14] The heaving multiplicity and perspectival variety of the world is therefore merely the external representation of the manufactured world's essential and monistic unity: "And as one and the same town viewed from different sides looks altogether different, and is, as it were, perspectively multiplied, it similarly happens that, through the infinite multitude of simple substances, there are, as it were, just as many different universes, which however are only the perspectives of a single one according to the different points of view of each monad."[15] Unity and multiplicity are the coterminous aspects of worldly monism.

Based on this premise, which is to be sure highly speculative, it is impossible not to admit that the everyday is a continual exfoliation of miraculousness. This is not to deny the repetitive, boring, perhaps even drab, nature of the everyday as ordinarily conceived, but that is not the point at all. Rather, the everyday is *strictu sensu* unthinkable within the perimeter of Leibniz's metaphysics, except as the continual and infinitely minuscule performance of an original and imperishable miracle.

Spinoza's everyday miracle

Until now we have neglected defining miracle, but it is now urgent that we touch upon Benedict Spinoza's original idea of that odd phenomenon. Before doing so, however, I would like to stress that Benjamin's historical

173

sketch of the loss of aura implicitly suggests that the miraculous vanishes
along with the irreducible singularity of the artwork. Endless technical
reproducibility evidently entails the annihilation of even the vaguest sense
of a miracle—the picture poster is produced in accordance with explicable
and well-known mechanical laws, whereas authentic artwork still hints at
the possibility of something practically incomprehensible being involved
in its creation. The actor in a theatre still embodies authentic presence,
whereas the film actor is torn apart, split and divided: "The situation can
also be characterized as follows: for the first time—and this is the effect of
film—the human being is placed in a position where he must operate with
his whole living person, while forgoing its aura."[16] This is the heart of the
distinction between creation and production. In what Max Weber famously
termed the 'disenchanted world,' miracles are decidedly a thing of the
past. The popular notion of miracles depict them as extraordinary breaches
of nature's laws, in effect as inexplicable states of exception; and the very
loss of a semantic horizon lead some—e.g., within the Catholic church—to
attribute the purportedly miraculous event to God's omnipotence.

In chapter six of *A Theologico-Political Treatise* (1670) pantheist, rationalist Spinoza powerfully rejects this notion. His central contention is that
miracles are nothing but natural events, thoroughly regulated in
accordance with the eternal and immutable laws of nature and our primary
ideas which are in turn established by God's divine intellect and omni-
potent will. The ignorant masses are susceptible to superstition and belief
in miracles, but when guided by the natural light of reason any sane and
educated person will quickly come to realize that miracles are essentially
mere natural occurrences: "a miracle, whether in contravention to, or
beyond, nature, is a mere absurdity; and therefore, that what is meant in
Scripture by a miracle can only be a work of nature, which surpasses, or
is believed to surpass, human comprehension."[17] Reason and nature are
intricately bound by the immeasurable force of God: "for whatsoever is
contrary to nature is also contrary to reason, and whatsoever is contrary
to reason is absurd, and, *ipso facto*, to be rejected."[18] All of this entails that
the miraculous is rooted in and is of the same fabric as the most everyday,

natural stratum: "miracles were natural occurrences, and must therefore be so explained as to appear neither new (in the words of Solomon) nor contrary to nature, but as far as possible, *in complete agreement with ordinary events*."[19] This implies that nothing is ever supernatural. Miracles are not out of the ordinary, rather they are emphatically ensconced in the midst of the realm of ordinariness. It further seems to imply that the miraculous is defined by its permanent state of exception.

Based on this natural and immanent ontology, the everyday miracle points toward a politics of power. 'Miracle' would then be the term accorded the standard extension of force in the natural and social stratum. In *Gilles Deleuze. An Apprenticeship in Philosophy*[20] Michael Hardt has brought to light the importance of this in relation to politics: "The expression of power free from any moral order is the primary ethical principle of society."[21] In chapter three Hardt performs an intensely Deleuzian reading of Spinoza. The relevant point in this context is that Hardt unearthed the bare outlines of miraculous politics in Spinoza; based partly on the premises that every body seeks to fulfill its ideal potential and that the chance encounter between bodies harbours the naked possibility of change: "The heart of Spinozian politics, then, is oriented toward the organization of social encounters so as to encourage useful and composable relationships."[22] Without touching on the notion of multitude,[23] my suggestion is that Spinoza's definition of miracle not only places it solidly within the confines of the everyday, but also contain *in nuce* a revolutionary potential—yet this very potential concerns the unexceptional state of exception, "in complete agreement with ordinary events." The everyday miracle would then be the malleable locus of a re-politicized concept of the aura. No longer the index of authentic genesis rooted in a tradition, but an interminably flexible and mobile trait within the expanding and contracting borders of all things made ordinary by time and routine use: film, the internet, cyberspace, Tupperware, cell-phones, etc. In that case, aura would be projective and prospective, directed towards a futurity filled with plastic configurations of monadism.

Rodolphe Gasché at one point polemically reminds us that for Benjamin the loss of aura entailed the disappearance of certain values, namely uniqueness, singularity and authenticity.[24] But seen in the light of a Spinozistic definition of miracles, this amounts to the achievement of something truly miraculous, i.e., the absence of great deeds or of anything out of the ordinary. In his "Theological-Political Fragment" Benjamin suggested that "nature is messianic by reason of its eternal and total passing away."[25] I would like to interpret this enigmatic statement of what Benjamin terms 'nihilism' (because everything, everywhere, forever is destined to pass into nothingness) as indirect acknowledgment of the emergence of interminable everydayness. For the everyday is precisely the withering away of time and things in a continuum bereft of great events.

If we accept Leibniz's postulates and premises as well as Spinoza's critique of the miraculous, we can comprehend why a certain reading of Benjamin's notion of aura may seem almost clichéd, based on what might be regarded as a nostalgic and reprehensible historico-philosophical platitude.[26] Such a rendering of Benjamin would fail to take into consideration his concept of 'natural history,'[27] but it would find support in a number of his crucial statements on history. Benjamin insisted on conceiving the historical stratum as capable of interruptions, revolutions, shocks, transformations of all kinds. In "On the Concept of History" Benjamin makes use of an explosion-metaphor several times to develop this point, e.g.: "What characterizes revolutionary classes at their moment of action is the awareness that they are about to make the continuum of history explode," and "Thus, to Robespierre ancient Rome was a past charged with now-time, a past which he blasted out of the continuum of history."[28] Also, in the 16th thesis he notes that: "He [the historical materialist] remains in control of his powers—man enough to blast open the continuum of history."[29] This sturdy materialist even "takes cognizance of it in order to blast a specific era out of the homogenous course of history; thus, he blasts a specific life out of the era, a specific work out of the lifework."[30] Indeed this is trivially true: history is amenable to change and is something other than the merely predetermined exposition of eternal laws.[31]

Continuum, however, is not determinism: Leibniz's cosmology and his notion of *petites perceptions* in no way entails a denial of the possibility of eruptive revolutions. It merely states that revolutions necessarily acquire the characteristics of a particularly violent fold, a variation upon the smooth surface of the world. Leibniz states as much in his famous image of the fishpond: "Thus nothing is fallow, sterile, or dead in the universe; there is no chaos, no disorder save in appearance. It is somewhat like what appears in a distant pond in which one might see the confused and, so to speak, teeming motion of the pond's fish, without distinguishing the fish themselves."[32] Monads are inextinguishable, but certainly allow for interruptions. They are also subject to change, with the proviso that this always comes about through internal machinations: "I also take it for granted that every created being is subject to change, and in consequence the created monad also, and even that this change is continuous in each one."[33] Leibniz added: "It follows from what has just been said that the natural changes of the monads proceed from an *internal principle* (that one can call an active force). For an external cause cannot influence their inner make-up [*son interieur*]. (And one can say, generally, that Force is nothing but the principle of change)."[34]

We seem, however, to be distant from Benjamin's conception of history as the medium of sudden transformation. The contrast becomes even more poignant by virtue of Benjamin's pointed inclusion of the monad as the formal figure of change: "Thinking involves not only the movement of thoughts, but their arrest as well. Where thinking suddenly comes to a stop in a constellation saturated with tensions, it gives that constellation a shock, by which thinking is crystallized as a monad. The historical materialist approaches a historical object only where it confronts him as a monad."[35] According to Benjamin, the monad is the frozen and arrested end-state of a process abruptly stopped in its tracks.

This directly counters Leibniz's theorem of continuity by which nothing in nature ever jumps or halts abruptly. In his "Foreword" to *New Essays on Human Understanding* Leibniz explicitly states that the enormous number of alterations of tiny particularities in nature is mostly unknown to us in that they come about via a multitude of *petites perceptions*, i.e., signs of change so small we only perceive the larger picture and never the complex, innumerable changes that taken together constitute the over-all image.[36] Leibniz compares this to our noticing the roll of the waves on the ocean— we are all instantly able to register their movement, but no one is capable of simultaneously perceiving the infinite number of minute changes that in unison compose the sea's movement. Thus even the most abrupt and violent wave discernable is the overt and external sign of a multitude of infinitesimal changes. This process is permanent and continuous, not prone to sudden variations that either freeze or decompose the interminable flow of nature. How then do we reconcile Leibniz's naturalist and rationalist monadology with Benjamin's philosophy of history? Additionally, the difference between the Leibnizian monad as a simple substance and the Benjaminian work of art, which is obviously and at the very least composite, is not yet surmounted. How can we align monad and work of art, aura and the everyday in the work of Leibniz and Benjamin?

Infinite interruption

By way of a circumspect answer, Peter Fenves has intriguingly brought to light Benjamin's debt to Leibniz, acknowledged in the "Epistemo-Critical Preface." Fenves initially quotes Benjamin: "The concept of philosophical style is free of paradox. It has its postulates. They are: the art of interruption in contrast to the chain of deductions; the endurance of the treatise in contrast to the gesture of the fragment; the repetition of motifs in contrast to shallow universalism; the fullness of concentrated positivity in contrast to negating polemics."[37] Fenves focuses on Leibniz's and Benjamin's respective theories of historical languages with special regard to their differing concepts of interruption. Fenves suggests that, "Leibniz and Benjamin mark out the limits of this study, in sum, because they both discover perspectives from which to grasp the infinite as they seek point of exit from the 'labyrinth of the continuum' in the course of perfecting the art of interruptive discourse."[38]

178

Both "grasp the infinite"—as a signpost for the following speculations. Aura is bounded and circumscribed, tied to the *hic et nunc*, as is all everyday life. Aura is tied to a particular object, any given life is mediate and finite. Yet aura is enmeshed in the continuous flow of manufactured objects (technical or handmade, endless or singular), while a life is embedded in the interminable motions of matter, constantly redistributing simple and complex substances. This connectivity implies an infinite realm of everyday, common, humdrum presence. Grasping the infinite means not least establishing a point from which to survey this all-inclusive movement bereft of exteriority. Fenves illuminates the mutual strategy tying Leibniz and Benjamin together when quoting Benjamin:

> And so the real world could be a task in the sense that it would be a matter of penetrating so deeply into everything actual that an objective interpretation of the world would disclose itself therein. Considered from the perspective of the task of such immersion, it does not appear puzzling that the thinker of the monadology was the founder of infinitesimal calculus. The Idea is a monad—that means, in abbreviated form: every idea contains the image of the world. The presentation of an idea must do nothing less than designate this image of the world in its abbreviation (*Verkürzung*).[39]

The foundation of this intuition and hypothesis—that the idea contains the image of the world—is Leibniz's assertion of universal causation and interconnectedness. The monad is said to be "without windows,"[40] it is an undisturbed entity, and yet it constantly interacts with all other substances in the universe: "Now this interlinkage [*cette liaison ou cet accomodement*] of all created things to each other, and of each to all the others, brings it about that each simple substance has relations that express all the others, and is in consequence a perpetual living mirror of the (whole) universe."[41]

What exactly does Benjamin mean by "The Idea is a monad"? A clue may lie hidden in a letter Benjamin sent his friend Florens Christian Rang on December 9, 1923, while still in the early stages of writing his

179

Trauerspiel-study.[42] The immediate context of Benjamin's ruminations concerns the question as to how works of art are related to historical life. Benjamin quickly brushes aside formal, neo-Kantian modes of analyzing works of art as well as naïve forms of art-historical analysis and abruptly introduces a distinction between the world of revelation and the taciturn world (*Welt der Verschlossenheit*). The world of revelation is extensive and temporal; it is the world of history. The taciturn world is intensive and is of nature and artworks alike. The work of art is a model of nature (*Modelle einer Natur*). Criticism of artworks is therefore the presentation (*Darstellung*) of an idea as monad: "Its intensive infinity characterizes ideas as monads."[43] The intensive infinity or interminability (*Unendlichkeit*) of ideas constitute their monadic being and this being is colored by the collapse of the difference between history and nature in Leibniz's monadology.

We now begin to ascertain one foundational similarity between Leibniz's monad and Benjamin's work of art and the aura (as well as his notion of an idea), namely that it is possible to comprehend both as mirrors of nature. Not a passive, ideational screen, such as Rorty once criticized,[44] but an emphatically living mirror, *miroir vivant*. The mirror *per se* only ever contains an abbreviated section of the universe's infinity. The moving, living mirror, in contradistinction, possess a gradual and pulsating spectrum of variable sections of the universe. Leibniz explains:

> To be sure, this representation is only confused regarding the detail of the whole universe. It can only be distinct in regard to a small part of things, namely those that are nearest or most extensively related to each monad. Otherwise each monad would be a deity. It is not in their object (namely the whole universe), but in the particular mode of knowledge of this object that the monads are restricted. They all reach confusedly to the infinite, to the whole; but they are limited and differentiated by the degrees of their distinct perceptions.[45]

This means that any abbreviation—e.g., one pertaining to a work of art or a mechanical reproduction—is flexible and mobile, the *Verkürzung* expands and dilates, contracts and distorts according to its mode of knowledge. Following this, my suggestion is that this description squares well with the technical peculiarities of film.

It is important to realize that this process never takes place in an isolated realm, but is located in the midst of life,[46] immersed "deeply into everything actual [...]" in that sphere where everything mirrors everything else by degrees and from specific positions. Leibniz adhered strongly to the idea of universal interdependence: "Certainly, in my opinion, there is nothing in the universe of creatures which does not need, for its perfect concept, the concept of every other thing in the universe of things, since everything influences everything else, so that if it were taken away or supposed different, all the things in the world would have been different from those that now are."[47] The name befitting this ubiquitous location and this global state of things is the everyday. The task of the everyday, what Stanley Cavell has termed "achieving the ordinary,"[48] is to immerse oneself maximally while accomplishing the abbreviation sufficient to grasp the infinite multitude and ordinariness of the everyday. This movement, if carried out successfully, is equally miraculous and auratic.

Seen from an Olympic vantage-point, the everyday obviously features a diffuse multitude of monads and aggregates of monads—objects, states of mind, constitutions, insects, persons, an infinite variety of extant physical and ideational and imaginary items.[49]

In *Everyday Life and Cultural Theory* Ben Highmore points to the curiously dual nature of the everyday. [50] On one hand, it is the very essence of tangibility and intimacy, the bedrock of our day-to-day existence, on the other, it may suddenly strike us as intolerably boring or agonizingly exciting. Yet in both instances the everyday is perhaps first and foremost characterized by its lack of distinguishing qualities: "the unnoticed, the inconspicuous, the unobtrusive."[51] The everyday is simultaneously ubiquitous and invisible. To the extent we cognize the everyday we may be bored or annoyed, find it blasé or delight with its homogenous stream of life. Highmore sought to enlist Benjamin as "theorist of the everyday"[52] in order to claim that "[t]he theme of everyday life as a problematic is central to Benjamin's work."[53] This comes about due to Benjamin's various analyses of modernity's staging of the everyday. Highmore depicts Benjamin as a sort of *Lumpensamler*, a ragpicker, scavenging among the debris of modernity, and quotes Richard Wolin on the philosophical underpinnings of Benjamin's method: "to reverse the terms of Western metaphysics by ceding pride of place in the field of philosophical inquiry to what had previously been merely derided and scorned: the ephemeral and transient aspects of the phenomenal world."[54] This rather sweeping passage is supplemented by Baudelaire: "By 'modernity' I mean the ephemeral, the fugitive, the contingent."[55] This comes close to casting Benjamin as a deluded nominalist, rooting about amidst the random and hitherto "scorned" contents of the dustbin of modern life's opulent production of material objects. Two things salvage Benjamin from this odious destiny: his attention to the dual temporality of the everyday and his conception of the dialectical image. Benjamin carefully explains: "Overcoming the concept of 'progress' and the concept of 'period of decline' are two sides of the same thing."[56] This ensures that Benjamin is neither trapped in an overly optimistic belief in progress nor caught wallowing in melancholy and pessimistic diagnoses of the decline of actuality. If we accept this general image of Benjamin as modernist adversary of debris and the *Jetzt-zeit* of the moment wrenched from the course of history, we need to revise a certain popular depiction of him as a melancholy figure bewailing the loss of aura and the decline of authentic tradition.[57] While at the same time underscoring the fact that Benjamin was emphatically not a one-sidedly blind optimist, he also was not a dialectical materialist and messianic knight in armor awaiting the revolutionary rise of the proletariat. Between these two extremes—pessimism and optimism—Benjamin wavers back and forth in the monadological mire of the everyday.

This revision might do well to regard anew the well-known comments on film made in the "Work of Art" essay and take note of the striking resemblance between film as media and Leibniz's notion of internal changes in the monad. Part of the backdrop for such a coupling would have to be the surrealist expression, *le merveilleux*, denominating, among other things, the secularized and everyday miracle of film as media; it would also include Stanley Cavell's fascination with film and its pertinence to the miraculousness of the everyday. Benjamin's fascination with sur-realism is well-known, but I would like to link this to Cavell's work not merely because Cavell shares Breton's love of film as an inherent part of the normal and everyday,[58] but additionally so as to underscore the inte-resting genealogy linking Breton, Benjamin and Cavell, a genealogy determined by their mutual engagement with the elusive and yet tangible realm of the ordinary and the everyday.

Inconspicuous filmic aura

What does Benjamin have to say of film as media and phenomenon in the "Work of Art"? In section eleven he initially notes that film tends to break down homogenous sequences into discontinuous moments or episodes, founded on the asymmetry between the reality of film-making and the perceived reality of film-viewing. What on the screen "appears as a swift, unified sequence" is in reality a "series of separate takes." As for the actor, his work is split "into a series of episodes capable of being assembled"[59] and is composed of many discrete performances. In this manner, art—or what at least poses as art—has become unhinged from the noble task of creating a beautiful and edifying image of reality: "Nothing shows more graphically that art has escaped the realm of 'beautiful semblance,' which for so long was regarded as the only sphere in which it could thrive."[60] In theatre live people perform on stage in an auratic—tradition bound and immediate—milieu. With the advent of film, however, this experiential link was broken and an insurmountable difference and distance developed between fragmented, episodic film-making and the organic, homogenous reality it was supposed to represent.

This quasi-Hegelian lament, curiously embedded in revolutionary fervor, is intense in section ten in which Benjamin scathingly criticizes the commercial aspects of the film-media: "Not only does the cult of the movie star which it fosters preserve that magic of the personality which has long been no more than the putrid magic of its own commodity character, but its counterpart, the cult of the audience, reinforces the corruption by which fascism is seeking to supplant the class consciousness of the masses."[61] The disenchanted and artificial culture-industry has appropriated film as the illegitimate heir to and hideous replacement for original, authentic art, as well as the truly revolutionary potential immanent to film.

The result was that art became democratized, but in a vulgar and shallow manner: "It is inherent in the technology of film, as of sports, that everyone who witnesses these performances does so as a quasi-expert."[62] Not even literature is exempt from this general, historical tendency: with the increasing predominance of the press and journalism, every reader is automatically turned into a writer: "At any moment, the reader is ready to become a writer. [...] Literary competence is no longer founded on specialized higher education but on polytechnic training, and thus is common property."[63] Benjamin's descriptive, historical survey is transformed into a massive, normative critique of modernity not unrelated to (though in no sense identical with) the Kierkegaardian disgust with 'nivelleringen,' the eradication of distinctive differences, as well as with the Heideggerian contempt for the planetary influence of technology.[64] What Benjamin finds abominable is the hollowing out of immediate reality, the gradual, insidious blurring of the threshold between artifice and reality: "The equipment-free aspect of reality has here become the height of artifice, and the vision of immediate reality the Blue Flower in the land of technology."[65] Benjamin's lament is congruent with that "colonization of the everyday" Henri Lefebvre later so bemoaned.[66]

What is interesting about Benjamin's essay is that he gradually veers from this initial domain and moves on to somewhat different terrain. Of course this does not ever amount to a liberalist embrace of new technologies or cheering the invisible hand of the market, but it perhaps implies a sullen affirmation and skewed appreciation of modernity in the shape of film. This most forcefully occurs in section sixteen and takes the byroad of innovations in technical apparatus and the findings of psychoanalysis: "Thanks to the camera, therefore, the individual perceptions of the psychotic or the dreamer can be appropriated by collective perception."[67] In oblique parallel with film, Freud's *The Psychopathology of Everyday Life* made clear the significance of the large number of minute, everyday occurrences hitherto practically ignored, namely slips of the tongue, etc. I want to stress that what Benjamin found noteworthy about film in this context was its ability to highlight hitherto unperceived aspects of everyday life: "This is where the camera comes into play, with all its resources for swooping and rising, disrupting and isolating, stretching or compressing a sequence, enlarging or reducing an object. It is through the camera that we first discover the optical unconscious, just as we discover the instinctual unconscious through psychoanalysis. Moreover, these two types of unconscious are intimately linked."[68] The field of perception is not directed towards the supernatural or the artistic, but expressly limited to and delimited by the horizon of the everyday. The everyday perceived as an area saturated with peculiarities, mishaps, double-entendres.

We might do well to consider the coincidental fact that Stanley Cavell shares Benjamin's antagonism towards Heidegger, not least as regards Heidegger's contempt of the ordinary. In Benjamin this is couched as a critique of Heidegger's notion of historicity: "What distinguishes images from the 'essences' of phenomenology is their historical index. (Heidegger seeks in vain to rescue history for phenomenology abstractly through 'historicity.')"[69] Cavell launches an attack from a slightly different angle. Quoting Heidegger's derisory remarks on the proliferation of acronyms or slang-like abbreviations in the language of modernity ("Uni," "Kino," "UN"), Cavell states:

> And then I think: Heidegger cannot hear the difference between the useful non-speak or moon-talk of acronyms [...] and the intimacy, call it nearness of passing colloquialisms and cult abbreviations [...]. But then I think: No, it must be just that the force of Heidegger's thought here is not manifest in his choice of examples any more than it is in his poor efforts to describe the present state of industrial society. [...] And as to his invoking of popular language and culture, Heidegger simply hasn't the touch for it, the ear for it.[70]

The affinity between Benjamin and Cavell as concerns the everyday is directly related to their immanent ontology, premised on the conception of the world as an infinite unity. This leads to a further exploration of the Leibnizian character of Benjamin's evocation of film.

In the *Monadology* Leibniz stated that the world was a plenum and that perception of the world in and through monads fluctuated between more or less distinct forms of apperception: "A created being is said to act externally insofar as it has perfection, and to react to (or 'suffer' by) another insofar as it is imperfect. Thus action is attributed to the monad insofar as it has distinct perceptions and reaction (passion) insofar as it has confused ones."[71] On the basis of this almost vitalistic idea Leibniz went on to explain the measured spectrum of distinctness with which any given monad is able to perceive things:

> It can only be distinct in regard to a small part of things, namely those that are nearest or most extensively related to each monad. [...] It is not in their object (namely the whole universe), but in the particular mode of knowledge of this object that the monads are restricted. They all reach confusedly to the infinite, to the whole; but they are limited and differentiated by the degrees of their distinct perceptions.[72]

This applies not only to the perception of individual souls, but also to the mode of perception put forward in film, for example. Benjamin implicitly recognized this:

> With the close-up, space expands; with slow motion, movement is extended. And just as enlargement not merely clarifies what we see indistinctly "in any case," but brings to light entirely new structures of matter, slow motion not only reveals familiar aspects of movements, but discloses quite unknown aspects within them—aspects "which do not appear as the retarding of natural movements but have a curious, gliding, float-ing character of their own."[73]

We should not forget that Leibniz linked perception with affect and its registration: "For a substance cannot perish, nor can it subsist without

186

some affection, which is nothing other than its perception."[74] Film is predominantly involved in the production of affect, moving and mobile perceptions and is thus—one could claim—the monadic medium par excellence. Broadly speaking, film also concerns the intricate manufacture of zones of distinct or indistinct images, toying in the same process with the viewers' perception of events and causal chains, in contrast to the frozen tableaux of paintings.

In the third version of the "Work of Art," Benjamin reasons on the basis of this hypothesis: "A similar deepening of apperception throughout the entire spectrum of optical—and now also auditory—impressions has been accomplished by film."[75] Benjamin compares filmed behavior with that depicted in painting: "filmed action lends itself more readily to analysis because it delineates situations far more precisely." This historical precision is related to the technological nature of film: "This circumstance derives its prime importance from the fact that it tends to foster the interpenetration of art and science."[76] This fruitful alliance concerns itself particularly with re-appropriating or re-arranging our mode of registering the everyday: "On the one hand, film furthers insight into the necessities governing our lives by its use of close-ups, by its accentuation of hidden details in familiar objects, and by its exploration of commonplace milieux through the ingenious guidance of the camera; on the other hand, it manages to assure us of a vast and unsuspected field of action."[77]

Before the advent of film we were 'locked up'—the prison metaphor is Benjamin's—in the customized mode of perceiving the humdrum quality of our most immediate surroundings, but: "Then came film and exploded this prison-world with the dynamite of the split second, so that now we can set off calmly on journeys of adventure among its far-flung debris."[78] This apparently world-shattering effect squares well with the aggressive-heroic cultivation of the notion of discontinuous history put forward in "On the Concept of History." Film is, then, the harbinger of revolutionary potential, despite its extensive expropriation and exploitation by the film industry.

What film technique first and foremost exposes is reality's decompos-

187

able and imaginary character: "With the close-up, space expands; with slow motion, movement is extended."[79] The borders and frameworks of reality are unsettled, the doors of perception are unmistakably ajar. In effect the camera eye functions exactly like Leibniz's 'living mirror': "This is where the camera comes into play, with all its resources for swooping and rising, disrupting and isolating, stretching or compressing a sequence, enlarging or reducing an object."[80] Compare Leibniz's statement on the mobile and fluctuating character of bodies: "For all bodies are in a perpetual flux, like rivers, and some parts enter into them and some pass out continually."[81] Thus conceived, the everyday is a terrain beset with minute, incessant movement (as well as uninterrupted continuity) and film is preeminently suited to represent this bare, yet delirious fact. Film thus incarnates the perspectivism cherished by Leibniz in section 57 of *Monadology*. In "The Formula in Which the Dialectical Structure of Film Finds Expression" (1935), Benjamin comes up with an enormously enlightening formula: "The formula in which the dialectical structure of film—film considered in its technological dimension—finds expression runs as follows. Discontinuous images replace one another in a continuous sequence."[82] This formula exactly reproduces the ontological structure of Leibniz's monadology, pointing out the infinite change and variability of single monads while respecting the theorem of continuity and the stream of *petites perceptions*. This exact overlap is no coincidence. It bears witness to Benjamin's intense engagement with Leibniz's monadology and reveals a profound complicity between Leibniz's metaphysics and Benjamin's ontology of film.

Exploring the revolutionary character of film, Benjamin distinguishes between distraction and contemplation as two separate modes of perception, one belonging to film and the everyday (urban) life of modernity, the other ensconced in the calm and measured absorption of the aura of the artwork. Film accommodates, even produces, shock, and is in that respect superior to the original artwork: "Film has freed the physical shock effect—which Dadaism had kept wrapped, as it were, inside the moral shock effect—from this wrapping."[83] Even early avant-gardism failed to fully appreciate the global, ubiquitous consequence of film's everyday monadology. Film's effect is intimately intertwined with enabling the mobilization of the masses via the distracted gaze: "Reception in distraction—the sort of reception which is increasingly noticeable in all areas of art and is a symptom of profound changes in apperception—finds in film its true training ground."[84] Distraction is the most widespread and frequent mode of perceiving the everyday, its *differentia specifica* being, precisely, the absence of any distinguishing marks or events.

Normal grace

We are now in a position to conclude that aligning Benjamin's notion of the migration and—according to this interpretation—transformation of the aura into the everyday domain of film brings to light the simple yet pervasive presence of Leibnizian monadology in Benjamin's concept of the aura. This presence betokens an inscription of the mundane and banal character of miraculousness à la Spinoza in Benjamin's depiction of film as the means to shock and distraction alike.

This is the point at which we are able, finally, to begin to glimpse the appearance of an everyday morality in Benjamin and Leibniz. If we regard Benjamin's shock-effect, his explosive philosophy of history, merely as violent waves in Leibniz's fishpond, we can perhaps dispense with Leibniz's God as well as Benjamin's messianism and yet retain a sense of the world's interminable and gracious changeability. The world is a monistic and endless terrain of the everyday. Perception of this peculiar everydayness, however, is prone to fluctuate in accordance with the construction and redistribution of technical means. Immersing oneself in the foreshortened and crystallized folds of the world is equivalent to eradicating the distance and difference between Leibniz's monadology and Benjamin's philosophy of history. The eradication of this difference assumes the form of two ideas: the world is a peculiar work of art interminably falling into nothingness and beauty is nothing but the name given to the wondrous and stupefying fact that this world exists given the countless multitude of equally possible versions. Beauty is thus a

189

profoundly indifferent modality and the original choice of God an incomprehensible and random event. 'Tradition' and 'presence' would by extension be mere names accorded specific and foreshortened measures of aura, 'shock,' 'grace,' 'perspectivism' a different set of names given to slightly varied folds and pleats of luminous matter.

And what of the morality of this global scenario? If monads are inescapable, if we are always and of necessity in the midst of the monad, then we would do well to strive after the ordinary. All of this amounts to the construction of monotonous banality, the bleakly utopian delineation of an endless everyday unfolding its terms in infinite series. Eliminating the horrors Voltaire sarcastically portrayed in *Candide* or eradicating the bloody trail left by fascism in the previous century would be tantamount to construing a world that might be unremarkable, positively boring, uneventful, a drab or delightful everyday Eden, bereft of catastrophe and cataclysm. This would be truly graceful and it perhaps merits attention as a modest proposal equally removed from Leibniz's sometimes bland optimism and Benjamin's infrequently sour melancholy. Unearthing the substratum subtending Leibnizian monadology and Benjaminian aura amounts to noticing the possibility of a new political program: the achievement of endless boredom and distracted jubilance as a first, negatively-defined criterion of immersion in worldly happiness. If ever realized, this would, perhaps surprisingly, constitute the dual materialization of Leibniz's law of continuity and Benjamin's permanent state of exception in a monstrously dilated *Jetzt-zeit*. Is not the everyday the very paragon of unbroken continuity? And would not the realization of permanent everydayness function as a shocking, interminable state of exception when seen in the light of humanity's tendency to produce abrupt tension and submit to nature's violence?

In a quite striking and off-handed manner Benjamin acknowledged this fact in October 1931 with a slight nod towards Leibniz's theory of the *petites perceptions*. Reading to children on the radio-channel *Berliner Rundfunk*, Benjamin recounted the story of the Lisbon earthquake of 1755–a great event if ever there was one.[85] Benjamin does not refrain from mentioning Kant's uncommon fascination with the earthquake and indeed he tells the children that Kant wrote an entire study of it, a study that "probably represents the beginnings of scientific geography in Germany. And certainly the beginnings of seismology."[86] In the course of doing so Benjamin delineated an entirely monadological perspective on everyday trepidation, the dual register of continuous change and infinitely small perceptions of it: "The extremely sensitive instruments that we have nowadays [...] are never entirely still. In other words, the earth experiences tremors all the time, but for the most part not so violently that we notice."[87] Living on the crust of everydayness means submitting to the absence of great events; in political terms it entails striving for a state in which the constant tremors of the earth pass unnoticed. Aligning Leibniz and Benjamin, conflating monad and aura, would then amount to being in the midst of the monad, i.e., abandoning ourselves to the endless task of procuring interminable, dreary and blissful everydayness.

Notes

[1] Samuel Beckett, *Endgame* (New York: Grove Press, 1958), 81.

[2] Walter Benjamin, "Theological-Political Fragment," in SW 3, 305. The editors note that the exact date of the fragment remains unknown, although it is suspected to lie somewhere between 1920 and 1937, (306). Although brief and enigmatic, both Adorno and Scholem "attached enormous importance to the text," (306).

[3] Benjamin, AP, 105 [D2,7].

[4] Benjamin, "Paralipomena to 'On the Concept of History'," in SW 4, 406.

[5] Keeping in mind Alexander Garcia Düttmann's interesting correlation between the traditional work of art and the language of names, in this article I put the vexed question of language aside. See Düttmann, "Tradition and Destruction. Walter Benjamin's Politics of Language" in *Walter Benjamin's Philosophy: Destruction and Experience*, eds. Andrew Benjamin and Peter Osborne (London: Routledge, 1994), 37, "The traditional work of art entails an effect of sacralization which refers back to a ritual function; in some sense it is a *name*."

[6] Benjamin, "The Work of Art in the Age of Its Technological Reproducibility (Second Version)," in SW 3, 104.

[7] Ibid., 104.

[8] Ibid., 105.

[9] Benjamin, OGT, 166.

[10] Rodolphe Gasché polemically notes the lack of nostalgia in Benjamin: "let me emphasize that for Benjamin the loss of aura in mechanically reproducible art is not something to be deplored as some of his Frankfurt School interpreters, in particular (Gasché is thinking of Susan Buck-Morss, mbz), have held." See "Objective Diversions. On Some Kantian Themes in Benjamin's 'The Work of Art in the Age of Mechanical Reproduction'," in *Walter Benjamin's Philosophy: Destruction and Experience*, 184. Although Gasché's essay is both persuasive and cogently argued, I beg to differ on the issue of nostalgia and melancholy. To be sure, the problem is muddled, but to claim that Benjamin is altogether bereft of melancholy seems to me somewhat less than true.

[11] My reading of Leibniz is heavily indebted to Gilles Deleuze, *The Fold: Leibniz and the Baroque* (Minneapolis: University of Minnesota Press, 1993).

[12] *G.W. Leibniz's Monadology*, bilingual edition, ed. Nicholas Rescher (Pittsburgh: University of Pittsburgh Press, 1991), 228.

[13] *G.W. Leibniz's Monadology*, 252–53.

[14] Leibniz means to say that the only true miracle, in the conventional sense, is God's originary act of creation not the ensuing consequences all of which are merely natural, i.e., ordered in accordance with the harmony preordained by God: "It is true there is miracle in my system of preestablished Harmony, and that God enters into it extraordinarily, but it is only in the beginning of things, after which everything goes its own way in the phenomena of nature, according to the laws of souls and bodies," *G.W. Leibniz's Monadology* 258.

[15] *G.W. Leibniz's Monadology*, 200–201.

[16] Benjamin, "The Work of Art," in SW 3, 112.

[17] Benedict Spinoza, *A Theologico-Political Treatise and A Political Treatise* (New York: Dover Publications, 1951), 87.

[18] Ibid., 92.

[19] Ibid., 97. Emphasis added.

[20] Michael Hardt, *Gilles Deleuze: An Apprenticeship in Philosophy* (London: UCL Press, 1993).

[21] Ibid., 109.

[22] Ibid., 110.

[23] Developed later on, in Michael Hardt and Antonio Negri, *Empire* (Cambridge, Mass.: Harvard University Press, 2000).

24 Gasché, "Objective Diversions," in *Walter Benjamin's Philosophy: Destruction and Experience*,184.

25 Benjamin, "Theological-Political Fragment," in SW 2, 306.

26 I have in mind Susan Sontag's rendering of Benjamin as merely *un triste*, in *Under the Sign of Saturn* (New York: Doubleday, 1991), 109–34.

27 See Beatrice Hanssen, *Walter Benjamin's Other History: Of Stones, Animals, Human Beings, and Angels* (Berkeley: University of California Press, 1998).

28 Benjamin, "On the Concept of History," in SW 4, 395.

29 Ibid., 396.

30 Ibid., 396.

31 Thus, Karl Popper and Benjamin could be said to be in agreement on this one point, see Popper's critique of historical determinism in, amongst other theories, vulgar Marxism, *The Poverty of Historicism* (London: Routledge, 1957). Popper's basic claim is that no scientifically valid laws predetermining history can be established and that history is thus essentially a realm of freedom. Obviously the liberalist Popper and the dialectical materialist Benjamin are fundamentally at odds on nearly all other counts.

32 *G.W. Leibniz's Monadology*, 231. At this juncture it might prove interesting to compare Leibniz's rather bland vision with Kant's disinterested gaze at the spectacle of the French Revolution.

33 *G.W. Leibniz's Monadology*, 66.

34 *G.W. Leibniz's Monadology*, 68.

35 Benjamin, "On the Concept of History," in SW 4, 396.

36 See G.W. Leibniz, *New Essays on Human Understanding*, eds. Peter Remnant and Jonathan Bennett (Cambridge: Cambridge University Press, 1982), 53–54.

37 Peter Fenves, *Arresting Language: From Leibniz to Benjamin* (Stanford: Stanford University Press, 2001), 8.

38 Ibid., 8–9.

39 Ibid., 9.

40 *G.W. Leibniz's Monadology*, 58.

41 Ibid., 198.

42 Benjamin, "Letter to Florens Christian Rang," in SW 1, 387–90.

43 Ibid., 389. The original reads: "Ihre intensive Unendlichkeit kennzeichnet die Ideen als Monaden." Benjamin, *Briefe I*, eds. Gershom Scholem und Theodor W. Adorno (Frankfurt am Main: Suhrkamp, 1978), 323.

44 Richard Rorty, *Philosophy and the Mirror of Nature* (New Jersey: Princeton University Press, 1980).

45 *G.W. Leibniz's Monadology*, 209–10.

46 See Eric Santner, *On the Psycho-Theology of Everyday Life* (Chicago: Chicago Univer-

sity Press, 2001), 11–24. Santner's extraordinarily rich intertwinement of Rosenzweig and Freud encircles the recalcitrant bonds we may pursue or escape in relation to being 'in the midst of life.'

47 G.W. Leibniz's Monadology, 258.

48 See Stanley Cavell, In Quest of the Ordinary (Chicago: Chicago University Press, 1988).

49 See Alfred Schutz's fascinating, phenomenological analysis of this difficult object in "Symbol, Reality and Society, part III," in Schutz, Collected Papers, ed. Maurice Natanson, vol. I (The Hague: Martinus Nijhoff, 1967), 207–356.

50 Ben Highmore, Everyday Life and Cultural Theory (London: Routledge, 2002).

51 Ibid., 1.

52 Ibid., 60.

53 Ibid., 61.

54 Wolin quoted in ibid., 63.

55 Baudelaire quoted in Highmore, Everyday Life, 65.

56 Benjamin quoted in Highmore, Everyday Life, 65.

57 Although this is the stand Benjamin took in his dispute with Adorno, I believe that a large number of passages on modernity and melancholy spread throughout Benjamin's oeuvre testifies to Benjamin's predilection towards what one might term the 'thesis of decay,' i.e., the mode of thinking that believes modernity is best comprehended as a fall from various earlier, allegedly more harmonious, forms of life.

58 See Stanley Cavell, Pursuits of Happiness (Cambridge: Harvard University Press, 1981) and Contesting Tears (Chicago: Chicago University Press, 1996).

59 Benjamin, "The Work of Art," in SW 3, 113.

60 Ibid.

61 Ibid.

62 Ibid., 114.

63 Ibid.

64 For the tangled network of resemblances and differences between Heidegger and Benjamin in this regard, see Samuel Weber, "Mass Mediauras; or, Art, Aura, and Media in the Work of Walter Benjamin," in Walter Benjamin: Theoretical Questions, ed. David S. Ferris (Stanford: Stanford University Press, 1996) 27–49.

65 Benjamin, "The Work of Art," in SW 3, 115.

66 See Henri Lefebvre, "Towards a Leftist Cultural Politics," in Marxism and the Interpretation of Culture, eds. Cary Nelson and Lawrence Grossberg (Chicago: University of Illinois Press, 1988), 75–88. Particularly page 80: "A revolution cannot just change the political personnel or institutions; it must change la vie quotidienne, which has already been literally colonized by capitalism."

67 Benjamin, "The Work of Art," in SW 3, 118.
68 Ibid., 117.
69 Benjamin, AP, 462 [N3,1].
70 Cavell, *In Quest of the Ordinary*, 159–60. Cavell quotes Heidegger from *What is Called Thinking* (New York: Harper and Row, 1968), 34.
71 *G.W. Leibniz's Monadology*, 168.
72 Ibid., 209–10.
73 Benjamin, "The Work of Art," in SW 3, 117. Benjamin's quote stems from Rudolf Arnheim, *Film als Kunst* (Berlin: Rowohlt, 1932), 130 and 138.
74 *G.W. Leibniz's Monadology*, 94.
75 Benjamin, "The Work of Art in the Age of its Technological Reproducibility (Third Version)," in SW 4, 265.
76 Ibid., 265.
77 Benjamin, "The Work of Art, (Second Version)," in SW 3, 117.
78 Ibid.
79 Ibid.
80 Ibid.
81 *G.W. Leibniz's Monadology*, 234.
82 Benjamin, "The Formula in Which the Dialectical Structure of Film Finds Expression," in SW 3, 94.
83 Benjamin, "The Work of Art, (Second Version)," in SW 3, 119. Emphasis removed.
84 Ibid. 120. Emphasis removed.
85 Benjamin, "The Lisbon Earthquake," in SW 2, 536–40.
86 Ibid., 538.
87 Ibid., 539.

The Afterlife of Judaism

From the Book of Splendor to Benjamin's Shooting Stars

Henry Sussman

Judaism, so the common myth runs, is the Abrahamic[1] religion devoid
of an afterlife. Where first Christianity and then Islam are quite explicit
regarding the determination of the life hereafter by the quality of the life
lived in this world, picturesque almost to the degree of luridness in
representing the conditions, qualities, and experience of Heaven and Hell
(and Purgatory, where applicable), Judaism hedges its bets, is far more
reticent in the sphere of eschatology.[2] The liturgy of the Days of Awe,
the New Year's festivals that stage the collective public acknowledgment
of mortal human vices, breeches in morality, and crimes, stresses a
judgment before God transpiring from year to year. The afterlife, in the
wake of this theology, is the ethical imprint that a person deposits in the
memory, communal and individual, of the survivors that s/he leaves
behind. If this is the Judaic afterlife, its image is as vague as personal
impressions of a fellow human being are idiosyncratic. Even Buddhism,
whose theology is far less individual-oriented and rule-driven than Judaism, envisions a much more particular and specific relation between past
lives and ones yet to emerge.

This familiar and time-honored cant makes the afterworld tantamount
to a place or lieu and a time apart. But if we divert our gaze to look past
this imagistic literality and allow ourselves to conflate the afterlife with
the spectral, Jewish theology has not been as eschatologically short-handed
as might first appear. It is true that Judaism fully realizes its own distinctive
version of the afterlife only after Christianity and Islam have established
and represented theirs. But once the Jewish afterlife has been inscribed,
for all its vagaries and in all the specifics of Christian and Muslim Paradise

and Hell that it in many respects evades, it disseminates itself to cultural sites far afield and insinuates itself into artifacts and cultural experiments in which its play and connivance have not been divined even in the present day. I would go even so far as to say that the Judaic afterlife, inscribed on the eve of European modernity,[3] and revising prior Jewish theology in keeping with the emerging lineaments of epistemic revolution, establishes a spectral setting or lieu, unmistakable in its particular sublimity, poetics, and rhetoric, leaving its imprint on artifacts as diverse as Kleist's tales, Büchner's prose poems, the Romantic speculations of the Schegels and Novalis, Kafka's sublime imagery, obviously, on Scholem's lifelong project, Benjamin's always-problematical Judaism, and Celan's poetry. The specifically Judaic provenance and imaginary surrounding this spectral scene of writing has been occulted over a significant segment of its 'run.' It is incumbent upon us as students of culture to extract and reconfigure this Jewish *revenant* or afterlife not in the name of nationalistic celebration or under the imperative of ethnic preservation, but in appreciation of the broad thoroughfare on which the three Abrahamic religions penetrated and revitalized each other's scripts and scenarios on the most profound and infrastructural levels. The platform common to the three major Western monotheistic religions, as well as the spectral abyss that haunts them,[4] has received an overdue upgrading, in terms of conceptual depth and rigor, in Jacques Derrida's religious explorations of the last three decades. In spite of, or even by dint of its occasional irreverence, Derrida's *parcours à la religion* opens significant possibilities for the ongoing cultural reception and debate of theology.

The 'full service' Judaic scenario of the afterlife is medieval in its provenance. The Judaic afterlife achieves its full configuration in the Zohar, the Book of Splendor, a major element of the mystical movement and literature in Judaism known as the Kabbalah. Gershom Scholem goes to some effort to deconflate Kabbalah from the Zohar. The Kabbalah, for one, is older. In its seminal moment, Jewish mysticism, according to Scholem,

197

did not aspire to an understanding of the true nature of God, but to a description of the phenomenon of the Throne on its Chariot as described in the first chapter of Ezekiel, traditionally entitled *ma'aseh merkabah*. [...] The 14th chapter of the Book of Enoch, which contains the earliest example of this kind of literary description, was the source of a long visionary tradition of describing the world of the Throne and the visionary ascent to it, which we find portrayed in the books of the Merkabah mystics. (*K*, 11)[5]

Although the Kabbalah claims direct roots in the Book of Ezckiel and the apocryphal book of Enoch, and encompasses such works as the 11th-century Sepher Yezirah, "a compact discourse on cosmology and cosmogony (a kind of *ma'aseh bereshit*, 'act of creation,' in a speculative form), outstanding for its clearly mystical character" (*K*, 23), and the early 12th-century Provençal *Sefer ha-Bahir*, it is in *Sefer ha-Zohar*, the Book of Splendor, where the Judaic afterlife achieves its full configuration. This multi-volume work is a compendium of Biblical commentaries or Midrashim "written mainly between 1280 and 1286 by Moses b. Shem Tov de Leon in Guadalajara, a small town northeast of Madrid" (*K*, 57). What the most rudimentary literary criticism makes obvious, an illumination betokening the compelling need at this juncture for broad-based literary scholars to return, in the sense of a *parcours*, to the canonical texts of a broad range of world religions, is that in the Zohar, the rabbinical contributors to the difficult and technical argumentation of the Talmud, names memorialized in the Mishna, Gemara, and the several registers of commentary around the Talmudic page[6] have been transformed into literary characters who are seen discoursing to each other (most often in pairs) as they wander through tangible earthly landscapes (sometimes furnished with geographical coordinates). In the Talmud, the rabbis who figure in the Zohar were remote and forbidding surrogates, distant in their conceptual and legal genius. In the Zohar, the myth of their genius is extended in the highly speculative thrust and tone of their comments and in their stunning capability to issue forth in metaphysical yet precise imagery (we shall explore some examples below).

The metamorphosis of rabbis into literary characters in the Zohar is a capital development in the cultural history of Judaism.[7] Already the Merkabah or Chariot literature of the Rabbinic period, the centuries straddling the birth of Christ, according to Scholem, "refers to historical figures, whose connection with the mysteries of the Chariot is attested by Talmud and Midrash. The ascent of its heroes to the Chariot [...] comes after a number of preparatory exercises of an extremely ascetic nature" (*K*, 15). The Zohar builds upon this tradition of narrativizing the theological paragons of Judaism. It is precisely the inclusion of the Amorim and Tannaim, the Talmudic commentators remembered for the logico-legalistic prose of their discourse, within the narrative episodes of the Zohar, that humanizes these rabbis, in the sense that Jesus humanizes the principles of Judaism by embodying, that is, by characterologically condensing them. Ironically then, the Zohar plays the New Testament to the Talmud's hopeless codification and obsessional qualification. And there is something surely otherworldly, spooky, I would say, but in a distinctly Judaic grain, in the proclivity of the Zohar's rabbis for imagery itself condensing the magical with the metaphysical. In the course of the Zohar's tales, we are made privy to the rabbis' gift for interweaving the logical and conceptually intriguing with imagery "riddled with light," breathtaking in luminosity. Scholem gathered this tendency and poetics of medieval Jewish script under the rubric of "Jewish mysticism." It may well be that the tenuous status of Palestine and Israel since the late 19th century combined with Scholem's urgency in establishing the Hebrew University forced him to impute a revealed foundation to his chosen literature, for his was surely a sophisticated literary and critical mind. Yet what distinguishes "Jewish mysticism" is far more the specific poetics and tonality of imagery that Scholem locates in such works as the Kabbalah, the Sefer Yezira, and the Zohar than the claim of direct revelation.

It is in the Zohar that the afterlife of Judaism is first fully revealed. The itinerant rabbis of the Zohar deliver up their images of splendor, which Benjamin would term their dialectical images,[8] in the aftermath of the formal commentaries delivered in the various registers of the Talmud. The rabbis of the Zohar expended themselves centuries before in

the intricate and obscure discursive involutions of that Talmudic compendium so vast that it is repeatedly described in oceanic terms.[9] Their
'life' in the Zohar is a *revenant*, a Second Coming. It is not only the rabbis
in the Zohar who are dead. At least figuratively, Judaism is dead as well.
It has died. The idyllic landscape the rabbis traverse as they discourse
on a more speculative and poetic level than ever before may be the heaven
of Jewish faith, but it is an afterlife. In figurative death, that is in exile,
and bound up in formalistic legal involution, Judaism is freer and more
vibrant than it ever was in life or as a sovereign nation. Many of the
Zohar's folktales take place at night.

Meteoric Figurations

For purposes of the present demonstration, I want to focus on the figure
of the stars, above all, because their figure resurfaces as a multifaceted
motif in Benjamin's criticism. There it ranges in its resonations from an
embodiment of metaphysical naiveté so indispensable to exegesis and
inscription at the same time that it cries out for debunking to a constellation, the configuration of anomalous and dissonant cultural counter-
forces emerging in the particular archive that every working critic
assembles and that becomes indistinguishable from her intellectual im-
primatur or signature. But within the framework of the mythopoetic
reconfiguration or reformation of Biblical and Talmudic sources that is
the Zohar, the stars are inscribed within a complex of other figures at
once poetically rich and hovering and instrumental to medieval Judaic
metaphysics, including nighttime, light, plants, bodies and vessels of water,
erotic desire, and clothes. Indeed, the stars form one point in a poetically
captivating constellation of images whose interaction lifts the curtain on
a modern, literarily full-fledged Judaism, and as a figure they become
key players in Benjamin's most resilient allegory of criticism. One could
well argue, moreover, that the Zohar's spectral, nocturnal narrative space,
in which everything is phantasmatically after the fact, preempts the
jarringly concussive space of post-modernity, in which the most disparate
and unrelated counterforce, formations and crystallizations coexist with

impunity and in mutual indifference. One of many possible fabulations from 20th-century literature that could be elicited as an instance of this Kabbalistic space, a phenomenon that could only transpire under the aegis of this specifically Judaic imaginary, would be the ironic coda and afterlife at the end of Bruno Schulz's *Sanatorium under the Sign of the Hourglass.* In the sanatorium highlighted by the title, the narrator is afforded one last encounter with his domineering yet vulnerable father. The father has died, yet is not yet gone. His affective and imaginary power over his son remains in effect. Their last interview transpires in an uncanny time-warp that is after life and before annihilation, during a temporal slowdown and deferral, one nonetheless very much in the province and provenance of language. In response to the narrator/son's incredulous question, Dr. Gotard, superintendent of the Sanatorium characterizes the father's status in the following terms:

> The whole secret of the operation [...] is that we have put back the clock. Here we are always late by a certain interval of time of which we cannot define the length. The whole thing is a matter of simple relativity. Here your father's death, the death that has already struck him in your country, has not occurred yet.[10]

This uncanny legend even goes so far as to suggest that there is something 'mystical,' in the Zoharic sense, in the temporality of Einsteinian physics, so much at home in the twentieth century. The radical deferral that has settled over the Sanatorium, itself a version of the afterlife, corresponds to the temporal setting of the particular folktales that among so many others were capable of riveting Scholem's attention.

The above will hopefully serve as a minimal context for a folktale from the commentaries in the Zohar directed at Exodus:

> Once Rabbi Eleazar and Rabbi Abba were sitting together, and then the dusk came, whereupon they got up and started toward a garden by the Lake of Tiberias. Going, they beheld two stars speed toward each other from different points of the sky, meet, and then vanish.

201

> Rabbi Abba observed: in heaven above and on the earth below, how great are the works of the Holy One, be blessed. Who fathoms it, how these stars come from different points, how they meet and disappear?
> Rabbi Eleazar answered: Nor did we need to see these two stars to reflect on them, for we have pondered on them, as we have on the multitude of great works that the Holy One, be blessed, is ever doing.
> Then quoting the verse, "Great is the Lord and mighty in power; his understanding is without number" {Ps. 147:5}, he went on to discourse: In truth, great and mighty and sublime is the Holy One, be blessed. (*ZBS*, 72–73)[11]

In a specific setting and location, indeed, in the specific site in the Galilee that was so crucial to the birth of Christianity, two of the seminal Jewish scholars and litigators of the Talmud meditate in solidarity and intimacy on the sublime phenomenon of the shooting stars that arise, coincide, and pass each other haphazardly outside the cadres of meaning or necessity. Indeed, the discussion is explicitly more about the very condition of such arbitrariness than it is about the most mercurial of the heavenly bodies, the shooting stars. The prerogative of thinking people to meditate on the shooting stars takes precedence over their actuality or veracity, just as the onto-theological mandate of Abrahamic religion, faith in a monotheistic divinity, transpires autonomously of the facts and of the prevailing sociopolitical formation, whose confirmation or approval it does not require. It is in this sense that the extraordinarily innovative and central Rabbi Eleazar can assure: "Nor did we need to see these stars to reflect upon them." He agrees with Rabbi Abba that it is ultimately unfathomable "how these stars come from different points, how they meet and disappear."

The shooting stars' enigmatic trajectory across the sky becomes a legend for a familiar Judaic outcome. The Lord is "great [...] and mighty in power [...]. In truth great and mighty and sublime is the Holy One, be blessed." The pretext and predetermined outcome of Jewish theology is faith in God, endlessly reaffirmed faith and commitment, in spite of the chance, accident, arbitrariness, and sublimity inscribed in the metaphysics and very image of the stars; indeed, this final conclusion known in advance is only strengthened by these extenuating circumstances. The formulaic Judaic response to the unmitigated arbitrariness of death, the Kaddish itself is a textual talisman whose repetition, thrice daily for a year after bereavement and thereafter at specific intervals, is above all a responsive series of attributions of omniscience and omnipotence to God.[12] The Judaic gut-reaction to death, in other words, consists largely of a subordination of personal loss, despair, outrage and related psychological reactions to a public figuration and affirmation of God's majesty.

However it might have been reached in advance, the Zoharic folktale registers a number of key modifications that have taken place in Judaic parlance on the way to this fatal if uplifting outcome. Rabbis Abba and Eleazar are literary characters, they are not sages or legal authorities, invested with quasi-divine intelligence and authority. On the Sea of Galilee, one of the primal scenes of Christianity, they have been raptured up from the Talmud and reborn as literary characters, where simply as such they have served as conduits or channels, a key Kabbalistic image, introducing several pivotal traits of modernity into Judaism. Indeed their rebirth as literary characters, under the enigmatic sign of the shooting stars, coincides with the entry of a Christian and Islamic notion of the afterlife into Judaism. In other words, the beloved sages of the Talmud, as avatars of all Judaism, must die in order to be reborn and their rebirth as literary characters coincides with the entrance of figured, depicted, represented death into the sanctuary of Judaism.

This is not all that is liberated and activated by Judaism's engagement with certain precepts, modalities, and scenes of representation that had been previously strictly other. The folktales of the Zohar may coincide with Judaism's acknowledgment of literary characterization and Western eschatology, of Greek as well as Christo-Islamic provenance, but they are also imprinted with a specifically Judaic poetics, one in which the categories of logic and classification are endowed with a vivid sublimity and then literally dance across the stage or abyss of representation, not unlike the track of the shooting stars against the backdrop of heaven.

203

The dance of the divinely inflected creatures or creations of logic across the scene of theological speculation as across the page anticipates by many centuries what Friedrich Schlegel would characterize as *parabasis*.[13] If the specifically Judaic afterlife and representation announced in the Zohar was embraced by and admitted into any mainstream European national culture it was into the domain of German letters and the German literary imaginary to a far greater degree than any other. This explains how Walter Benjamin could have credibly set out on his life's work as a herald and scribe of German-Jewish literary relations, although this vocation was ultimately torpedoed by the politico-historical events taking place during his lifetime.

A very fine display of the poetics accompanying the rebirth of the rabbis as literary figures is encompassed by our legend of the shooting stars:

> Acting as guardians over this world are all the stars of the firmaments, with each individual object of the world having a specially designated star to care for it. The herbs and the trees, the grass and the wild plants, to bloom and increase much have the power of the stars that stand over them and look directly at them, each in its particular mode. The great number of the plants and stars of all kinds emerge at the beginning of the night and shine until three hours minus a quarter after midnight. Thereafter only a small number are out. It is not without purpose that all the stars shine and serve. Some, being at their duty the whole night through, cause the plant which is their special ward to spring up and flourish. Others begin their activities at the advent of night and watch over their own objects until the hour of midnight. [...] So it was with the stars which we saw, which appeared briefly for their set task. When their task is accomplished, such stars vanish from this world. (*ZBS*, 74–75).

In this vignette, each herb, tree, plant, and variety of grass is the "ward" of a particular star. The sublime multiplication of the stars, and by implication, the vastness of the heavens, are infused into the domestic world of cultivation by means of this dedicated stewardship. In the passage above, for instance, each of the elements in the vegetable kingdom is activated at a different moment in the course of the night. Based on this stately progression of nocturnal vegetable awakening, God has scientifically coordinated a succession of stars to best oversee the worldly garden. What is stunning about this image is the juxtaposition between earthy plant-life and unreachable stars, impeccable divine planning, and spaces and schemes of inconceivable vastness. We are speaking here of 'guardian stars,' if not guardian angels. The passage builds toward a Foucauldian analogy or similitude between the inconceivable architecture of the heavens and the vegetable biosphere.[14] The poetic effect of this coincidence between two realms, which are, from a human point of view, both inconceivable and uncontrollable, is a specific form of Kabbalistic magic, magical reverie, not realism. By means of such a figure as the stars, the Book of Splendor marshals the vastness of the universe in the service, and representation, of God. The Judaic divinity functions not merely as the transcendental signifier of the work; the *Shekhinah*[15] or divine presence manifests itself in a specific poetics. This poetics choreographs a dance, delirious in its exoneration from the constraints of rationality, but also in its deployment of logic, between the things of our world and the grandeur, multiplication, and endless extension and proliferation characterizing the holy guardians charged with overseeing them, that is, manifesting unwavering attentiveness and intimate, total understanding of them.

> The book of the higher wisdom of the East tells us of stars with trailing tails. Comets, which from the skies hold sway and direct the growth of certain herbs on earth, of the sort known as "elixirs of life," and influence also the growth of these is brought about by the flash of that luminous tail trailing after these stars across the firmament. (*ZBS*, 75)

Not only is the magnificent, ineffable design of the universe scored into the earth, literally implanted, under the sign of the guardian stars; the heavens, particularly as expressed by the comet's tail, take on a worldly ephemerality within the framework of otherworldly movement and time. Indeed no figure could intensify fleeting intransience more fully than a comet's instantaneously disappearing traces. The sweep of the comet's tail gives full evidence that the dance which is the exemplary figure for the radiation of divine, that is to say mystical insight throughout the universe, the dance trips across the heavens as it does the earth.

The dance of mystical Judaic poetics, a choreography that is the pre-eminent poetic trait reaching across a liturgical literature, transpires in a scene or theatre that is an afterlife. The dance between the plenitude of this world and the ineffable predestination of the divine plan is rendered all the more vital by the fact that it is staged in a spectral setting in which all telling figures and characters are long dead. This prior death, the transpiration of Jewish mysticism's most striking figures in an afterlife, infuses all Judaic eschatology with an irreducible pretext of irony. This is an irony situated on the very threshold between life and death. Indeed the very contemplation by Judaism of final things becomes a life-and-death matter whose endless potential for humor can be taken in exactly the opposite way. It is one thing for Judaism to suspend certain discursive preoccupations and roles it has assigned to some of its key players in an ironic afterlife; quite another for it to be apprehended as a culture that has prospectively, through some bizarre collective death-wish, accommodated its own demise or demission.

Yet if we need any further proof that when Judaism succumbs to the overall Abrahamic tendency toward eschatology it does so with particular vehemence and intensity, we need only examine certain of the folktale commentaries to Genesis in which the afterlife is explicitly invoked. In one of the "basic readings from the Kabbalah" that Scholem translates and assembles in his thin collection of Zoharic folktales, Rabbi Simeon, who appeals directly to God, manages to fend off Rabbi Isaac's impending death, but only for a while. Scholem furnishes this story with the title "The Great Feast," a "parabolic expression of death." In a dream, Rabbi Isaac's father telegraphs ahead his "portion" in the "world to come." The landscape that Rabbi Isaac is about to inhabit has been fitted out with

seventy crowned places which are his, and each place has doors which
open to seventy worlds, and each world opens to seventy channels and
each channel is open to seventy supernal crowns, and thence are ways
leading to the Ancient and Inscrutable One, opening on a view of that
celestial delight which gives bliss and illumination to all, as is stated, "to see
the pleasantness of the Lord and to visit His temple" {Ps. 27:4}. (*ZBS*, 29)

The kernel of this Zoharic fabulation is once again a Biblical verse, a
relatively bland celebration of the Lord's temple and of visiting him there.
The extract from the Psalm is merely a pretext to a celestial panorama of
immense splendor multiplying itself by a constant factor of seventy. In
the approach to the ineffable that Judaic poetics make through multiplication and illumination, the latter term embodying Benjamin's highest hope for commentary, a channel is opened to the iconography of
Indian religions. The channels of the Zohar, like the passages that Kafka
conspicuously installs in the various Court settings of *The Trial* and in
the burrow creature's labyrinthine subterranean refuge, function both as
features in an expansive architecture and as rhizomatic nodes of textual
convergence and displacement.[16]

We need to remember that this splendiferous abode, whose channels
and crowns belong to the *Sefiroth* or formal spheres of Kabbalistic
cosmology,[17] belongs to an afterlife, a setting whose Being and opening
is conditioned on prior annihilation, the demise not only of particulars,
but of all. The sweep of the comet's tail, the limitless domain of the
channels, and as we shall see the splendiferous garment of the days gain
their sense only in the face of this death which may be negotiable to a
point but whose priority and eventuality are final. The only recompense
that Judaism offers for the trials and sufferings of this world is a collective
splendor, a state of exegetical as well as cosmological luminosity conditioned on the undergoing of not a particular, time-specific death, but
an ongoing death, a death inhabiting an ecology and a condition. The
Zohar figures both our entry to the domain of life and our departure
from it as a display of days, days represented not as invisible units of
time but as graphic markers, as signs or posters.

> Rabbi Judah said: Men's ears are shut to the admonitions of the Torah [...] in not realizing that in the day on which a human being appears in the world there appear all the days assigned to him, and these swarm about the world and then each in turn descends to the man to warn him. And if the man, being so warned, yet transgresses against his Master, then that day in which he transgressed ascends in shame and stands isolated outside, bearing witness, and remains thus until the man repents [...]. (*ZBS*, 39)

The days swarm like falling leaves caught in the wind. They are frail and ephemeral, yet occupy the two-dimensionality of paper and other surfaces of inscription. At the outset of life, according to Rabbi Judah, they foreshadow the successive sequence of life and forewarn of the inscriptive consequences of our deeds. Our actions will be collected in a transcript of days, and these in turn will determine whether we will be inscribed in the Book of Life or the Book of Death. The swarm of days is thus the pages of a yet unbound book, the book of our moral profile. On its basis we may be well booked by the highest authorities.

The Zohar also figures our private book of days as a garment, a covering, but one with intense symbolic and sociological significance. The poor quality of an ethical life translates into an inferior mystical garment:

> Woe to the man that has lessened his days before the Almighty, nor left himself days wherewith to crown himself in the other world and draw near to the holy King. For being worthy, he ascends by virtue of those days, and those days in which he did righteously and sinned not become for his soul a garment of splendor. Woe unto him that has lessened his days above, for the days damaged by his sins are lacking when it comes time to be garbed in his days, and his garment is therefore imperfect; worse is it if there are many such, and then he has nothing at all for garb in the other world. (*ZBS*, 39–40)

More significant than the moralistic dress-code enforced by the seaming together of the days that unfold in splendor at the beginning and end of life are the poetic and leaps making the scenario altogether possible. The days first of all coalesce out of an otherwise purely abstract and nonrepresentational dimensionality of time into markers and signboards of human life and spirituality. The metaphor of paper or woven days is then literalized to allow their configuration as clothes or garments, garments with a message far more spiritual than experiential. The textual days swirl and dance about in the cosmic motion that the Zohar has established as the very tenor of mystical apprehension and revelation. The swirling of the days and the radiance of the garments they form join in a *danse macabre*, for the hyper-vitality of movement and illumination is possible only in the extended afterlife of Judaism, within the framework of the death that Judaism has, metaphysically and aesthetically, admitted into itself. In keeping with its economy of closed allegorical reading, the Zohar puts a moral point on the possible outcomes that the garment of days can signal.

> The righteous are the happy ones, for their days are in store with the holy King and make a splendid attire for clothing themselves in, in the other world. This is the secret meaning of the verse, "and they knew that they were naked" {Gen. 3:17}, which is to say, glorious vestments composed of those days had been ruined and no day was left to be clothed in. (*ZBS*, 40)

Poetically however, the Zohar and the Judaism that it would presume to revise, have established a figuration and a topography they cannot contain; indeed, no specific religious culture could. Set in an afterlife of extended death, the radiance of comets' tails, the palace of proliferating portals and channels, and the garments of days demarcate a distinctive cultural landscape and poetic idiom, but one that was readily transferable to other cultures, theological spheres, and literary and discursive genres. The diaspora of these figures and the imaginary and metaphysical space they inhabit may have illumination to shed on historical outcomes as well as cultural phenomena far afield from Talmudic and Kabbalistic formulation. The figures and their tortuous trajectory are obscured by the general inaccessibility of these sources. But the comets' tails of the Zohar sparkle over a widely diverse but intrinsically interconnected trail of cultural artifacts.

Auratic Stars: From the Zohar to Benjamin

The trajectory of the shooting stars in The Book of Splendor is the dawn of the flight of the Angel of History,[18] who inscribes his markings on the mystical notepad of the sky. Benjamin's fascination with stars and their aurioles, constellations, and messianic angels, angels whose transformative vision of the world consists in their criticism, is both the endpoint of the modern Judaic reconfiguration of death and redemption in the Zohar and the taking off point for issues still captivating us today. The comet's tail invoked by Jewish mysticism sweeps over German literature—Goethe's "Egmont" and Elective Affinities, and Büchner's "Lenz" comprise only a few of its ports of call—effecting the multifaceted Judeo-German cultural graft noted above, and 'touching down,' if only briefly, as a posture of radical exegetical credulity in Benjamin and as a key feature in the abyssal poetic landscape carved out by Paul Celan.

History has taught us that Benjamin's stake in resuscitating a wonder at the heart of the Jewish imaginary with powerful extensions into the German Romantic imagination was a serious matter. It was to have nothing less than life-and-death consequences. The auratic wonder that Benjamin professed in relation to so many intellectual experiences and sites of thinking and creativity—it dawned upon him in conjunction with children's playthings, collecting peasants' wares on Moscow streets, the sensorium of modernistic life as it first evolved in nineteenth-century Paris, twentieth-century technological gadgetry—was first and foremost a splendid guise for an exemplar and relentless advocate for cultural sensibility. Yet there was something more, something strategic to this protean professed wonder, one unequalled, perhaps, by any other critic save Roland Barthes. Auratic magic exercised the capacity to span several facets of Benjamin's experience that the commonplaces of history sundered from one another: the Judaic and the German, the studied and the popular, the solitude of thinking and the mass-experience of twentieth-century life. Under the tutelage of Buber and Scholem, the latter of whose favorite Zoharic passages were collected in a slim volume still in print, Benjamin could trace the diaspora of an aura dawning in a distinctly

Judaic environment into a network of German letters to which he was every bit as committed. The splendors of figuration in the Zohar cast a messianic glow. Benjamin accesses the messianic powers of cultural wonder, narrative craft, and exegetical creation in German as well as Jewish sources. Indeed, one powerful flank of the Benjaminian messianism is the wish that the shooting stars setting out in the Zohar could cast their tails over German letters and affect the miracle of the edifying integration of Judaism into German cultures.

The pivotal irony here is that German Romantic literature could transpire in an abyss ultimately configured by Kabbalistic messianism even where it appeals to the trappings of evangelical theology and, on occasion, anti-Semitic folklore (as abounds, for instance, in Büchner's "Woyzeck"). The 'Judaic' feature of this literary space is nothing explicit; it is the irony inhering to the afterlife that persists after the claims of law and sovereignty have been exhausted, including those actions taken in their name. It is in this spirit that Jakob Michael Reinhold Lenz, Goethe's "poetic twin" (*CWL*, 161)[19] can go "through the mountains" on January 20, 1778 in search of Johann Friedrich Oberlin (1740–1826), the well-known spiritualist and healer, also the inspiration for Oberlin College in Oberlin, Ohio. Büchner, in recounting Lenz's ascent to the highlands where the simplicity of rural life continues unabated, and his quest, amid states of incipient madness, for psycho-spiritual healing, indeed 'fills in' the low road or dark side of mainstream Romanticism, with its polymorphous negotiations of the transcendental so magisterially announced by Goethe. In Lenz's wanderings through the mountains, Frankenstein finally meets his younger brother. The power of Büchner's fragmentary tale (it really is an extended prose poem) derives from many sources, among them its explicit appropriation of the visual effects of the sublime as it irradiates Romantic imagery, particularly in the paintings of Caspar David Friedrich. One could argue in parsing the following description, that one of Büchner's primary motives is to furnish Friedrich's landscapes (or Turner's seascapes, or Courbet's caves) with a textual caption in the medium of Romantic prose:

211

> Huge masses of light gushing at times from the valley like a golden river, then clouds again, hanging on the highest peak, then climbing down the forest slowly into the valley or sinking and rising in the sunbeams like a flying silvery web; not a sound, no movement, no birds, nothing but the wailing of the wind, sometimes near, sometimes far. Dots also appeared, skeletons of huts, boards covered in straw, a somber black in color. People, silent and grave, as though not daring to disturb the peace of their valley, greeted them quietly as they rode past. (*CWL*, 142)

This is a visual landscape configured by the vastness of its zones and the tensions between them. Its sublimity transpires unabated by 'human touches' designed to furnish it with scale, the miniscule human figures in Friedrich's "Morning in the Riesengebirge," or in this verbal canvas, the trail of snowflakes following from a bird, the train or sequence to Kabbalistic comets. "No movement in the air except for a soft breeze, the rustle of a bird lightly dusting snowflakes from its tail." (*CWL*, 143).

Within this setting, Lenz and Oberlin make an ironic if not comical pair, both dwarfed by the prospect of reining in Lenz's recurrent madness. Their partnership, even if its terms are christological and the redemption it attempts to effect manifestly Christian in its metaphysics, makes sense only in a context of prior ambulatory rabbinic dialogues hopelessly after the fact, the fact of exile, the fact of madness, the fact of endless wandering. This Judeo-German wedding of resources shimmers though the explicitly Christian settings of "Lenz" like the snow-crystals illuminating the highland landscape. Oberlin's work is indeed framed by this landscape. The extended description immediately above continues:

> The huts were full of life, people crowded around Oberlin, he instructed, gave advice, consoled; everywhere trusting glances, prayer. People told of dreams, premonitions. Then quickly to practical affairs. [...] Oberlin was tireless. Lenz his constant companion, at times conversing, attending to business, absorbed in nature. It all had a beneficial and soothing effect on him, he often had to look in Oberlin's eyes, and the immense peace that comes upon us in nature at rest, in the deep forest, in moonlit, melting summer nights seemed even nearer to him in these calm eyes, this nobler,

serious face. He was shy, but he made remarks, he spoke. Oberlin enjoyed his conversation and Lenz's charming child's face delighted him. But he could bear it only as long as the light remained in the valley; toward evening a strange fear came over him, he felt like chasing the sun; [...] he seemed to be going blind; now it grew, the demon of insanity sat at his feet. (*CWL*, 143)

In Büchner's cinematography the engagement between the two men transpires in the flashes of their two countenances rather than in the exegetical conundrums they ponder. But an ineffable and fatal intimacy prevails between them. It too is grounded in their having entered, at least for the moment, a mystical engagement with each other signaled by a loss of boundaries between them. Enigmatically, the text does not specify who was "toward evening" overcome by a "strange fear." It is Lenz whose emotional state is turbulent, but Oberlin who may experience limits in the delight exerted by Lenz's "charming child's face." The highlands are a place where, very much in a spirit of Christian compassion, Oberlin assumes the burden of Lenz's madness, yet they are also a Kabbalistic afterlife in which madness and meticulous human reform or *Tikkun* are one, in which the shimmering dance of nature is also an allegory of understanding and cultural literacy.

The importance of this text as an interface between Jewish and Christian mystical poetics is not lost on Paul Celan. It is precisely as a Lenz

that the Jew, the Jew and the son of a Jew, and with him went his name, the inexpressible, sets out on his wanderings through the mountains. He went then, one heard about it, he went one evening, a number had already descended, he went under cloud cover and shadow that were his own and foreign—since the Jew, you know it, whatever he has already, whatever belongs to him, that wasn't borrowed, lent out and never returned—so he went out and came there, came to the road, of the beautiful, the incomparable, like Lenz, through the mountains, who would have been allowed to reside below, where he belongs, in the lowlands, he, the Jew, came and came.[20]

213

His name may be this Jew's only possession, everything else having been "borrowed, lent out, and never returned." Celan alludes to a moment when the landscape has been largely emptied of Jews. The mountains remain, but not the Jews of the lowlands. This Jew, the Jew of the prose poem, resides in a spectral afterlife. It is only in this sense that his advent, his arrival, could be multiple and ongoing. He "came and came." Whether belatedly and indirectly or not, this Jew comes bearing his only property, his name, which walks with him and beside him. This figure consists, precisely, in a word, an element of language, the nominative, mystically transformed into a figure, a character, one free to dance and play, like days woven into garments, to dance within a world suffused with mystical meaning, a world defined by its role in a consummate exegesis by God. This Jew doesn't encounter many interlocutors. One is the figure of Büchner's Lenz. And of course, the remnants of a family, his cousin and his *Geschwisterkind*: with them he will join a chatter haunting the sublime landscape filled with Jews as absences and memories as well as voices and figurations.

If Celan is free in his own post-disaster poetics to resume both a practice and setting for figuration established in the Zohar, it is Walter Benjamin who, in his own wanderings on the frontier between Judaic and German letters, elaborates the terms and theory of this grafting, makes it historically explicit. Benjamin is long a careful reader of the stars. Since the onset of *The Arcades Project*, he has pursued their spectral sway over Paris, in Baudelaire's expletives, and in Grandville's cosmic cartoons.[21] Benjamin, in what is arguably his first full-fledged work of literary criticism, his essay on Goethe's *The Elective Affinities*, in which he effects a full cross-over between his philosophical readings and his critical ambitions, is exquisitely sensitive to the shooting stars' role within the narrative of the Goethean novel. As late as "On Some Motives in Baudelaire," he still charts the trajectory as the shooting stars thread the seam between loss and redemption, ritual and industrial time, and poetic inspiration and shock.

Benjamin volunteers himself as the astronomer of the mystical Kabbalistic heavens in the turbulent domain of advanced modernity. He will

214

not allow his readers to overlook Goethe's caption for the last moment in *The Elective Affinities* when romantic love might win out over social convention, when desire might realize itself instead of capitulating to diversions and dissimulations: "Hope shot across the sky above their heads like a falling star."[22] This burst of hope, set in one of German literature's most resonant and suggestive novels, is all the more poignant for being destined to extinction amid the truisms of *Sittlichkeit* and the economics of bourgeois domesticity. Its short-lived flash reminds us that the broad swathe of German letters in Goethe's wake is susceptible to Messianic time. The final of two afterthoughts Benjamin appended to his "On the Concept of History," characterizes this openness: "For every second of time was the straight gate through which the Messiah might enter." Not only does this brief note characterize the hope that briefly flares for the love-crossed modern prisoners of desire in *The Elective Affinities*: it reminds us of Benjamin's explicit desire, also not realized, to pursue messianic mysticism into the nexus of modern urbanity and shock. This aspiration, which might seem out of character with his secular sophistication, his commitment, first and foremost, to letters, and his receptivity to social as well as conceptual revolutions of the mind, is spelled out where we are not afraid to read its legend. Given the "On the Concept of History's" commitment to fragmentary utterance, to dialectical imagery, and to epigrammatic closure, it is not by chance that in their aftermath, Benjamin should signal his own prior meditations on the afterlife of Judaism:

> We know that the Jews were prohibited from investigating the future. The Torah and the prayers instruct them in remembrance, however. This stripped the future of its magic, to which all those succumb who turn to the soothsayers for enlightenment. This does not imply, however, that for the Jews the future turned into homogenous, empty time.[23]

The Jewish future here becomes an afterlife of hope, not of projection. And indeed, Benjamin enlists the words of Joubert to characterize the messianic hope that still suffuses the modern world. "'Time is still found in eternity; but it is not earthly, worldly time ... It does not destroy; it merely completes.'"[24] This time is still accessible in a modernity that has largely degraded the "crowning of experience" consummated by the fulfillment of the wish.[25] This is a modernity in which the folkloric wish embodied by the falling star has been supplanted by "The ivory ball which rolls into the *next* compartment, the *next* card which lies on top," in gambling.[26] In this degraded but captivating time, the wish is served by the one-armed bandit, operated by a spasmodic gesture carried over from the assembly line. "On Some Motifs in Baudelaire" is, after all, a miniature crystallization of the materials gathered in *The Arcades Project* and a roadmap to their many convergences, departures, and collisions. The world configured by both works, the former at an extreme of poetic condensation in critical discourse and the latter at an extreme of archival dispersion, is nothing other than the complex of late-modern commercial, urban, communicative, and technological forces first coinciding in Paris under the Second Empire. Benjamin makes Joubert the mouthpiece for a radical messianic temporality that persists into this configuration. Yet Benjamin is explicitly, ironically, and morbidly aware of its Kabbalistic provenance. Many were the dreams that failed to be realized in the 20th century, a period of unprecedented violence, genocide, and the disregard of life. Yet the blueprints for these dreams survive. In the fictive topography configured by a set of obscure medieval rabbis and in certain of the tropes they tripped into motion the likes of Benjamin and Scholem accessed a *Genizah*, a repository for disrupted dreams whose very parameters mirrored, reenacted, and extended their life.

Notes

[1] The notion of three core Abrahamic religions, Judaism, Christianity, and Islam, is a conceptual matrix and platform that Derrida uses to culturally far-reaching effects in his writings on religion of the past three decades. This construct reminds us that the major Western religions, studied from a rigorous philosophical point

of view, are in a far more intimate exchange and communication than the history of religious persecutions, expulsions, and genocide would allow us to suspect. For some of Derrida's major writings in this sphere, see his *Acts of Religion*, ed. Gil Anidjar (New York: Routledge, 2002); also, *On the Name*, (Stanford: Stanford University Press, 1995). Also see Hent de Vries, *Philosophy and the Turn to Religion* (Baltimore: Johns Hopkins University Press, 1999).

2   A useful overview of Jewish positions on the afterlife is to be found in "The Domain of Heaven and the Domain of Hell," a chapter in Ben Zion Bokser, *Judaism: Profile of a Faith* (New York: Alfred A. Knopf, 1963), 131–60.

3   My own efforts to come to some productive terms with modernity are contained in my *The Aesthetic Contract: Statutes of Art and Intellectual Work in Modernity* (Stanford: Stanford University Press, 1997).

4   Among the many contributions furnished by Derrida's writings on Western religion is a full extrapolation of the otherworldly, spectral, abyssal, ghostly, and uncanny constructs and figures, including the *revenant* appearing in this very paragraph, upon which the edifice of the Abrahamic religions literally stands. Derrida places this sometimes downright flaky underside to our canonical faiths in full relief, and this in turn allows us to question their claim to have initiated an age of rationality, principle, and disinterest in religion and the communities of Judeo-Christianity and Islam. Derrida's highly nuanced recognition of the spectral dimension of the core Western religions has helped me instrumentally in discerning the traits of the Jewish afterlife as it is staged in the Zohar. See Jacques Derrida, *Acts of Religion*, 62, 83–84, 87, 91–92, 100, 141, 151, 191, 198–203, 208, 210, 213–18, 222–23, 252–53, 258–59, 276–79, 296, 382, 384, 387, 399, 405, 413.

5   In sheer scholarly terms, Gershom Scholem's annotations and elucidations are indispensable to any approach to the Kabbalah. The fact that he was an intimate and lifelong friend of Benjamin's, having met him in 1912, at the age of seventeen, means that there is an important imaginary confluence of their views, although their opinions diverged on many essential theological points. This citation, as well as the others that are so helpful to me in launching the present exploration, comes from Scholem's *Kabbalah* (New York: Meridian, 1978). The abbreviation "*K*" refers to this edition.

6   I have explored the Talmud's status as a multi-register text, above all in relation to Benjamin's *Arcades Project*, but also in conjunction with Derrida's *Glas*, in "Between the Registers: The Allegory of Space in Benjamin's Arcades Project," in *Benjamin Now: Critical Encounters with The Arcades Project, boundary 2*, 30 (2003), 169–90.

7   The thinker whose work most closely and persistently tracks the theoretical impact of narrative in its multifarious aspects is, of course, J. Hillis Miller. In a Millerian context the transformation of the quasi-transcendental rabbis of the Talmud into

creatures of fictive narrative is of necessity a catacysmic event. Among the many points in the theoretically vibrant topography of reading that Miller has charted relevant to the present essay are the following: his overall survey of death as a literary construct—above all as negotiated by the trope of prosopopoeia—in *Versions of Pygmalion* (Cambridge: Harvard University Press, 1990). His careful exegeses of James, Melville, and Blanchot are particularly relevant in this respect. Also incisive and generative are his readings of the Book of Ruth and of Derrida's theoretical topography in *Topographies* (Stanford: Stanford University Press, 1995), 291–337; and, his lucid overview of narrative sequence and continuity in *Reading Narrative* (Norman: University of Oklahoma Press, 1998), 46–83.

8   For the notion of the dialectical image, see Benjamin, AP, 13, 70, 150, 317, 388–89, 391–92, 396, 406, 417, 459–70, 473-76.

9   "The Talmud has been compared to the sea; you never enjoy swimming anywhere until you've gotten used to the water." Robert Goldenberg, "Talmud," in *Back to the Sources*, ed. Barry W. Holtz (New York: Simon & Schuster, 1984), 168.

10 Bruno Schulz, *Sanatorium under the Sign of the Hourglass*, (New York: Penguin, 1979), 117.

11 *Zohar: The Book of Splendor: Basic Readings from the Kabbalah*, ed. Gershom Scholem (New York: Schocken, 1963), henceforth abbreviated, "ZBS." It makes all the difference to the present essay and intellectual exercise that Scholem selected and edited the slim compilation of Zoharic tales and elucidations making my own extrapolations possible. The choice of texts in this slim volume is indeed selective: in English, it narrows the five-volume Soncino Edition down to less than a hundred pages. The folktales that Scholem included must have indeed enjoyed special resonance to the groundbreaking elucidator of Jewish mystical literature.

12 For a comprehensive and personally compelling account of this prayer, one entwining the pivotal aspects of the Judaic approach to death, see Leon Wieseltier, *Kaddish* (New York: Alfred A. Knopf, 1998), xiii, 4–11, 96–124, 264–95, 355–68.

13 The *Athenaeum Fragments* comprise a privileged site, one whose significance Benjamin fully recognized, for the theoretical working-through of the poetic figurations of key philosophical issues explored, among different literatures, in Jewish mysticism. Benjamin's aspirations to an integration of Judaic images and narratives and German letters were not merely the stuff of wishes. They were founded on the 'hard' data and solutions furnished by the likes of Fichte, the Schlegels, and their peers. See, above all, Friedrich Schlegel's *Lucinde and the Fragments*, (Minneapolis: University of Minnesota Press, 1971), 175–77, 191–98.

14 In *The Order of Things*, Michel Foucault earmarks analogical thought and imagery, capable spanning vast distances of plane, realm, and category, a thinking not incompatible with the author(s) of the Zohar, with the *épistème* (or linguistically

218

configured world-view) of the European Renaissance. This cultural moment is for him a domain saturated with radical similitudes. See Michel Foucault, *The Order of Things*, (New York: Vintage, 1973), 17–77.

[15] See Gershom Scholem, *Major Trends in Jewish Mysticism* (New York: Schocken, 1961), 217–35; also, *On the Kabbalah and its Symbolism* (New York: Schocken, 1965), 130–53.

[16] Given that Kafka does so much to dramatize and perform the twentieth-century cultural imaginary of texts and textually-configured environments and institutions, it can be no accident that Deleuze and Guattari dedicated a book to his fiction and the philosophical notions that can be extracted from it. Two of Kafka's novels, *Amerika* and *The Trial*, and an extended late animal fable, "The Burrow," devote particular attention to the construction and performance of extended, interconnected, involuted, self-enclosing environments and architectures. Dedicated readers of Kafka, Deleuze, and Guattari owe much of their sense of a rhizomatic, schizo- (that is, non-hierarchically) interconnected cultural landscape to Kafka's projections and imaginings. See Franz Kafka, *Amerika*, (New York: Schocken, 1974), 4, 11, 41, 74–75, 108–10, 196–99; *The Trial*, (New York: Schocken, 1974), 34–35, 63–67, 99, 116, 119–21, 142–45, 155, 213–14; "The Burrow," in *The Complete Stories*, ed Nahum N. Glatzer (New York: Schocken, 1971), 326–28, 337, 339–40, 343–49. Deleuze and Guattari, above all in their "Capitalism and Schizophrenia" diptych, translate, in a Benjaminian sense, Kafka's images and tropings into a rhetoric of rhizomes and an architecture of "planes of consistency" and assemblages. For an introduction to this rhetoric, see Gilles Deleuze and Félix Guattari, *A Thousand Plateaus*, (Minneapolis: University of Minnesota Press, 1987), 3–18, 40–45, 49–57, 141–48, 208–27, 351–74.

[17] For the Sefiroth, see Gershom Scholem, *Major Trends in Jewish Mysticism*, 204–15, 268–73; also, *On the Kabbalah and its Symbolism*, 94, 96–105.

[18] I refer here of course to the character of the Angelus Novus, culled from one of Klee's drawings (and once owned by Benjamin), a figure for the cultural redemption attainable only through the 'tasks' of close exegesis, translation, collecting, and dedicated archival work. This image, as its possibility, rises to its full aura and eloquence in IX of the "On the Concept of History," in SW 4, 392–93.

[19] Citations from "Lenz" derive from Georg Büchner, *Complete Works and Letters*, The German Library, 23 (New York: Continuum, 1986), 139–59, abbreviated "*CWL.*"

[20] This is my translation of a passage from Paul Celan, "Gespräch im Gebirg," in *Gesammelte Werke* (Frankfurt am Main: Suhrkamp Verlag, 1983), III, 169.

[21] Benjamin, AP, 25–26, 64–65, 112–19, 337, 339–40, 343, 347–49, 357, 462–64, 466, 470, 475, 540.

[22] Benjamin, "Goethe's Elective Affinities," in SW 1, 354–56, 357n.

219

[23] Benjamin, "On the Concept of History" in SW 4, 397.
[24] Benjamin, "On Some Motifs in Baudelaire" in SW 4, 331.
[25] Ibid.
[26] Ibid.

The Decay of Aura / The Aura of Decay

Erik Steinskog

In the essay "Experience and Poverty," Walter Benjamin writes: "Objects made of glass have no 'aura.'"[1] This single sentence contains several important notions for discussing Benjamin's understanding of modernity. First, there are objects or things. What to understand by 'objects' in Benjamin is quite difficult to determine, though of no little importance. His late work on the Parisian arcades, *The Arcades Project*, might be seen as a movement 'back to the things,' though in a quite different sense than what Edmund Husserl's famous dictum intended.[2] Second, there is in the sentence a reference to glass—to objects made of glass, but also glass related to architecture, to the arcades as well as glass architecture more generally. And then, third, Benjamin refers to aura, marking the term, but also using it to point to something the objects made of glass lack. Unfolding this single sentence, then, will explicate dimensions related to things, glass, and aura. But given the title of the essay to which the sentence belongs, the primary focus here will be on modernity's different modes of experience and on the possibilities of expressing or making sense of these experiences.

One possible entry-point for such a discussion is architecture, and in particular its process of becoming-ruin. Aura is, in important senses, of the past. All we have left are traces of aura, the memories of what the auratic used to be. These traces testify to the present absence of the auratic. The aura is in a constant process of decay, for the traces tell us that it has not disappeared altogether. In this sense, the aura resembles a ruin. All architectural structures are, from their moment of construction— or even from the blueprint—in a dialectical process of becoming-ruin and becoming-repaired. The process of ruination may extend over centuries

221

and be almost invisible, or it may be swift and traumatic. Buildings are in a process of decay, and disappear altogether if this process is completed. The ruin thus exists only within this very process, with decay as a necessary dimension. What interests me here is the long process, what Benjamin in *The Origin of the German Tragic Drama* terms 'nature-history':

> When, as in the case in the *Trauerspiel*, history becomes part of the setting, it does so as script. The word "history" stands written on the countenance of nature in the characters of transience. The allegorical physiognomy of the nature-history, which is put on stage in the *Trauerspiel*, is present in reality in the form of the ruin. In the ruin history has physically merged into the setting. And in this guise history does not assume the form of the process of an eternal life so much as that of irresistible decay.[3]

There are, however, other dimensions to the ruin, which seem to have attached to them something resembling an opposite to aura, what Benjamin terms 'trace': "Trace and aura. The trace is appearance of a nearness, however far removed the thing that left it behind may be. The aura is appearance of a distance, however close the thing that calls it forth. In the trace, we gain possession of the thing; in the aura, it takes possession of us."[4] The ruinous process itself takes place between the trace and the aura, as a quivering standstill. There is, therefore, both a decay of trace and a trace of decay as well as a decay of aura and an aura of decay.

Sense and Architecture

Architecture is in many ways different from other art forms. It is not simply something we experience at a distance, with the kind of detached look often described as the proper aesthetic attitude towards for example the pictorial arts. A painting or a sculpture is exhibited, in the etymological sense of being 'held out,' for a subject to perceive. Experiencing an architectural artifact—a building—we are, on the contrary, in the midst of it. In this direct engagement with the work of art, any preference for the detached gaze is challenged. When perceiving exhibited works of art with the detached attitude that used to be the norm of aesthetic perception, the relation between the work of art and the beholder is a mediated one. The work of art is mediated, first through the senses, and secondly through the language used in discussing it. Being in the work of art, as we are when experiencing architecture, is at the same time a mediated and an immediate experience. Dwelling within the work—or being-in-the-work—thus challenges fundamentally the privilege of the detached attitude. In Kant's famous discussion of the beautiful and the sublime, these dimensions are not attributes of the objects, but refer back to the subject who constructs the objects as beautiful or sublime in the reflective judgment of taste. Thus, these features are not attributes of the objects, but feelings or experiences of pleasure or displeasure in the judging subject. Both the beautiful and the sublime—that is, any possible content of an aesthetic judgment—is detached from the object.[5] It is here that Benjamin's understanding of subject and object demands a different aesthetics than the Kantian framework.[6]

Dealing with architecture, one has to discuss experience differently than in relation to other kinds of artworks. It is not that there is no common ground. On the contrary, experiencing works of art is always intimately related to sensation, to sensing the works and making sense of them. But it is the problem of representation that specifies the difference. How is it possible to move from the act of sensation to the act of making sense? The different modalities of experience in architecture and exhibited artworks question the being of the relation between aesthetics and epistemology: sense as in sensation and sense as in meaning-making.

Traditionally, works of art have often been considered monosensorial, implying that whenever a work is perceived through several senses at once, severe discursive difficulties arise. Architecture is not the only art form where several senses are at play simultaneously. But architecture is perhaps the oldest artform that requires a sensibility prior to the diversification of senses.[7] In this respect, the experience of architecture is comparable to other, more modern kineasthetic experiences, such as cinema and urban life. The bodily dimension of these sensations—reminding us that we experience as whole bodies—is important for understanding aesthetics in modernity; and here architecture might become a model for discussing other art forms.

This has important consequences for how to read Benjamin's discussion of art. In "The Work of Art in the Age of Its Technological Reproducibility," Benjamin writes about architecture:

> Buildings have accompanied human existence since primeval times. Many art forms have come into being and passed away. [...] But the human need for shelter is permanent. Architecture has never had fallow periods. Its history is longer than that of any other art, and its effect ought to be recognized in any attempt to account for the relationship of the masses to the work of art. Buildings are received in a twofold manner: by use and by perception. Or, better: tactilely and optically. [...] On the tactile side, there is no counterpart to what contemplation is on the optical side. Tactile reception comes about not so much by way of attention as by way of habit. The latter largely determines even the optical reception of architecture, which spontaneously takes the form of casual noticing, rather than attentive observation.[8]

The fact that buildings have accompanied human existence since primeval times, that they are part of the primal history (*Urgeschichte*) of mankind, implies that the old philosophical question "What is a human being?" is intimately related to what it means to build and dwell. However, as Benjamin reminds his readers again and again, even questions that have been part of the quest of humans since time immemorial are still historical questions. They change throughout history, and must thus be asked anew. In Benjamin's time, the historicity of these eternal questions related to architecture. Siegfried Giedion referred to how architecture, when it towards the end of the eighteenth century became part of the *l'Ecole des beaux arts*, simultaneously became linked to the plastic arts.[9] This was "a disaster for architecture," but according to Benjamin it also "indicates that architecture was historically the earliest field to outgrow the concept of art, or, better, that it tolerated least well being contemplated as 'art'."[10] The category of contemplation is here distinct from habitual experience, following Benjamin's argument in the "Work of Art" for an immediate, tactile dimension of architecture. In "Little History of Photography" Benjamin discusses art in similar terms as in relation to architecture. With photography "something new and strange" comes into being, and Benjamin argues that there is something in photographs that "will never consent to be wholly absorbed in 'art'."[11]

What makes the sensation of architecture different from that of many other works of art is that buildings are received in a twofold manner. Architecture is received by bodily use as well as by visual perception, tactilely as well as optically. These two faculties have spatial characters that Benjamin discusses in the essay on Surrealism: "an image space and, more concretely, a body space."[12] The "body- and image-space" is conceptually close to how architecture is described in the "Work of Art"— a coexistence of two different spaces or two different modes of perception, one related to the gaze, the other to the body. And, as Benjamin reminds us in "Surrealism," "the collective is a body, too,"[13] thus including the discussion of the collective or the masses, categories also found in the "Work of Art."

The twofold reception of architecture has consequences for sensation. Being-in-the-work means that contemplation cannot be the sole way of relating to art. Contemplation or attention has since Kant been related to the detached gaze and therefore been highly valued aesthetically. Use, on the other hand, has not been valued as an aesthetic dimension. With the notions of body space, photography and architecture—all related to use—Benjamin fundamentally challenges the opposition between artworks and artifacts, the sphere of art and the culture of everyday life. This also engages new questions of technology.[14] As Howard Caygill writes, "architecture provides the main site for the interaction of technology and the human, a negotiation conducted in terms of touch and use."[15] This reference to architecture and technology relates the "Work of Art" to "Experience and Poverty," where Benjamin wrote about how soldiers from the First World War returned from the trenches, not richer but poorer in communicable experience due to technological developments,

225

and where he further claimed that a completely new poverty had descended on mankind.

> No, this much is clear: experience has fallen in value, amid a generation which from 1914 to 1918 had to experience some of the most monstrous events in the history of the world. Perhaps this is less remarkable than it appears. Wasn't it noticed at the time how many people returned from the front in silence? Not richer but poorer in communicable experience? And what poured out from the flood of war books ten years later was anything but the experience that passes from mouth to ear. No, there was nothing remarkable about that. For never has experience been contradicted more thoroughly [...]. A generation that had gone to school in horse-drawn streetcars now stood in the open air, amid a landscape in which nothing was the same except the clouds and, at its center, in a force field of destructive torrents and explosions, the tiny, fragile human body.[16]

This poverty of experience, Benjamin argues, is "not merely poverty on the personal level, but poverty of human experience in general."[17] He claims that this indicates "a new kind of barbarism," one, however, that should not necessarily be taken as something negative. He wants to "introduce a new, positive concept of barbarism," one forcing the barbarian "to start from scratch; to make a new start."[18] These "new barbarians" are what Benjamin calls "constructors;" they think on the drawing table. For Benjamin, the most important ones seem to be Paul Klee, Adolf Loos, Paul Scheerbart, and Karl Kraus. What binds them together is a certain kind of purification or drawing of distinctions, where "Loos's first concern [was] to separate the work of art from the article of use," whereas for Kraus it was "to keep apart information and the work of art."[19]

What is perhaps most important in Benjamin's description of the soldiers coming home from the trenches is the notion of "communicable experience." It is thus not "experience" per se (if there is such a thing), but the communicable experience that is at stake. The silence of the returned soldiers was not the absence of experience, even if it might seem close, but rather the absence of a language suitable to render those experiences. This lack may for Benjamin be remedied by the "completely new language" found in Scheerbart, where "what is crucial [...] is its arbitrary, constructed nature, in contrast to organic language."[20] This is the same language described in "Karl Kraus" as "stellar Esperanto."[21]

The new barbarians are very specific about their buildings, their "glass-covered dwellings":

> To return to Scheerbart: he placed the greatest value on housing his "people"–and, following this model, his fellow citizens–in buildings befitting their station, in adjustable, movable glass-covered dwellings of the kind since built by Loos and Le Corbusier. It is no coincidence that glass is such a hard, smooth material to which nothing can be fixed. A cold and sober material into the bargain. Objects made of glass have no "aura." Glass is, in general, the enemy of secrets. It is also the enemy of possession.[22]

Objects made of glass have no aura. This is due to qualities intrinsic to glass. Glass is a hard and smooth material, as well as cold and sober. It is also the enemy of secrets and possession. Glass architecture "dissolves the distinction between interior and exterior" and replaces it "with the single, continuous concept of transparency."[23] That Benjamin's discussion of glass and the mentioning of aura in this context take place within a discussion of architecture as well as objects is significant.[24] The most fundamental feature of glass is its transparency, where any secret becomes impossible. The secret is a key dimension of aura.

Glass is the enemy of secrets and the same might be said about photography, but in a somewhat different sense. Given the transparency of glass, secrets become impossible. The photograph, on the other hand, reveals secrets through a new way of perception, a perception based in the apparatus, which, in a sense, works better than the eyes. "Photography, with its devices of slow motion and enlargement, reveals the secret," Benjamin writes in "Little History of Photography."[25] Through photography we discover the existence of the "optical unconscious," comparable to how the instinctual unconscious is discovered through psychoanalysis.[26]

The decay of aura brought about by photography might thus be compared to the absence or lack of aura in objects made of glass. There are other similarities as well. The new architecture of glass and iron, which Benjamin describes in *The Arcades Project,* was built to last. The same is said about the earliest portrait photographs: "Everything about these early pictures was built to last."²⁷ This, then, seems to be in accordance with glass and iron architecture, where the lasting dimension is inscribed in the buildings as their refusal to become ruins.

Hand and Eye

When, in the developments of the nineteenth century, lithography gave way to photography, an alteration of the senses took place as well. Benjamin describes this as a kind of detachment of the hand from the eye, which is related to industrial as well as technological developments of the pictorial arts: "For the first time, photography freed the hand from the most important artistic tasks in the process of pictorial reproduction—tasks that now devolved upon the eye alone."²⁸ This argument points to an altered understanding of the work of the artist. The artist once was a craftsman doing handicraft and the hand and the technologies extending the hand were of severe consequence—indeed necessary—for reproduction to be possible. Considering technologies as extensions of the human body has been common to, among others, Sigmund Freud in *Civilization and Its Discontents* and Marshall McLuhan in *Understanding Media.* For Benjamin it means that in the case of artistic reproduction, the technological extensions move from the hand to the eye—the opposite direction than in perceiving a work of art. In Benjamin's argument, lithography should be seen as an extension of the hand, whereas photography becomes an extension of the eye. And as Freud and McLuhan seem to agree upon; "any invention of technology is an extension or self-amputation of our physical bodies,"²⁹ contributing to what Freud describes as "a kind of prosthetic God."³⁰

The process Benjamin describes with the movement from lithography to photography resembles another process described in the same chapter of the "Work of Art": the invention of the printing press.³¹ This process, the movement into the "Gutenberg Galaxy," impinges on the senses.[32] In McLuhan's *Understanding Media*, the 'invention' of writing, or the written word itself, is presented under the heading "An Eye for an Ear."[33] With the invention of the printing press and movable type, however, the hand becomes increasingly important. McLuhan argues that writing is an extension of sight whereas numbers are extensions of touch, an argument further emphasizing the differentiation between these senses. "Just as writing is an extension and separation of our most neutral and objective sense, the sense of sight, number is an extension and separation of our most intimate and interrelating activity, our sense of touch."[34] He then develops this argument, taking it into the twentieth century with Paul Klee as an example:

> This faculty of touch, called the "haptic" sense by the Greeks, was popularized as such by the Bauhaus program of sensuous education, through the work of Paul Klee, Walter Gropius, and many others in the Germany of the 1920s. The sense of touch, as offering a kind of nervous system or organic unity in the work of art, has obsessed the minds of the artists since the time of Cézanne. For more than a century now artists have tried to meet the challenge of the electric age by investing the tactile sense with the role of a nervous system for unifying all the others. Paradoxically, this has been achieved by "abstract art," which offers a central nervous system for a work of art, rather than the conventional husk of the old pictorial image.[35]

Touch is here in opposition to any division of the senses. Touch reintegrates the senses into a kind of super-sense.[36] By keeping in touch with the objects, things are perceived kinesthetically, in accordance with McLuhan's understanding of the haptic.

That photography frees the hand from the mode of image production seems contrary to William Henry Fox Talbot's understanding of "the pencil of nature," and "words of light," which indicates a continuation of writing with other means.[37] However, a kind of automatism is indeed inscribed in the process of photography, eliminating, as McLuhan writes, "the syntactical procedure of pen and pencil."[38] McLuhan seems to echo Benjamin's description of something different coming into being with photography. Where Benjamin argues that "photography freed the hand from the most important artistic tasks in the process of pictorial reproduction—tasks that now devolved upon the eye alone,"[39] McLuhan writes that "the step from the age of Typographic Man to the age of Graphic Man was taken with the invention of photography."[40] Drawing out the consequences of McLuhan's statement, by comparing it with Benjamin, testifies to a cultural transformation from the (written) word to the image.[41] The historical event of photography thus marks the culture of images. The illiterates of the future will be those who do not know how to read images.[42] This statement has become a kind of truism, but it shows a transformation from writing to image taking place within modernity, a transformation with crucial consequences for the traditional arts. "The painter could no longer depict a world that had been much photographed" and thus instead turned to inner processes and abstraction, McLuhan argues;[43] and Benjamin writes, in "Little History of Photography," that "the real victim of photography [...] was not landscape painting but the portrait miniature."[44]

Freeing the hand and substituting it with the eye implies alterations of temporality, or, more precisely, speed. The slowness of the hand makes it obsolete, or rather; temporally unfit for the fast speed of modernity. "The eye perceives more swiftly than the hand can draw," Benjamin observes, and "the process of pictorial reproduction was enormously accelerated, so that it could now keep pace with speech."[45] The accelerating speed of modernity further implies that when writing becomes too slow, speech takes over. In these developments visual media attain prophetic qualities, already containing seeds of the coming, as in Benjamin's argument that "the illustrated newspaper virtually lay hidden within lithography," and that "sound film was latent in photography."[46]

The work of the hand is part of the history of reproduction. When Benjamin describes the development from lithography to photography as an alteration from the hand to the eye, this is simultaneously a trans-

230

formation from manual to technological reproduction. Works of art have in principle always been reproducible, but the means of reproduction alter over time. This, however, impacts on the relation between original and copy:

> But whereas the authentic work retains its full authority in the face of a reproduction made by hand, which it generally brands as forgery, this is not the case with technological reproduction. [...] technological reproduction is more independent of the original than is manual reproduction. For example, in photography it can bring out aspects of the original that are accessible only to the lens (which is adjustable and can easily change viewpoint) but not to the human eye; or it can use certain processes, such as enlargement or slow motion, to record images which escape natural optics altogether.[47]

Thus, manual and technological reproductions differ. The differences not only have to do with the means of reproduction but also with perception. Technological reproduction challenges 'natural optics' in such a way that it makes possible perception of what was previously unperceivable; that is, it makes the invisible visible. The senses are thus expanded, strengthening sensation beyond the 'natural.'[48] The optical unconscious is due to the camera being able to expand both space and time: "With the close-up, space expands; with slow motion, movement is extended."[49] In this, and Benjamin highlights slow motion here, what was previously invisible becomes visible. With the help of the camera we can see new things. The unconscious dimension of this new optics also implies alterations in the psychic structure of perception. The two different versions of the unconscious—the optical and the instinctual—are, according to Benjamin, intimately linked.[50] There are two reasons for this: first, "the diverse aspects of reality captured by the film camera lie outside of the *normal* spectrum of sense impressions," and second, "thanks to the camera [...] the individual perceptions of the psychotic or the dreamer can be appropriated by collective perception."[51] Thus the camera alters the relation between the individual and the collective, not

231

only concerning sense impressions, but mental or abstract reception as well. Sensations give impressions to the mind and, due to the camera and the optical unconscious, differences between the individual and the collective break down.

The difference between the hand and the eye is notable in Benjamin's comparison between the camera operator and the painter and its related argument about the surgeon and the magician. The magician heals the sick person by laying on of hands, which differs from the surgeon, who makes an intervention into the patient. This is a question of distance:

> The magician maintains the natural distance between himself and the person treated; more precisely, he reduces it slightly by laying on his hands, but increases it greatly by his authority. The surgeon does exactly the reverse: he greatly diminishes the distance from the patient by penetrating the patient's body, and increases it only slightly by the caution with which his hand moves among the organs.[52]

For Benjamin, this is analogous to the relation between painter and cinematographer: "Magician is to surgeon as painter is to cinematographer."[53] It is not, however, clear how this analogy is supposed to work. In the description of the magician and the surgeon, the hand, and the work of the hand, is highlighted. But the main difference between painter and cinematographer, at least in the overall context of artistic production is the movement from the hand to the eye. Furthermore, cutting, common to both surgeon and cinematographer, is both similar and different. The surgeon cuts open the human body, that is, opens up the interior of the body, and makes visible what he is operating on, in contrast to the magician who heals from a distance, in the sense of putting his hands on the outside of the human body, on the skin. The surgeon's opening into the interior is thus different from what the cinematographer does, where the surface is dominating. Even though the cinematographer too cuts, and his whole art is dependent upon cut and montage, is it a different kind of cutting.

232

The Mark of History

As the strange weave of time and space suggests, there is a dimension of historicity associated with the aura. Things that have aura have a mark of history:

> In even the most perfect reproduction, *one* thing is lacking: the here and now of the work of art—its unique existence in a particular place. It is this unique existence—and nothing else—that bears the mark of the history to which the work has been subject. This history includes changes to the physical structure of the work over time, together with any changes in ownership.[54]

Benjamin's argument implies that something unique is inscribed in the original work of art. The notion of original is in itself problematic; one might argue that there are no originals before there are copies, in other words, that the copies constitute the very precondition of the original. However, what Benjamin describes here is something lacking in reproductions but found in the original work of art, and this is its here and now. The here and now is a moment both in time and space, although it also describes something outside of time and space, bringing, in a certain sense, time and space to a standstill. Thereby it resembles the caesura described in Benjamin's reading of Goethe's *Elective Affinities*.[55] The "unique existence" of the work of art, coextensive with its here and now, is "the mark of the history to which the work has been subject," and "this history includes changes to the physical structure of the work over time."

Such changes are of particular interest for a discussion of ruins. A ruin is in a sense defined by changes to physical structure; for a building is a becoming-ruin, and its physical structure changes over time.[56] This change makes a ruin, or, in other words, actualizes the building. Ruins are thus the very embodiment of history, understood as changes to the physical structure. As such they have an "existence in a particular place," but not a here and now in the sense of a specific time-space of the now. The historicity of the ruin is incompatible with the here and now, but at the same time points to the very process of history. However, the marks of history are inscribed in the process of ruinosity in such a way that the ruin becomes the emblem, the very mark, of history.[57]

There is no reason to say that the ruin resembles a copy even if it lacks the here and now. Rather, the ruin resembles the original, but it is a resemblance only. The ruin replaces the absent original without being a copy. What is always absent is the original building before history; in other words, the original is always lost in an irreducible past.[58] This dimension of the past is history from the point of view of the Angel of History, in that the Angel sees a "pile of debris before him" growing toward the sky.[59] The past, at which the Angel stares, is "one single catastrophe, which keeps piling wreckage upon wreckage and hurls it at his feet."[60] The Angel sees ruins upon ruins, and these ruins constitute the past from the point of view of the Angel. This point of view shows history, in a concrete sense, as a process of ruination. The ruin relates to buildings as the traces of history to a work of art. That does not challenge Benjamin's critique of authenticity related to the original's here and now. However, it does challenge the usefulness of terms like 'authenticity,' and 'the original,' when it comes to architecture.[61] This is due to the particular kind of perception we employ when experiencing architecture, but also to architecture's relation to art. "The authenticity of a thing is the quintessence of all that is transmissible in it from its origin on, ranging from its physical duration to the historical testimony relating to it."[62] Such a historical testimony relates both to authenticity and to the here and now. Physical duration is pointed out as important, but the "changes in the physical structure" unworks this very duration. It is finally critical that Benjamin describes the work's circumstances: when circumstances change, the work changes as well.[63] These different dimensions are shown in the ruin. When a building becomes a ruin, its surroundings are not necessarily altered. Rather it is the relation between building and surroundings that changes, although arguably the work of art itself, marked by the passing of history, changes the most. The ruin challenges the here and now, and instead points to historicity as inherent in it. Watching a ruin we see the work of history, and we do so in a concrete way. The ruin testifies to a process of history, comparable to how a still life painting testifies to the inevitability of death. When Benjamin claims that terms such as here and now and authenticity can be focused in the notion of the aura, and "what withers in the age of the technological reproducibility of the work of art is the latter's aura,"[64] it is on the basis that ruinosity structurally antecedes both the aura and its decay. With regards to what could be postulated as the aura of architecture or the aura of a building, a tricky question arises about how to describe the decay of aura when the auratic work of art we are describing has always been in a state of (physical) decay. The historicity of buildings points to such processes of physical decay as inevitable.

The particular problem of description involves a general development away from experience towards information. According to Benjamin, the reason for "the isolation of information from experience is that the former does not enter 'tradition'."[65] Information is contrary to experience, and this is significant for how different media has worked throughout history:

> Historically, the various modes of communication have competed with one another. The replacement of the older relation by information, and of information by sensation, reflects the increasing atrophy of experience. In turn, there is a contrast between all these forms and the story, which is one of the oldest forms of communication. A story does not aim to convey an event per se, which is the purpose of information; rather, it embeds the event in the life of the storyteller in order to pass it on as experience to those listening. It thus bears the trace of the storyteller, much the way an earthen vessel bears the trace of the potter's hand.[66]

Again there is an analogy to works of art made by hand, or handicraft. The potter and the storyteller are similar in the sense that traces of them both are part of what they communicate or make. The story bears the traces of the storyteller; the vessel bears the traces of the potter's hand.[67] Here, then, emerges the trace, which in *The Arcades Project* is opposed to aura. When Benjamin mentions "the possibility of reproducing the story," a necessary reproducibility is implied, and inscribed in the very form of

235

storytelling, and this depends upon memory, "the epic faculty par excellence."[68] But as is clear from "On Some Motifs of Baudelaire," when Benjamin discusses Proust as a latter-day storyteller, the structure of memory has altered within modernity. The alterations include sensation, as storytelling also has its sensory aspects. Quoting Paul Valéry, Benjamin writes about a connection between the soul, the eye, and the hand, describing a practice which is no longer familiar:

> The role of the hand in production has become more modest, and the place it filled in storytelling lies waste. (After all, storytelling, in its sensory aspect, is by no means a job for the voice alone. Rather, in genuine storytelling what is expressed gains support in a hundred ways from the work-seasoned gestures of the hand.) That old co-ordination among the soul, eye, and hand which emerges in Valéry's words is that of the artisan which we encounter wherever the art of storytelling is at home. In fact, one might go on and ask oneself whether the relationship of the storyteller to his material, human life, is not in itself a craftsman's relationship— whether it is not his very task to fashion the raw material of experience, his own and that of others, in a solid, useful, and unique way.[69]

The interrelation of the themes discussed here—the soul, the eye, and the hand—is an important reason for the decline of storytelling. This is shown by the lesser importance of the hand in production, not only industrial production, but also in art, including the art of storytelling. The immediacy of the storyteller, in the implicit orality, includes bodily gestures but these gestures are removed both in the writing of novels and in the information of the newspapers. It would thus seem that the removal of the hand is a consistent theme that runs throughout the history of media.

After having observed that the art of storytelling is "coming to an end," Benjamin adds: "It is as if a capability that seemed inalienable to us, the securest of our possessions, has been taken from us: the ability to share experiences."[70] This argument is similar to that in "Experience and Poverty" about communicable experience. It concerns the coexisting development of technology, of the mode of experience as well as the socially determined questions of experience. Benjamin even repeats, almost verbatim, the discussion of soldiers coming home from the trenches from "Experience and Poverty."[71] In between these two texts, the "Work of Art" was written. Comparable to the withering of the aura, "the communicability of experience is decreasing."[72] Even if Benjamin, in "On Some Motifs in Baudelaire," argues that Proust undertakes "the effort it took to restore the figure of the storyteller to the current generation,"[73] it seems clear that this will have to be a new, previously unknown, version of storytelling. The old "essential features of every real story," that "it contains, openly or covertly, something useful,"[74] have become impossible. And this is why giving or receiving counsel (*Rat*) begins to have an old-fashioned ring to it. Counseling has become impossible, a main reason being the new perceptive mode determined by the optical unconscious. This unconsciousness alters storytelling too. In another domain, the newspapers testify to the same alteration with their focus upon informational montage of text and images.[75]

A different mark of the decline of storytelling is the rise of the novel.[76] The novel, dependent upon the printing press and the individual (in contrast to storytelling with its dependence upon the oral and the collective),[77] becomes vital in the construction of the middle class. And from the novel-reading middle class a new mode of communication emerges. This form of communication ultimately "confronts storytelling as no less of a stranger than did the novel, but in a more menacing way; furthermore, it brings about a crisis in the novel. This new form of communication is information."[78] The decline of storytelling is intimately related to the rise of information. "If the art of storytelling has become rare, the dissemination of information has played a decisive role in this state of affairs."[79]

The Face of Death

The decay of aura is furthermore associated with death. This relation is best described with the image of the human face, and the various possibilities of preserving its features:

237

In the cult of remembrance of dead or absent loved ones, the cult value of
the image finds its last refuge. In the fleeting expression of a human face,
the aura beckons from early photographs for the last time. This is what
gives them their melancholy and incomparable beauty.[80]

Early photographs have something they should not have. There is an
aura in these photographs and it would seem, not least if compared with
Benjamin's discussion of the baroque—and such a comparison makes
sense given the introduction of the theme of melancholy here—that these
photographs are a latter-day version of death masks. Atget's photographs
of the streets of Paris alter this. With these images, the human beings
withdraw from the images—a process that coincides with the disappearance
of cult value and the rise of exhibition value. The absence of human
beings is another token of death. In this context, Benjamin again refers
to Valéry with a quotation claiming a "decline of the idea of eternity"[81]

The idea of eternity has always had its strongest source in death. If this
idea declines, so we reason, the face of death must have changed. It turns
out that this change is identical with another—the one that has diminished
the communicability of experience to the same extent as the art of
storytelling has declined. It has been evident for a number of centuries
how, in the general consciousness, the thought of death has become less
omnipresent and less vivid. In its last stages this process is accelerated.
And in the course of the nineteenth century, bourgeois society—by means
of medical and social, private and public institutions—realized a secondary
effect, which may have been its subconscious main purpose: to enable
people to avoid the sight of the dying. Dying was once a public process in
the life of the individual, and a most exemplary one [...]. In the course of
modern times, dying has been pushed further and further out of the
perceptual world of the living.[82]

"The face of death" has indeed changed, and not only in terms of public
and private. The images of the face of the dead have changed as well,
from the death-mask of the baroque to the photography of the modern.
This change may be expressed in terms of proximity and distance, for

instance in the social proximity of death in earlier times. The death-mask too has this proximity to the dead person—it is a direct imprint of the dead person's face. Photography, on the other hand, has a distance inscribed in its very apparatus. The face of death is different; it has been mediated by the photographic apparatus.

The absence of death is also one reason for the decline of storytelling. "Death is the sanction for everything that the storyteller can tell. He has borrowed his authority from death."[83] Thus, when death becomes a thing of the past, or at least a thing removed from everyday life, so, it follows, must storytelling:

> Within the decisive category of time, the introduction of which into this field of semiotics was the great romantic achievement of these thinkers, permits the incisive, formal definition of the relationship between symbol and allegory. Whereas in the symbol destruction is idealized and the transfigured face of nature is fleetingly revealed in the light of redemption, in allegory the observer is confronted with the *facies hippocratica* of history as petrified, primordial landscape. Everything about history that, from the very beginning, has been untimely, sorrowful, unsuccessful, is expressed in a face—or rather in a death's head.[84]

Given the central position of the death's head in Benjamin's discussion of baroque allegory, the "decline of death" in modernity, and the relationship between images and death, it makes sense to see photography as a latter-day version of the figure of the death's head.[85]

Sensations and the Masses

Sense-experiences and their conditions are intrinsically historical and thus change over time. The ways in which our senses are organized are also, Benjamin claims, historical. The conditions for sensation in modernity are different compared to other historical periods, meaning that one has to relate discussions of aesthetic experience to the historical circumstances. The senses, and thus also sense-experiences, are both natural and histo-rical. They are inscribed in the process of history, and change "over long

239

historical periods."[86] Human perception, as media, is conditioned both by nature and by history, which means that perceptions are historically alterable. Benjamin refers to Alois Riegl and Franz Wickhoff, whose writings testify to historically coinciding and interrelated alterations in art, modes of perception, and social structures. He then moves on to argue for similar alterations taking place in his own time.[87] "Today, the conditions for an analogous insight are more favorable. And if changes in the medium of present-day perception can be understood as a decay of the aura, it is possible to demonstrate the social determinants of that decay."[88]

Perception is here a translation of the German term *Wahrnehmung*, a term Benjamin quite obviously plays with in this text as well as others. Perception is about grasping (*nehmen*) the truth (*die Wahrheit*). In *The Arcades Project*, Benjamin expands this play on words to include the commodity (*die Ware*). The commodity, and its relation to the thing, suggests a continuation of this strategical play into other domains, for example into a new allegorization where the baroque allegory is substituted by a new, modern allegory. What happens to commodities (or things) in the process of intensified technological reproducibility is that our perception of them alters. The perception (*Wahrnehmung*) of the commodities (*Waren*) alters the truth (*Wahrheit*) of things.[89]

But there are breaks or discontinuities in the history of perception, meaning both that perception has to be rethought historically and that contemporary modes of perception have to be addressed. And it is here that we may return to the interactions between cinema and architecture. At first sight this relation might seem paradoxical. Connected to time and space, one would assume cinema to be related to time and architecture to space. However, for Benjamin time and space are clearly not primarily to be understood in opposition. This is not least due to alterations in the forms of perception, that is to say, in the very historicity of perception. The tactile dimension in aesthetic perception comes to the fore and challenges the culture of contemplation. Instead of contemplation—or, perhaps better, in addition to contemplation—there is another mode of aesthetic perception, a perception where the tactile and kinaesthetic

240

dimensions are significant. Here, the notion of shock, so central for the modern aesthetic, is of importance, as is the notion of anesthesia.[90] Both shock and anesthesia affect the senses, either overwhelming or sedating them. Under these alterations, the psychic or mental relation to works of art alters as well. During the increased impact on the senses, one cannot any longer react traditionally, since the very reaction, and implicitly the bodily impact of sensations, are both altered.

Benjamin returns to discuss the different reception of painting and cinema, where it is not least the difference between the single viewer and the masses that is decisive:

> A painting has always exerted a claim to be viewed primarily by a single person or by a few. The simultaneous viewing of paintings by a large audience, as happens in the nineteenth century, is an early symptom of the crisis in painting, a crisis triggered not only by photography but, in a relatively independent way, by the artwork's claim to the attention of the masses.[91]

Photography and even more so film address themselves to the masses, and a new mode of reception comes into being. But with a twist to the argument, Benjamin shows that this is not necessarily a wholly new mode. Architecture is not an art form for the single viewer any more than cinema is. Contrasting painting, as something perceived primarily by the single person, with other art forms received collectively, Benjamin points to a kind of genealogy, including architecture, epic poem, and film.[92] In this, architecture shows us dimensions of how to perceive film, since it has always been an object of collective reception. What architecture shows is an integral way of perceiving, a perception based on several senses at the same time.

> From an alluring visual composition or an enchanting fabric of sound, the Dadaists turned the artwork into a missile. It jolted the viewer, taking on a tactile [taktisch] quality. It thereby fostered the demand for film, since the distracting element in film is also primarily tactile, being based on

241

successive changes of scene and focus which have a percussive effect on the spectator.[93]

Film is a tactile medium. It is primarily related to shock, a notion Benjamin makes palpably present in the essay "Experience and Poverty." Here is where Benjamin sees the possibility of communication in modern culture, where visual and other sensual stimuli are simply too strong for ordinary experience.

The masses' relation to the work of art is also a result of the collectivity of experience. The masses imply totally new ways of experience, also in the case of works of art.

> The masses are criticized for seeking distraction [*Zerstreuung*] in the work of art, whereas the art lover supposedly approaches it with concentration. In the cases of the masses, the artwork is seen as a means of entertainment; in the case of the art lover, it is considered an object of devotion.–This calls for closer examination. Distraction and concentration form an antithesis, which may be formulated as follows. A person who concentrates before a work of art is absorbed by it; he enters into the work, just as, according to legend, a Chinese painter entered his completed painting while beholding it. By contrast, the distracted masses absorb the work of art into themselves. Their waves lap around it; they encompass it with their tide. This is most obvious with regards to buildings. Architecture has always offered the prototype of an artwork that is received in a state of distraction and through the collective. The laws of architecture's reception are highly instructive.[94]

There are two different processes at stake here: one is distraction, the other concentration. They are antithetical, and as such exclude each other. Furthermore, they follow from the distinction between the collective on the one hand, and the individual on the other. Concentration is what the individual art lover does in front of an artwork. The collective is, on the other hand distracted, either in the cinema or within a work of architecture. In the act of concentration the person is absorbed into the work of art, whereas in the act of distraction the masses absorb the work into

242

themselves. Thus, the two processes indicate two different relations between audience and work, and two different ways of engagement between what used to be known as subject and object.

It is, however, of interest that Benjamin highlights buildings and architecture. This is, as he himself underlines, not a new art form. On the contrary, it might seem to be one of the oldest; it has "accompanied human existence since primeval times."[95] At the same time, however, it tells us something general about how the contemporary masses relate to works of art. Architecture is "the prototype of an artwork that is received in a state of distraction and through the collective." Thus we can learn a lot from architecture, since it can be seen as a prototype for the work of art, or an aesthetic, where reception is collective and distracted. But the masses challenge the discussion of aesthetic experience and perception. Traditional theories of aesthetic experience relate to the single person's experience. However, as Benjamin makes clear again and again, an essential feature of modernity, within the aesthetic as well as the political sphere, is the mass.[96] However, the question Benjamin rises does not only concern the possibility of such collective experiences, but even more their possible communication. So what, then, does the vanishing of communicable experience mean? This question definitely challenges any hope for the possibility of communication or sharing of experience. Communal experiences are, however, deeply imbedded within the very vocabulary of Benjamin's thinking in the "Work of Art." The 'mass' is just one of the words of importance, others being found with the dimension of religion, or cult, seeming to be included in the notion of aura. This notion of the "communal" is of course also related to the common and to communication.

Beyond Beauty

In "Surrealism" Benjamin writes about living in a glass house as "a revolutionary virtue par excellence."[97] Glass architecture does not have any aura, or so it would seem following Benjamin's statement in "Experience and Poverty." The transparency of glass in one sense implies

243

alterations not only in the buildings themselves, but also in our perception. Is this a place where the optical and the tactile grow apart? In other
words, is this an architectural form where the lowered visibility—the fact
that we are seeing through the building—alters also what we are able to
see? Could glass architecture be seen as relating to the optical unconscious
in the sense that we are looking at something we cannot see, something
that is hidden in its very visibility? The notion of transparency is important
not least in *The Arcades Project* where Benjamin relates it to Le Corbu-
sier.[98] Comparable to photography, but still very differently, glass architecture shows us a completely new, also a historically new, visibility.

Another question concerns whether the reason that "things made out
of glass have no 'aura'" is because glass architecture cannot become ruins.
Architecture made of glass must somehow decay differently than architecture made of stone. The withering or decay of aura seems in important
ways to be related to a potential ruinosity, that is, to a becoming-ruin.
The process when buildings fade relates to a particular auratic dimension in architecture. Important for this version of the auratic is similarities
found between between Benjamin's discussion of aura in his later works
and the discussion of the ruin in *The Origin of German Tragic Drama*. "The
Ruin" is a central category in *The Origin of German Tragic Drama*, designa-
ting a dynamic and synaesthetic form, a building marked by natural
history. This marking is one of the reasons for the ruin becoming central
to the notion of allegory. In *The Arcades Project*, and in the study of Baudelaire, it is more as if the allegorical is primarily related to commodities.
Thus, there is a movement from buildings to things, from the ruin to the
commodity. However, the ruin was always related to things. As the already
quoted passage from *The Origin of German Tragic Drama* has it:

> When, as is the case in the *Trauerspiel*, history becomes part of the setting,
> it does so as script. The word "history" stands written on the countenance
> of nature in the characters of transience. The allegorical physiognomy of
> the nature-history, which is put on stage in the *Trauerspiel*, is present in
> reality in the form of the ruin. In the ruin history has physically merged
> into the setting. And in this guise history does not assume the form of the

process of an eternal life so much as that of irresistible decay. Allegory thereby declares itself to be beyond beauty. Allegories are, in the realm of thoughts, what ruins are in the realm of things.[99]

The ruins categorically determine the being of things, which constitute the material world as such, but also become the commodities which within the context of *The Arcades Project* are related to the allegorical. Here, however, it would seem that allegory primarily functions as an epistemological category, in that it is related to "the realm of thoughts."

"Allegory declares itself to be beyond beauty," writes Benjamin. What does it mean to be beyond beauty? Within the context of *The Origin of German Tragic Drama*, it seems to be a new kind of beauty:

> Its [the *Trauerspiel's*] outer form has died away because of its extreme crudity. What has survived is the extraordinary detail of the allegorical references: an object of knowledge which has settled in the consciously constructed ruins. Criticism means the mortification of the works. By their very essence these works confirm this more readily than any others. Mortification of the works: not then—as the romantics have it—awakening of the consciousness in living works, but the settlement of knowledge in dead ones. Beauty, which endures, is an object of knowledge. And if it is questionable whether the beauty which endures still deserve the name, it is nevertheless certain that there is nothing of beauty which does not contain something that is worthy of knowledge.[100]

This beauty, then, which most likely does not deserve the name of beauty still, is the new beauty, related to the allegorical and thus to the ruin. In the very process of decay, when the buildings wither away, there thus arises a new beauty. And this new beauty—the beauty beyond beauty—is still worthy of knowledge. It is comparable to Benjamin describing how the art of storytelling is coming to an end since wisdom is dying out:

> This, however, is a process that has been going on for a long time. And nothing would be more fatuous than to wish to see it as merely a "symptom of decay," let alone a "modern symptom." It is, rather, only a concomitant

245

of the secular productive forces of history—a symptom that has quite gradually removed narrative from the realm of living speech and at the same time is making it possible to find a new beauty in what is vanishing.[101]

A new beauty in what is vanishing at the same time suggests that there is a beauty in and of decay. Related to the ruin, this is part of its natural history, and perhaps there is a similar natural history of aura, implying that even if there is a decay of aura within modernity, there is, simultaneously, within the historicity of aura, an aura of decay.

Notes

[1] Walter Benjamin, "Experience and Poverty," in SW 2, 734.
[2] See Edmund Husserl, *Logical Investigations, Volume 1,* ed. Dermot Moran (London: Routledge, 2001), 101.
[3] Benjamin, OGT, 177–78.
[4] Benjamin, AP, 447 [M16a,4].
[5] See Immanuel Kant, *Critique of Judgement* (Oxford: Oxford University Press, 1989), 41–42: "The judgement of taste, therefore, is not a cognitive judgement, and so not logical, but is aesthetic—which means that it is one whose determining ground *cannot be other than subjective.* Every reference of representations is capable of being objective, even that of sensation (in which case it signifies the real in an empirical representation). The one exception to this is the feeling of pleasure or displeasure. This denotes nothing in the object, but is a feeling which the Subject has of itself and of the manner in which it is affected by the representation."
[6] There are good reasons to read Benjamin's texts related to Kant, but his understanding of subjects and objects shows some of the problems at stake in reading Kant together with Benjamin. For an interesting discussion of these themes, see Rodolphe Gasché, "Objective Diversions: On Some Kantian Themes in Benjamin's 'The Work of Art in the Age of Mechanical Reproduction,'" in *Walter Benjamin's Philosophy: Destruction and Experience,* eds. Andrew Benjamin and Peter Osborne (London: Routledge, 1994), 183–204.
[7] Such a diversification or differentiation of the senses is discussed thoroughly by Jean-Luc Nancy in *The Muses* (Stanford: Stanford University Press 1996), in

particular in chapter 1, "Why Are There Several Arts and Not Just One?" This discussion is strongly related to the question of art versus the arts, and as such any question of singularity within the aesthetic field.

8 Benjamin, "The Work of Art in the Age of Its Technological Reproducibility (Second Version)," in SW 3, 120.

9 In this process technology and art were separated as well, making the polytechnic and the artistic separate spheres. Architecture thus becomes part of the Beaux-Arts, ceasing to be engineering and construction. See Susan Buck-Morss, *The Dialectics of Seeing: Walter Benjamin and the Arcades Project* (Cambridge, Mass.: The MIT Press, 1989), 126.

10 Benjamin, AP, 155 [F3,1].

11 Benjamin, "Little History of Photography," in SW 2, 510.

12 Benjamin, "Surrealism: The Last Snapshot of the European Intelligentsia," in SW 2, 217.

13 Ibid.

14 The different threads woven together here might suggest a possible comparison with Martin Heidegger's "The Origin of the Work of Art," in Heidegger, *Off the Beaten Track* (Cambridge: Cambridge University Press, 2002). Such a comparison, however, is beyond the scope of the present article.

15 Howard Caygill, *Walter Benjamin: The Colour of Experience* (London: Routledge, 1998), 116.

16 Benjamin, "Experience and Poverty," in SW 2, 731–32.

17 Ibid., 732.

18 Ibid., 732.

19 Benjamin, "Karl Kraus," in SW 2, 434.

20 Benjamin, "Experience and Poverty," in SW 2, 733.

21 Benjamin, "Karl Kraus," in SW 2, 456.

22 Benjamin, "Experience and Poverty," in SW 2, 733–34.

23 Caygill, *Walter Benjamin*, 32.

24 The constellation of objects, language, glass, aura and architecture is related to Scheerbart, whose book on glass architecture Benjamin refers to in the 1935 Exposé to *The Arcades Project*, See Benjamin, AP, 4.

25 Benjamin, "Little History of Photography," in SW 2, 510.

26 Ibid., 519. See also "The Work of Art," in SW 3, 117.

27 Benjamin, "Little History of Photography," in SW 2, 514.

28 Benjamin, "The Work of Art," in SW 3, 102.

29 Marshall McLuhan, *Understanding Media: The Extensions of Man* (London: Routledge, 2002 [1964]), 49.

30 Sigmund Freud, "Civilization and Its Discontents" (1930), in Sigmund Freud:

The Standard Edition of the Complete Psychological Works of Sigmund Freud, ed. James
Strachey (London: Vintage, 2001), 21: 91–92.

31   See Benjamin, "The Work of Art," in SW 3, 102.
32   This phrase is of course taken from Marshall McLuhan, *The Gutenberg Galaxy: The
Making of Typographic Man* (Toronto: University of Toronto Press, 1962). See also
Norbert Bolz, "Swanengesang der Gutenberg Galaxis," in *Allegorie und Melancholie,*
ed. Willem van Reijen (Frankfurt am Main: Suhrkamp, 1992), 224–60.
33   McLuhan, *Understanding Media,* 88.
34   Ibid., 116.
35   Ibid., 116–17.
36   A similar argument, albeit from a very different tradition is presented by Jean-Luc
Nancy. For more on Nancy and sensation, see my article "Being Touched by Art:
Art and Sense in Jean-Luc Nancy," in *Sense and Senses in Aesthetics,* eds. Per Bäckström and Troels Degn Johansson (Göteborg: NSU Press, 2003), 21–49.
37   See Eduardo Cadava, *Words of Light: Theses on the Photography of History* (Princeton:
Princeton University Press, 1997), xvii. "*Words of light.* With these words from a
notebook entry of 3 March 1839, William Henry Fox Talbot names the medium
of photography. [...] Photography is nothing else than a writing of light, a script of
light, what Talbot elsewhere called 'the pencil of nature.'"
38   McLuhan, *Understanding Media,* 206.
39   Benjamin, "The Work of Art," in SW 3, 102.
40   McLuhan, *Understanding Media,* 206.
41   A similar argument is also made by Vilém Flusser, where "the invention of linear
writing" and "the invention of technical images" testify to two watersheds in the
history of human culture. See Vilém Flusser: *Towards a Philosophy of Photography*
(London: Reaktion Books, 2000).
42   This is almost identical to Benjamin's statement in "Little History of Photography,"
in SW 2, 527, where he, without acknowledging it, quotes László Moholy-Nagy.
See Cadava: *Words of Light,* 21.
43   See McLuhan, *Understanding Media,* 211.
44   Benjamin, "Little History of Photography," in SW 2, 514.
45   Benjamin, "The Work of Art," in SW 3, 102.
46   Ibid., 102.
47   Ibid., 103.
48   Compare with Freud from "Civilization and Its Discontents," 90–91.: "By means
of spectacles he [man] corrects defects in the lens of his own eye; by means of the
telescope he sees into the far distance; and by means of the microscope he overcomes
the limits of visibility set by the structure of his retina. In the photographic camera
he has created an instrument which retains the fleeting visual impressions."

[49] Benjamin, "The Work of Art," in SW 3, 117.

[50] This dimension is perhaps nowhere as clear as in what Benjamin writes in the Third Version of "The Work of Art," where he refers to Freud's *Psychopathology of Everyday Life* (1901), a book which "isolated and made analyzable things which had previously floated unnoticed on the broad stream of perception," something which Benjamin then compares to how new impressions become possible with film. See Benjamin, "The Work of Art in the Age of Its Technological Reproducibility (Third Version)", in SW 4, 265.

[51] Benjamin, "The Work of Art" (Second Version), in SW 3, 118.

[52] Ibid., 115.

[53] Ibid., 116.

[54] Ibid., 103.

[55] Benjamin, "Goethe's Elective Affinities," in SW 1, 340–41.

[56] There is of course the exception here of buildings built as ruins. Such buildings might be seen as challenging this interpretation in their different conceptions. However, within a framework of 'natural history' I would argue that this challenge is minimized. For another interpretation of ruins in Benjamin, see Manfred Schneider, "Der Barbar der Bedutung: Walter Benjamins Ruinen," in *Ruinen des Denkens–Denken in Ruinen*, eds. Norbert Bolz and Willem van Reijen (Frankfurt am Main: Suhrkamp, 1996), 215–36.

[57] It seems necessary here to differentiate between buildings becoming ruins through a slow historical process on the one hand and ruins being a result of catastrophes, such as for example war, on the other. However, even related to catastrophes, some kind of 'natural history' might be thought, as exemplified by W. G. Sebald's *On the Natural History of Destruction* (London: Penguin, 2003), a book also quoting Benjamin's "On the Concept of History", 68.

[58] This argument might seem to reduce the complexities of the philosophy of history within Benjamin's oeuvre, but if comparing with the notion of 'original' as found in his philosophy of language, in particularly related to translation, then all that is transmissible, what seems to outlive the here and now, might become somewhat easier to grasp.

[59] Benjamin, "On the Concept of History," in SW 4, 392

[60] Ibid.

[61] Such an understanding is challenged when dealing with architectural reconstructions, where the original blue-prints are highly valued. However, given the argument that decay is inscribed in the building even when it is only on the drawing table, the 'original' is already marked.

[62] Benjamin, "The Work of Art," in SW 3, 103.

[63] "These changed circumstances may leave the artwork's other properties untouched,

but they certainly devalue the here and now of the artwork." Ibid.

[64] Ibid., 103–4.

[65] Benjamin, "On Some Motifs in Baudelaire," in SW 4, 316.

[66] Ibid., 316.

[67] See Benjamin, "The Storyteller," in SW 3, 149.

[68] Benjamin, "The Storyteller," in SW 3, 153. Compare also an earlier statement: "For storytelling is always the art of repeating stories, and this art is lost when the stories are no longer retained," 149.

[69] Ibid., 161–62.

[70] Ibid., 143.

[71] See ibid., 143–44.

[72] Ibid., 145.

[73] Benjamin, "On Some Motifs in Baudelaire," in SW 4, 316.

[74] Benjamin, "The Storyteller," in SW, 3, 145.

[75] The newspapers and their relation to photography are one of the main reasons for the development of this whole story of the modern mass media, detached from experience, where older relations are replaced by information, reflecting "the increasing atrophy of experience." Benjamin, "On Some Motifs in Baudelaire," in SW 4, 316.

[76] See Benjamin, "The Storyteller," in SW 3, 145.

[77] See ibid., 156.

[78] Ibid., 147.

[79] Ibid.

[80] Benjamin, "The Work of Art," in SW 3, 108.

[81] Valéry, quoted in Benjamin, "The Storyteller," in SW 3, 150.

[82] Benjamin, "The Storyteller," in SW 3, 150–51.

[83] Ibid., 151.

[84] Benjamin, OGT, 166.

[85] The relation between these different domains become even clearer when Benjamin, in "The Storyteller," continuing the argument about how the storyteller borrows his authority form death: "In other words, his stories refer back to natural history." Benjamin, "The Storyteller," in SW 3, 151.

[86] See Benjamin, "The Work of Art," in SW 3, 104.

[87] Such similarities, or correspondences, between different periods of history are also part of the arguments being made in *The Origin of German Tragic Drama*, where Benjamin points to similarities between the German baroque and his own, contemporary, Weimar republic.

[88] Benjamin, "The Work of Art," in SW 3, 104.

[89] As Graeme Gilloch writes in his *Walter Benjamin: Critical Constellations* (Cambridge:

Polity Press, 2002), 209: "The afterlife of the object is exactly that process of decay and decomposition in which the spell of the fetishized commodity, resplendent in the fashionable arcades, is broken. The commodity is destined to ruination. In this despised form, the commodity, like allegory, gestures towards the catastrophic truth of the unredeemed world."

90 See Susan Buck-Morss, "Aesthetics and Anaesthetics: Walter Benjamin's Artwork Essay Reconsidered," *October*, 62 (1992), 3–41.

91 Benjamin, "The Work of Art", in SW 3, 116.

92 "Painting, by its nature, cannot provide an object of simultaneous collective reception, as architecture has always been able to do, as the epic poem could do at one time, and as film is able to do today." Benjamin, "The Work of Art," in SW 3, 116.

93 Ibid., 119.

94 Ibid., 119–20.

95 Ibid., 120.

96 This is the case even if this collective, or the mass, cannot be understood as a new transcendental subject. The notion of concentration employed here in relation to the mass thus seems necessary to be distinguished from the concentration of the detached gaze with reference to the Kantian aesthetic.

97 Benjamin, "Surrealism," in SW 2, 209.

98 See Benjamin, AP, 419 [M1a,4].

99 Benjamin, OGT, 177–78.

100 Ibid., 182.

101 Benjamin, "The Storyteller," in SW 3, 146.

The Phantasmagoria of the Spectacle

A Critique of Media Culture

Jae-Ho Kang

Walter Benjamin's essay, "The Work of Art in the Age of its Technological Reproducibility" has been celebrated as one of the most original contributions to the study of cinema, film and visual culture, and his conception of aura has been highlighted as the nucleus of the essay. The decay of aura has been widely employed to describe how technical reproduction changed the nature of art and aesthetic experience. Together with the general appreciation of Benjamin's insight, however, there have also been critical questions about its contemporary applicability: whether his account is predicated upon the early development of media technology and thus relevant only for his own historical epoch or whether it is still valid and useful in order to understand the more complex contemporary media-scape. For instance, in the "Work of Art" essay, Benjamin relates the distracted but simultaneously critical attitude of the cinema audience to the coincidence of the camera's position and the audience's viewpoint. However, given the multi-camera positions of contemporary films, which render many different perspectives possible, Benjamin's account of the rise of the critical audience seems restricted to the infancy of cinematography. It is questionable whether cinematic collective experience will bring forth a new subjectivity to the extent that Benjamin believed. Thus some key ideas in the "Work of Art" seem obsolete when applied to the substantial transformations in contemporary media culture known as the digital revolution and the information society.

Although a great deal of attention has been paid to the concept of aura, its close relation to phantasmagoria in *The Arcades Project* has not been sufficiently examined. It should be noted that in *The Arcades Project*, Benjamin rarely uses the notion of aura, but instead employs the term phantasmagoria as a central category. In the 1935 exposé, where Benjamin outlines the categories to be used in *The Arcades Project*, the term phantasmagoria is particularly employed to circumscribe the distinctive characteristics of modernity, for example: "the phantasmagoria of capitalist culture"; "the phantasmagoria of the interior"; "the phantasmagoria of cultural history"; "the phantasmagoria of space"; and "the Commune puts an end to the phantasmagoria holding sway over the early years of the proletariat."[1] In the revised 1939 exposé we observe an even more expanded use of the concept. It is now located at the center of his approach to modernity. Benjamin outlines the overall theoretical aim in the introduction:

> Our investigation proposes to show how, as a consequence of this reifying representation of civilization, the new forms of behavior and the new economically and technologically based creations that we owe to the nineteenth century enter the universe of a phantasmagoria. These creations undergo this "illumination" not only in a theoretical manner, by an ideological transposition, but also in the immediacy of their perceptible presence. They are manifest as phantasmagorias.[2]

In his conclusion, Benjamin characterizes modernity as "the world dominated by its phantasmagorias."[3] With respect to Benjamin's main concern—how modern experience is historically constituted in accordance with the development of technology—his analyses of the decay of aura and of modernity as phantasmagoria share several affinities. However, the existing conceptual discontinuity between aura and phantasmagoria also raises questions as to whether Benjamin used the notion of aura only in his accounts of aesthetic experience. Further speculation is also needed about whether his analysis of the decline of the communicability of experience (*die Mitteilbarkeit der Erfahrung*) is related only to changes in aesthetic perception; another urgent question is to what extent the emergence of mass culture, what he calls 'the entertainment (or pleasure)

253

industry' (*die Vergnügungsindustrie*), is related to the decay of aura. Reading the transformation of aesthetic experience in the broader context of his analysis of the entertainment industry, I seek to develop the actuality of Benjamin's auratic and post-auratic experiences in conjunction with his investigation of nineteenth-century mass culture. In so doing, I call into question whether Benjamin's analysis of the spectacle can still be said to be relevant today for the purposes of developing a critical theory of media culture.

The Distracted Collective

The "Work of Art" essay primarily explores the transformation of aesthetic experience under the impact of particular technologies such as photography and cinematography. Benjamin conceived aesthetics not as a theory of fine art, but as a study of perception. Aura delineates a way of perceiving a work of art; in his terminology, it is the experience of "a strange weave of space and time" which entails "the unique appearance or semblance of distance, no matter how close it may be."[4] What technological advancement diminishes is a spatial experience which comprises the unique and authentic manifestation of distance—a distance that implicates inapproachability. Benjamin's account of the change of aesthetic experience was not, however, welcomed by his contemporary fellows. As is widely known, Adorno criticized Benjamin's view of the decay of aura for being overly optimistic and technologically determined. He thought that Benjamin undervalued the autonomous attribute embodied in a work of art and overestimated the radical promise of film and photography.[5] Brecht, by contrast, regarded Benjamin's approach to art as non-materialist, describing his use of aura as "mysticism under the guise of antimysticism."[6] These criticisms overlooked Benjamin's lifelong concern with the relationship between experience and technology which was at the core of his analysis of modernity. His understanding of experience is composed of critiques of two philosophical traditions—the overly rational version of *Erfahrung* and the alleged immediacy and meaningfulness of *Erlebnis*—and is therefore distinct from predecessors such as Kant and Dilthey. In his exploration of the structural transformation of experience, Benjamin paid appreciable attention to the historical and anthropological grounds bound up with the development of technology. By "technological reproducibility" he referred to two important aspects of the reproduction process: In a narrow sense it designates specific techniques involved in the multiple reproductions of artworks; in a broader context it connotes the reproduction of social relations, that is, the reproduction of the masses. Examining the impact of technology on experience, Benjamin assumed that all experiences are, in a sense, technological if the term technology signifies the artificial organization of perception. Benjamin's recognition of experience as historically specific and technologically conditioned enabled him to avoid the shortcomings embedded in the dichotomy between *Erfahrung* and *Erlebnis* and led him to systematically examine the process of the reproduction of social relations.

The discussion of technologically mediated experience in the "Work of Art" essay distinguishes between two main forms of perception: attention and distraction. At the center of auratic experience lies contemplation, which implies attentive perception. The decay of aura reflects a crisis in attentive perception and the replacement of individual contemplation with collective distraction. Unlike an individual viewer's contemplation of a painting, the masses absorb works of art in a distracted manner. To fully appreciate the complexities of Benjamin's speculations about a transformed perception—its relation to technology as well as to the human senses—one should consider a variety of properties he associated with modern experiences, such as different subject formations (individual or collective and private or public), various modes of communication (printing or electronic), and other related faculties (mimesis, remembrance and oblivion). A narrow understanding of the decay of aura—such as Adorno's and Brecht's—stems from a tendency to oversimplify Benjamin's idea of the relationship between contemplation and distraction. This relationship is itself interwoven in a complex way with technological advancement.

Michael Taussig has aptly characterized distraction as "the type of

255

flitting and barely conscious peripheral vision perception unleashed with great vigor by modern life."[7] From Georg Simmel's explication of shock experience of modern urban life, Benjamin drew special attention to the optical disruption. However, when he addressed distraction and concentration as an antithesis, he was mainly concerned with the tactile dimension of distraction.[8] Drawing upon Alois Riegl's seminal study of spatial perception in *Die spätrömische Kunst-Industrie* (1901), Benjamin further underlined the tactile mode of distraction as the primary relation of the masses to art. "Buildings are received in a twofold manner: by use and by perception. Or, better: tactilely and optically. Such reception cannot be understood in terms of the concentrated attention of a traveler before a famous building. On the tactile side, there is no counterpart to what contemplation is on the optical side."[9] The aura embedded in traditional works of art is perceived through the single sense of vision. New non-auratic artworks, however, communicate with an audience via the multiple sensorial of the body. Considering architecture as a quintessential form of the new mode of artwork, Benjamin envisaged a transition of the nature of artistic activity from aesthetic creativity to construction as a technical manifestation. As a result of this transformation, the artist now appears primarily as an engineer or a producer. This transformation signifies that the production and appropriation of artworks is set in the broad and complex web of social relations.

Distraction is connected not only with instantaneous and spontaneous attributes but also with a long-term change of behaviour: "Tactile reception comes about not so much by way of attention as by way of habit. The latter largely determines even the optical reception of architecture, which spontaneously takes the form of casual noticing, rather than attentive observation. Under certain circumstances, this form of reception shaped by architecture acquires canonical value."[10] Habit, which distracted behaviour naturally creates, turns into "a paradigm of non-contemplative practical memory" carried out collectively.[11] It is noteworthy that Benjamin found the emancipatory potential of distraction not in the level of consciousness underpinned by optic contemplation, but in the tactile dimension embodied in habitual practice: "*For the tasks which face the human apparatus of perception at historical turning points cannot be performed solely by optical means—that is, by way of contemplation. They are mastered gradually— taking their cue from tactile reception—through habit.*"[12] Hence, Benjamin's account of the decline of aura cannot be simplified as the displacement of contemplation by distraction. Rather, it points to the transformation of experiences from individual, private, and attentive modes, via the visually distracted mode, to a collective, public and tactile distraction.

The Experience of Phantasmagoria

Benjamin's examination of various forms of the entertainment industry in *The Arcades Project* (department stores, industrial exhibitions, panoramas, and so on) demonstrates his endeavor to explore several dimensions of experience as linked to various forms of technological advance. Overshadowed by the concept of commodity fetishism, the notion of phantasmagoria in the *Arcades Project* has received a good deal less attention. The debates focusing on objectification, reification, and commodity fetishism no doubt represent key facets of the theoretical fulcrum of Western Marxism. However, they have marginalized Marx's use of the notion of phantasmagoria which describes the reified relationship between people mediated by commodities. In *Capital,* he wrote: "This fetish character of the commodity world has its origin in the peculiar social character of the labour that produces commodities [...]. It is only the particular social relation between people that here assumes, in the eyes of these people, *the phantasmagorical form of a relation between things.*"[13] Rolf Tiedemann argues that, "the concept of phantasmagoria that Benjamin repeatedly employs seems to be merely another term for what Marx called commodity fetishism."[14] It needs to be emphasized that inter- pretations like Tiedemann's are at best tenuous, and strictly at odds with *The Arcades Project's* Convolute X, where Benjamin employs phantas- magoria to examine the relevance of a Marxist categorical framework for the analyses of cultural dynamics.

257

> The property appertaining to the commodity as its fetish character attaches as well to the commodity-producing society—not as it is in itself, to be sure, but more as it represents itself and thinks to understand itself whenever it abstracts from the fact that it produces precisely commodities. The image that it produces of itself in this way, and that it customarily labels as its culture, corresponds to the concept of phantasmagoria.[15]

Benjamin revealed his intention to concentrate particular attention on the concept of phantasmagoria in a letter to Gretel Adorno in March 1939: "I have busied myself, as well as possible in the limited time, with one of the basic concepts of the 'Arcades,' placing at its core *the culture of the commodity-producing society as phantasmagoria*."[16] Benjamin also acknowledged the critical implications of commodity fetishism and reification that are explicated not only in Marx's *Capital* but also in Lukacs's *History and Class Consciousness*[17] but he was, at the same time, well aware of the deficiencies in their analyses of the relationship between the capitalist system and cultural phenomena. Benjamin's phantasmagoria seems to be associated with a critical concern for the theoretical blind-spots in the Marxist analysis of culture. Hence what is needed today is to clarify how Benjamin's application of phantasmagoria differs from a Marxist analysis of culture in terms of commodity fetishism.

The Oxford English Dictionary gives the following meaning to the word phantasmagoria in the late eighteenth and early nineteenth centuries: "a shifting series or succession of phantasms or imaginary figures, as seen in a dream of fevered condition, as called up by the imagination, or as created by literary description."[18] Terry Castle notes that the term phantasmagoria was frequently used by later Romantic and symbolist writers such as Edgar Allan Poe, Arthur Rimbaud and Charles Baudelaire.[19] In tales of the supernatural, Poe employed the phantasmagorical figure "as a way of destabilizing the ordinary boundaries between inside and outside, mind and world, illusion and reality."[20] According to Castle, phantasmagoria was a favorite metaphor for the heightened sensitivities and often tormented awareness of the Romantic visionary: "delirium, loss of control, the terrifying yet sublime overthrow of ordinary experience."[21]

The term phantasmagoria (*fantasmagorie* in French) was originally coined by Etienne-Gaspard Robertson—a Belgian physicist and student of optics—and named the ghost show that he performed for the first time in Paris in 1797. These shows were illusionist exhibitions, a type of public entertainment in which ghosts were produced with the use of magic lanterns. The *Gentlemen's Magazine* vividly described the first ghost show in London in 1802: "Dark rooms, where spectres from the dead they raise [...]. An awful sound proclaims a spectre near, And full in sight behold it now appear. [...] Such are the forms Phantasmagoria shows."[22] The success of the show fundamentally hinged upon the fact that the ghost was conceived to be very real and consequently to have a powerful effect to shock the unwary.[23] This spectacle rapidly became a staple of popular entertainment in most large European cities. However, Benjamin's use of the term seems to indicate a decline in the communicability of experience: a transformation from communication involving co-presence to communication with an absent other. In this vein, the notion of phantasmagoria also indicates a transition of communication forms, for instance, the demise of narrative communication through storytelling in the growing predominance of information industry.

Benjamin places considerable emphasis on the social features of the emergence of mediated communication. In "The Storyteller" (1936), written as "a companion piece" to the "Work of Art,"[24] Benjamin explores the shift from storytelling to the novel. Here he reflects in particular upon the movement from auratic communication, based upon face-to-face companionship between participants, to the mediated communication of the solitary writer and the isolated reader. This change is bound up with the disintegration of community. It marks the transition from a collective community to individualist social relations, from *Gemeinschaft* to *Gesellschaft* in Ferdinand Tönnies' terminology. Concomitant with this social transition in which information came to be the dominant mode of communication, the individual lost the ground from which to claim uniqueness. The value of information is not decided by means of personal stories; on the contrary, information is imposed on the individual in terms of public opinion. In a modern society the individual is standardized and represented in terms of a functional entity which is constantly reproducible.

By placing the notion of phantasmagoria at the center of his analysis of mediated experience, Benjamin established a new theoretical basis upon which to develop a more systematic analysis of post-auratic culture. Theoretically, he managed to avoid the crucial limitation embodied in two conventional concepts: ideology and commodity fetishism. For Benjamin the fundamental limitation of Marxist theories of art and culture was rooted in the idea of ideological superstructure, an idea that consequently formed a key tenet of the doctrine of *Ideologiekritik*. Benjamin tried to keep a substantial distance from Marxist analysis arguing that such approaches constituted "a deductivist aesthetic."[25] In his view, if theorization of art followed the logic of a causal relationship between superstructure and base it would inevitably sink into the vulgar reduction of art as a mere commodity. These deductive aspects are derived from Marx's fundamental failure to acknowledge the relationship between the appearance (*der Schein*) and the mechanical character of visual representation. It is widely acknowledged that in *The German Ideology* Marx makes the concept of ideology more mechanical by discussing it in terms analogous to the camera obscura: "If in all ideology men and their circumstances appear upside down as in a *camera obscura*, this phenomenon arises just as much from their historical life-process as the inversion of objects on the retina does from their physical life-process."[26] The camera obscura has been a pivotal emblem of visual representation technology since its advent in the Renaissance. The wide use of this optic machine in areas such as art and science was motivated by the firm belief that it enabled the true representation of objects. Marx's understanding of ideology as a sort of "optical inversion as in a camera obscura" shows that he took for granted the stable and honest reflection of objects. He believed, however, that ideology presents the world upside-down, leading to misrecognition. In this respect Marx's epistemological base differs little from the theory of knowledge that underpins the Enlightenment.

For Benjamin, however, the optical analogy of ideology as camera obscura gave rise to a fundamental problem and, furthermore, rendered Marx's notion of critical activity questionable. Marx's formula did not explain how a true or objective world could be represented or recognized. Benjamin challenged those understandings which held that the outside world is reflected in the subject's consciousness in the same way as an image is reflected in a camera obscura. For Benjamin, who was familiar with illusionist technology, the mirroring function of the superstructure appeared very doubtful. Hence the initial question was not 'what' but 'how' an object was to be represented and perceived.

Phantasmagoria illuminates certain forms of experience that raise doubts about the supposedly rational nature of the human subject. In the experience of phantasmagoria, the Cartesian divide between subject and the objective world becomes questionable. Benjamin found that the experience of phantasmagoria coincides with a very central attribute of modern experience, one which specifically depicts the shock penetrating into everyday life and the following break-down of communication. Phantasmagoria indicates neither a partial nor a transient but a general mode of experience arising from the expansion of commodification to all social relations.

It is widely recognized that in his later work, and most notably after *Capital*, Marx implicitly changed his emphasis on ideology and focused more on the idea of the fetish character of the commodity. His later account of commodity fetishism is increasingly concerned with illustrating the interrelated problems of representation and consciousness. Benjamin was aware of the fact that the notion of fetish appears in Marx's account as a way to understand the transformation of perception against the backdrop of the development of the capitalist system: "In his chapter on the fetish character of the commodity, Marx has shown *how ambiguous the economic world of capitalism seems. It is an ambiguity* considerably heightened by the intensification of capital management—as we see exemplified quite clearly in the machines which aggravate exploitation rather than alleviate the human lot."[27] What Benjamin drew from Marx's insight was that the experience of commodity culture is less akin to 'mechanical' reflection

261

than to 'ambiguous' attributes. Benjamin placed particular emphasis on the motif of ambiguity embodied in the meaning of the fetish, which stands in opposition to the concept of ideology. While the notion of ideology is derived from the scientific understanding of representation and assumes the possibility of highly realistic images, fetish has been referred to as the antithesis of the scientific image. Yet even more important is the fact that Benjamin's appropriation of Marx's introduction of the concept of fetishism led him to expound a more distinct understanding of social structure. Opposing the Marxist concept of superstructure as the reflection of the base, Benjamin offered his own formula, emphasizing the expressive role of superstructure.

> On the doctrine of the ideological superstructure. It seems, at first sight, that Marx wanted to establish here only a causal relation between super-structure and infrastructure. But already the observation that ideologies of the superstructure reflect conditions falsely and invidiously goes beyond this. The question, in effect, is the following: if the infrastructure in a certain way (in the materials of thought and experience) determines the superstructure, but if such determination is not reducible to simple *reflection*, how is it then—entirely apart from any question about the originating cause—to be characterized? As its *expression. The superstructure is the expression of the infrastructure.* The economic conditions under which society exists are expressed in the superstructure—precisely as, with the sleeper, an overfull stomach finds not its reflection but its expression in the contents of dreams, which, from a causal point of view, it may be said to "condition." The collective, from the first, expresses the conditions of its life. These find their expression in the dream and their interpretation in the awakening.[28]

In this formulation, expression seems to indicate the autonomous character of superstructure as opposed to its inversion or mechanical reflection. At this point Benjamin's application of phantasmagoria hardly seems reconcilable with Marx's original understanding of fetishism.[29] Benja-min understood that the role of the base was to "condition" the expression—not by means of the mechanical power of production but by technological reproducibility, which reproduces the masses through a transformation of collective experience. Phantasmagoria in Benjamin's work illuminates those ambiguous aspects of collective experience that are expressed as cultural phenomena and conditioned by a particular mode of technological advancement.

Mechanical Reproduction of Aura

In parallel with his critique of Marxist analyses of culture, Benjamin also intended to replace the common theories of cultural history: "Cultural history presents its contents by throwing them into relief, setting them off. Yet for the historical materialist, this relief is illusory and is conjured up by false consciousness. [...] If the concept of culture is problematic for historical materialism, it cannot conceive of the disintegration of culture into goods which become objects of possession for mankind. [...] The concept of culture [...] has a fetishistic quality. Culture appears reified."[30] Whereas the Marxist critique of culture reduces art to the ideological superstructure, cultural history uproots the object of study from social relations. By characterizing cultural phenomena as the ambiguous expressions of collective experience conditioned by technological development, Benjamin set himself radically apart from those two theories. Herein lies one of the crucial affinities between the decay of aura and modernity as phantasmagoria. Distancing himself from the subjectification of culture epitomized in cultural history, Benjamin did not lose sight of the commodity character of the artwork. At the same time, however, unlike a traditional Marxist criticism of art, his concern with commodities does not gravitate towards an economic interpretation whose central terms are use- and exchange-value; instead, he formulates a new approach based on two new terms; cult value (*Kultwert*) and exhibition value (*Ausstellungswert*).

While cult value denotes the ritualistic features of art, exhibition value refers to the aspects of art on display. The critical aspects of the shift from cult value to exhibition value are elaborated by considering two different dimensions of the quantitative changes in art and the qualitative transformation of its nature. Regarding quantitative change, cult value refers to the invisible and closed nature of art, emphasizing a restricted accessibility except for a certain group. The development of technological reproducibility increases the artwork's potentials for being exhibited, and facilitates thus public access.[31] The revolutionary role of photography rests on the fact that it democratizes the reception of visual images by bringing an artwork, which had been characterized by its inapproachability and uniqueness, to the masses. Photography fulfils "*the desire of the present-day masses to 'get closer' to things spatially and humanly*" and enables technologically mediated experience across the whole social scale.[32] The authenticity and the uniqueness of the artwork are destroyed because technological reproducibility allows endless copies to be made. This lack of authenticity is not restricted to the realm of art; it is also effective in social relations where a subject is stripped of individuality by means of representational technology.

The qualitative transformation of art is linked to the changing function of the artwork. While the nature of art in prehistoric times was "an instrument of magic," with the predominance of exhibition value it became a political instrument.[33] In the "Work of Art" essay, however, Benjamin's analysis of the functional change of art is sometimes evasive and important questions still remain. In his discussion of the qualitative change in the nature of artworks it remains unclear as to whether aura no longer functions as a value of post-bourgeois art. Similarly, when he places special emphasis on exhibition value it is uncertain whether he is referring to the end of art's autonomy. The extent to which aesthetic experience and political consciousness are interrelated in the artwork's political function is also unclear. These issues can be illuminated only when careful consideration is given to his account of the political attributes of technological reproducibility.

Referring to Eduard Fuchs, Benjamin quoted: "'Every age has very *specific techniques of reproduction* corresponding to it. These represent the prevailing standard of technological development and are [...] the result of a specific need of that age. For this reason, it is not surprising that any *historical upheaval which brings to power* [...] *classes other than those currently ruling* [...] *regularly goes hand in hand with changes in techniques of pictorial reproduction.*

264

This fact calls for careful elucidation.'"[34] Seen from this perspective, Benjamin's pivotal notion of reproducibility does not imply the end of aura or the end of art. The invention of photography by no means signified the destruction of aura *per se*; rather, it pointed to the emergence of technological conditions that disturbed aura. Benjamin saw technological apparatuses such as the camera enabling a discontinuous retrieval of aura, as exemplified in the emergence of the '*Führer* cult' during the Nazi era.[35] At the same time, he praised the close-up technique of cinematography as the destructive power to undo the distance and eradicate aura. However, as vividly exemplified in Leni Riefenstahl's *Triumph des Willens* (1934), this technique employed in political propaganda or documentary newsreels appeared to revive and magnify aura. Within a close-up shot the image remains distant and thereby aura is mechanically reproduced.[36] The replacement of cult value by exhibition value demonstrates that from now on art's primary function is to be placed on display and above all directed towards its political function. The increasing presentability of art and its social function converge into the growing visibility of power. Likewise, the analysis of the predominance of exhibition value provides the ground upon which to examine the phantasmagoria of politics in a broader context.

The change noted here in the mode of exhibition—a change brought about by reproduction technology—is also noticeable in politics. *The crisis of democracies can be understood as a crisis in the conditions governing the public presentation of politicians.* Democracies exhibit the politician directly, in person, before elected representatives. The parliament is his public. But innovations in recording equipment now enable the speaker to be heard by an unlimited number of people while he is speaking, and to be seen by an unlimited number shortly afterward. This means that priority is given to presenting the politician before the recording equipment. Parliaments are becoming depopulated at the same time as theaters. Radio and film are changing not only the function of the professional actor but, equally, the function of those who, like the politician, present themselves before these media. The direction of this change is the same for the film actor and the politician, regardless of their different tasks. It tends toward the exhibition of controllable, transferable skills under certain social conditions, just as sports first called for such exhibition under certain natural conditions. This results in a new form of selection—selection before an apparatus—from which the champion, the star, and the dictator emerge as victors.[37]

As outlined in this passage, Benjamin's analysis of the political function of art found the origin of mediated politics bound to the technological reproduction of political figures. He focused on the transformation of government—the collapse of parliamentary democracy—in terms of a transformation of the visibility of power, that is, the representation of the ruler. Benjamin saw these transformations as part of a broader transition in the nature of politics grounded upon the private/public dichotomy in Western political discourse. In his account the crisis of bourgeois democracy and the emergence of fascism correspond with the decay of aura, in much the same way as bourgeois art and aesthetic experience are replaced by the entertainment industry and a new mode of collective experience. In the "Work of Art," Benjamin raised the central question of whether the increasing visibility of power and the new possibilities brought about by communication media lead to a "crisis of representative democracy" or to more democratization. He believed that increases in the visibility of power, together with a corresponding growth of accessibility and openness, do not guarantee democratization; rather he feared it might be increasingly possible to manipulate the representation of the ruler and thereby to control the collective experience of the audience. If politics depends on the exposure and control of the body (or its image), it is possible to consider mediated politics as exemplary of all politics or the dominant mode of political communication, at least in the period following the emergence of electronic media. Viewed from the broader context of mediated politics, it becomes evident that his well-known thesis concerning the "aestheticization of politics" is not simply about the employment of art for political propagation. Rather, it illuminates the dynamics of political communication consonant with the key principles of the entertainment industry, that is, the predominance of exhibition value in the transformation of public spaces.

Adorno's Phantasmagoria

The phantasmagorical, material base, with its relation to analyses of mediated politics and its distinct position from *Ideologiekritik*, becomes further explicit in the critical debates between Adorno and Benjamin. In contrast to Horkheimer's positive, encouraging response to Benjamin's 1935 exposé, Adorno was severely critical of the project. Adorno believed that Benjamin's central concepts were too closely associated with the 'reactionary theories' of Carl Jung's psychology and Ludwig Klages's social anthropology. In a letter to Benjamin dated August 2, 1935, Adorno ascribed to Benjamin's approach an "overvaluation of machine technology and of machines in general."[38] Ironically, parts of Benjamin's analyses of the phantasmagorical experience had their source in Adorno's own writings.

Referring to Adorno's manuscript, *"Fragmente über Wagner,"* (published in the *Zeitschrift für Sozialforschung* late in 1939), Benjamin argued that Adorno offered a "definition of phantasmagoria."[39] Benjamin was well aware of the affinities between Wagner's *Gesamtkunstwerk* and certain phantasmagoric features of early nineteenth-century entertainment, such as the panorama.[40] If the underlying principles of all forms of filmic exhibition rely on elements such as "projection, darkened auditorium, and spectatorial immobility," the main principles of Wagner's operas have a great number of affinities with the cinematic form.[41] In a passage from the 1935 exposé Benjamin characterized Wagner's *Gesamtkunstwerk* as a prototype of aesthetic phantasmagoria, emphasizing the way in which technological development increases the commodity character of art.[42]

Adorno had explored the phantasmagoric character of Wagner's operas in his first musical monograph, *In Search of Wagner.*[43] In the sixth chapter, "Phantasmagoria," Adorno analyzed Wagner's operas in detail by means of the term phantasmagoria, showing that "the great phantasmagorias that recur again and again occupy a central position in his work."[44] Adorno generally considered Wagner the paradigmatic figure of the post-1848 period, focusing on those technological aspects that present Wagner's operas as a timeless and ahistorical myth.[45]

267

Three central attributes characterize Adorno's particular uses of phantasmagoria. First, the term underlines the techno-aesthetics of Wagner's operas. To Adorno, the most distinctive feature of Wagnerian phantasmagoria derived from the utilization of every technology, in order to create an aesthetic totality. Wagner's theatrical illusion is achieved through the technical effects of sound and is magnified by innovations in opera settings like lighting, stage design, etc.[46] The predominance of sound is the "outcome of the articulation of the phantasmagoria and the rhythm of its dissolution."[47] This artificially created totality constitutes the primary attribute of the *Gesamtkunstwerk*, which reflects the industrialization of time and space. As Andreas Huyssen has argued, Adorno believes that the experience of this total artwork delineates the atomization and the "devaluation of the individual vis-à-vis this totality."[48]

Second, the phantasmagoric quality of Wagner's operas lies not in its magic but in its "inauthentic sense of theatrical illusion."[49] Yet this illusion appears as real; the audience cannot identify it as unreal. By employing technological advancements, Wagner was able to create a new form of realism which was established upon "the daily reality of a reified society."[50] In this artificial reality the distinction between real and representation collapses entirely; the traditional aesthetic categories that derive from the stable representation of the object and its recognition cannot survive as originally conceived. As Jonathan Crary points out, Wagner's aim was to establish a "theatron," a "place for seeing" by means of "the collective act of seeing."[51] Wagner adopted the theatrical apparatus in order to "do away with the autonomy of the audience" and to "control sensorial perception" by "isolating and compelling attention and fixing the gaze."[52] This feature coincides with the simulacra of the magic lantern shows, which projected images that the audience thought were real. Technological reality provides the basis from which the audience's perceptions are controlled. This is the key aspect of the phantasmagoric experience, through which the autonomous agency of the individual audience member is undermined and the audience is transformed into 'a mythic community.' Adorno's analysis of the *Gesamtkunstwerk* as phantasmagoria placed particular emphasis on the alienation of the human sensorium which sought to prevail over critical consciousness.

Third, Adorno underlined the commodity character of Wagner's operas. For Adorno, Wagner's operas were prototypes of the culture industry in which art is merely a commodity that satisfies the needs of the culture market in the age of consumer culture: "In Wagner's day the consumer goods on display turned their phenomenal side seductively towards the mass of customers while diverting attention from their merely phenomenal character, from the fact that they were beyond reach. Similarly, *in the phantasmagoria, Wagner's operas tend to become commodities*."[53] Adorno constructed the edifice of his theory of the culture industry upon ascribing a predominance of exchange value to the commodity character of phantasmagoria: "As a commodity it purveys illusions. *The absolute reality of the unreal* is nothing but the reality of a phenomenon that not only strives unceasingly to spirit away its own origins in human labour, but also, *inseparably from this process and in thrall to exchange value*, assiduously emphasizes its use value, stressing that this is its authentic reality, that it is 'no imitation'—and all this in order to further the cause of exchange value."[54] Here, Adorno uses the term phantasmagoria to indicate the quasi-totality and homogenization of an artwork brought about by the magical combination of sound and visual effects. This total artwork overwhelms the rational reception of the audience, organizes their experience in terms of forgetting, fragmentation and atomization, and disciplines their sense perception, thereby establishing the basis upon which to transform their desire into a cultic community.

Despite similarities with Benjamin's analysis of the entertainment industry as phantasmagoria, Adorno confessed to the inadequacy of his phantasmagoria chapter in a letter to Benjamin dated November 10, 1938: "The phantasmagoria chapter of my book on Wagner has certainly not succeeded in resolving them [the problems of mediation in historical materialism] yet."[55]

Benjamin's concern with the notion of phantasmagoria derived from his methodological perspective. His non-conceptual approach to modernity

269

initially attracted Adorno, especially since it seemed to offer a radical alternative to historical ontology, that is, to Heidegger's notion of history as the basic structure of *Dasein*.[56] Later, in formulating his understanding of fetishism, Adorno deliberately distanced himself from both Lukács' reification and Benjamin's phantasmagoria. In Adorno's account, as Gillian Rose points out, "Lukács' concept of reification presupposes the reconcilement of subject and object and thus relapses into idealism and fails to found a truly materialist dialectic."[57] By contrast, Adorno's objections to Benjamin's conceptualization of dialectical images stemmed from the danger he saw in "subjectivising the phantasmagoria."[58] Deeply suspicious of psychologistic subjectivism and ahistorical Romanticism, Adorno complained that Benjamin inappropriately subjectivised the Marxist category of commodity fetishism by converting it from an "objective structure of exchange value" into a mythological consciousness.[59] Adorno made his objection explicit in the letter of November 10, 1938:

> It seems to me that this pragmatic introduction prejudices the objectivity of phantasmagoria [...] as much as the approach of the first chapter reduces phantasmagoria to characteristic types of behaviour in the literary *bohème*. You need not fear that I would suggest that phantasmagoria should simply survive in your text in unmediated form, or that the study itself should assume a phantasmagorical character. But the liquidation of phantasmagoria can only be accomplished in a truly profound manner if they are treated as an objective historico-philosophical category rather than as a 'vision' on the part of social characters. It is precisely at this point that your own conception differs from all other approaches to the nineteenth century.[60]

In Adorno's view "the dialectical image must therefore not be transferred into consciousness as a dream, but rather the dream should be externalised through dialectical interpretation and the immanence of consciousness itself [should be] understood as a constellation of reality."[61] On a methodological level, Adorno's main critique centered on Benjamin's substantial lack of mediation. Adorno sought to formulate the theory of reification as an objective social category by which cultural

270

traits are understood as the total social process. He seems to have reached the conclusion that the notion of phantasmagoria cannot be applied successfully to his large-scale analysis of modernity. Instead, he tried to turn the concept of reification into an empirical category in order to aid his sociological examination of the culture industry. For this reason Adorno relied heavily on Marx's theory of commodity value. And henceforth, Benjamin and Adorno's respective understandings of Marx's use of commodity fetishism diverged substantially. While Benjamin elucidated the term phantasmagoria on the basis of the prevalence of exhibition value embodied in the commodity feature of the artwork, Adorno conversely sought to develop objective categories via the theory of commodity value, predicated by the exclusive dominance of exchange value. In "On the Fetish Character in Music and the Regression of Listening" (1938) Adorno argued that Marx defined the fetish character of the commodity as "the veneration of the thing made by oneself which, as exchange value, simultaneously alienates itself from producer to consumer—'human beings.'"[62] In his view the decay of the aural faculty fundamentally derived from the commodification of music, which with the help of sound-recording technology in the age of consumer culture constantly damaged music's authenticity: "If the commodity in general combines exchange value and use value, then the pure use value, whose illusion the cultural goods must preserve in a completely capitalist society, must be replaced by pure exchange value, which precisely in its capacity as exchange value deceptively takes over the function of use value. The specific fetish character of music lies in this *quid pro quo*."[63]

At this point there is no alternative but to accept that Adorno's emphasis on the predominance of exchange value over use value is closer to 'classical' Marxism than previously assumed, since it construes the theory of commodity value as an objective science of political economy. He is, in fact, fascinated by the theory of exchange value because he hopes it will enable him to establish a universal theory of aesthetics with which he might fully analyze the transformation of aesthetic appearance and grasp the totality of commodity culture in capitalism. Adorno's use of

271

exchange value appears highly abstract, however, and as a result his critique of commodity culture encompasses a very broad historical period. This is one of the reasons why Adorno's later work shifted from a critique of capitalism to a critique of dominance and mastery of nature. As Markus describes, Adorno's desire to develop a universal aesthetics is "over-charged."[64] Adorno's incomprehension of the social attributes of techno-logical reproducibility resulted in analyses that neglect significant dimensions of commodity culture.

Towards a Materialist Critique of Culture

Although Benjamin took some of Adorno's advice regarding the structure of his 1935 exposé, he firmly defended his own use of phantasmagoria.[65] By means of phantasmagoria Benjamin sought to illuminate the quintessential attribute of modern experience—shock-based distraction through technologically created illusion—in other words, the media-spectacle. For Benjamin, post-auratic cultural phenomena expressed the reified communicability of collective experience, itself interwoven in a complex way with politics and the entertainment industry. In this vein the phantasmagoria of modern experience is linked to a fundamental question of knowledge: "The particular difficulty of doing historical re-search on the period following the close of the eighteenth century will be displayed. *With the rise of the mass-circulation press, the sources become in-numerable.*"[66] Furthermore, Benjamin's understanding of images raises a crucial methodological issue concerning the object of social and cultural studies. Benjamin dissociated himself from both Hegel and Heidegger's notions of time and history but followed Baudelaire's delineation of modernity as "the transitory, the fugitive, and the contingent."[67] As David Frisby notes, this position led cultural critics such as Simmel, Kracauer and Benjamin to the methodological conundrum that the object of study itself disappears and social relations are caught up "in a state of flux, in motion, in ceaseless movement."[68] Benjamin's epistemological doctrine outlined a critique of culture where history in general (or at least parti-cularly in the age of mass communication) breaks down into images.

272

The key attributes of materialist critique of culture are discussed in the Convolute N of *The Arcades Project:*

(1) An object of history is that through which knowledge is constituted as the object's rescue.
(2) History decomposes into *images*, not into stories.
(3) Wherever a dialectical process is realized, we are dealing with a *monad*.
(4) The materialist presentation of history carries along with it an *immanent critique of the concept of progress.*
(5) Historical materialism bases its procedures on long experience, common sense, presence of mind, and dialectics.[69]

At the center of his materialist critique of culture lies the concept of the dialectical image. Reflecting on the development of the media industry—in particular the growth of information and entertainment industries from the middle of the nineteenth century—Benjamin conceptualized the dialectical image as the elementary doctrine of materialist historiography. This stood in opposition to the epistemological grounds of any other kind of historicism. Benjamin's concern with the ambiguous nature of experience was consonant with the central features imposed by the experience of modernity itself. He believed that the dialectical image illuminates the instantaneous nature of the collective experience conditioned by time: "The past can be seized only as an image that flashes up at the moment of its recognizability, and is never seen again."[70] The key attribute of the dialectic image lies in its ambiguity; every image of the past that is not recognized by the present disappears irretrievably.

The materialist way of presenting history constructs the historical object as ambiguous fragments. Benjamin's materialist historiography aims to present history as "imagistic" (*bildhaft*).[71] The famous doctrine, "I needn't *say* anything. Merely show [*zeigen*],"[72] illustrates well the figural aspect of his materialist critique of culture. His analysis of modernity as phantasmagoria in *The Arcades Project* presents these fragmented objects in a figurative and imagistic constellation in which objects dislodged from the past become the present story.

273

The fact that it is through distraction and not contemplation that the dialectical image is perceived is of substantial relevance to the analysis of contemporary media culture. Benjamin's comprehension of distraction resists the main principles of *Ideologiekritik*, since he questioned whether reflective or critical consciousness was possible in the age of media culture. He had no faith in the procedures of *Ideologiekritik* which assumed a substantial distance between the object and subject of reflection. The phantasmagoria of experience implied that the configuration of images, time and space reshaped with the new modes of communication and that consequently, the boundary between the cognitive subject and its object dissolved. If all experience were saturated by the phantasmagoria of media, attentive perception and rational thinking would be untenable. Through his analyses of arcades, department stores, world exhibitions and panoramas, Benjamin offered a detailed picture of how the entertainment industry utilized new representation technologies and how it configured a new mode of perception, that is, collective tactile distraction. In so doing Benjamin identified a substantial breakdown of communicable experience and a blurring of the boundaries between subject/object, rational/irrational, and private/public—dichotomies upon which conventional *Ideologiekritik* depended. The phantasmagoria of the entertainment industry denied the clear and innocent representation, which classical Enlightenment thought presumed.

While his idea of the decay of aura is more concerned with the transformation of aesthetic experience in the context of classical notion of art, the phantasmagoria of modernity unfolds key attributes of the transformation of the sentient bodily collective. Seen from this broader context, Benjamin's concern with cinema in the "Work of Art" identifies the quintessential space for the formation of a new subjectivity by means of technological innervation. Cinema is a multi-functional techno-space where new perceptions are constituted, reconstructed and shattered, not only through visual experience, but more decisively through distracted bodily behavior. Benjamin's central idea of the decay of aura and the main facets of post-auratic culture can be more fully grasped in conjunction with his broader analysis of phantasmagoria, through which he endeavoured to demonstrate the transformation of collective experience.

Notes

1 Benjamin, "Paris, the Capital of the Nineteenth Century: Exposé <of 1935>," in AP, 8–12.
2 Benjamin, "Paris, Capital of the Nineteenth Century: Exposé <of 1939>," in AP, 14.
3 Ibid., 26.
4 Benjamin, "Little History of Photography," in SW 2, 518.
5 Theodor W. Adorno, *Aesthetic Theory* (London: The Athlone Press, 1997), 56. See also Adorno, letter to Benjamin, March 18, 1936, in *Theodor W. Adorno–Walter Benjamin: The Complete Correspondence 1928-1940*, ed. Henri Lonitz (Cambridge: Polity, 1999), 131.
6 Bertolt Brecht, *Arbeitsjournal (1938 bis 1942)*, ed. Werner Hecht (Frankfurt am Main: Suhrkamp, 1973), 16.
7 Michael Taussig, *The Nervous System* (New York: Routledge, 1992), 143.
8 Benjamin, "The Work of Art (Third Version)," in SW 4, 268.
9 Ibid.
10 Ibid.
11 Heiner Weidmann, *Flânerie, Sammlung, Spiel* (München: Wilhelm Fink, 1992), 71.
12 Benjamin, "The Work of Art (Third Version)," in SW 4, 268.
13 Karl Marx, *Capital* (New York: International Publishers, 1967), vol. 1, 76–77. Emphasis added. The original German word *phantasmagorische* has been translated as "fantastic" in the English versions. Benjamin pays particular attention to this passage, quoting it in AP, 182 [G5,1], from Otto Rühe's book, *Karl Marx* (Hellerau, 1928).
14 Rolf Tiedemann, "Dialectics at a Standstill," in *On Walter Benjamin*, ed. Gary Smith (Cambridge, Mass.: The MIT Press, 1988), 277.
15 Benjamin, AP, 669 [X,13a].
16 Benjamin, GS V, 1172. Emphasis added.
17 See Benjamin, letter to Gerschom Scholem, September 16, 1924, in *Briefe* 1, eds. T. W. Adorno and G. Scholem (Frankfurt am Main: Suhrkamp, 1966), 355.
18 *The Oxford English Dictionary*, vol. XI (Oxford: Oxford University Press, 1998), 658.
19 Terry Castle, "Phantasmagoria: Spectral Technology and the Metaphorics of Modern Reverie," in *Critical Inquiry*, 45 (1988), 48.

[20] Ibid., 50.

[21] Ibid., 48.

[22] The *OED*, vol. XI, 658. The OED also quotes from the magazine *National Magic* of 1831: "An exhibition depending on these principles was brought out by M. Philipstal in 1802, under the name of the Phantasmagoria [...] Spectres, skeletons, and terrific figures [...] suddenly advanced upon the spectators, becoming larger as they approached them, and finally vanished by appearing to sink into the ground."

[23] Castle describes that "the bizarre, claustrophobic surroundings, the mood of Gothic strangeness and terror, the rapid phantom-train of images, the disorientation and powerlessness of the spectator" were all characteristics of the magic lantern show. Castle, "Phantasmagoria," 43.

[24] See Benjamin, letter to Scholem, May 3, 1936, in Corr., 528.

[25] Benjamin, "False Criticism," SW 2, 408.

[26] Karl Marx and Friedrich Engels, *The German Ideology*, ed. R. Pascal (New York: International Publishers, 1947), 14. For a detailed analysis of the relationship between Marx's concept of ideology and the camera obscura, see W. J. T. Mitchel, *Iconology: Image, Text, Ideology* (Chicago: University of Chicago Press, 1987).

[27] Benjamin, AP, 395 [K3,5]. Emphasis added.

[28] Benjamin, AP, 392 [K2,5]. Emphasis added.

[29] As Gyorgy Markus points out, "the content of such representations was quite narrowly circumscribed by the requirements of their pragmatic efficacy and economic functionality." Gyorgy Markus, "Walter Benjamin or the Commodity as Phantasmagoria," in *New German Critique*, 83 (spring/summer, 2001), 25.

[30] Benjamin "Eduard Fuchs, Collector and Historian," in SW 3, 267. Benjamin criticizes cultural history for being rooted in the Hegelian concept of *Zeitgeist*, and positivist perspectives on history. For the German origin of cultural history, see Peter Burke, *Varieties of Cultural History* (Cambridge: Polity, 2001), 21–23.

[31] Benjamin, "The Work of Art (Third Version)," in SW 4, 257.

[32] Ibid., 255.

[33] Ibid., 257.

[34] Benjamin "Eduard Fuchs," in SW 3, 283. Emphasis added.

[35] Benjamin, "The Work of Art (Third Version)," in SW 4, 269.

[36] For a detailed analysis of the artificial aura in the film, see Graeme Gilloch's essay in this volume.

[37] Benjamin "The Work of Art (Second Version)," in SW 3, 128.

[38] Adorno, letter to Benjamin, August 2, 1935, in *The Complete Correspondence*, 110. In 1936, Adorno suggested that Benjamin investigate Jung's and Klages's work in more detail, in order to clarify the differences between the archaic image and the

dialectic image. Benjamin, who was unfamiliar with these works, did not write on this issue. However, in the revised version of his Baudelaire study, "On Some Motifs in Baudelaire," there is a notable loss of the strength of the original "The Paris of the Second Empire in Baudelaire." In this modified version, for instance, Dilthey is dismissed, and Jung and Klages consigned to the camp of fascism, while Freud is incorporated through extensive use of the notion of shock drawn from *Beyond the Pleasure Principle*. See *Aesthetics and Politics*, ed. Roland Taylor (London: Verso, 1980), 105.

[39] Benjamin, AP, 669 [X,13a]. In a review of 1933, "Kierkegaard: The End of Philosophical Idealism," in SW 2, 703–4, Benjamin had already characterized Adorno's book *Kierkegaard* as phantasmagoric: "The extremely precise and exhaustive analysis and description of these formations gives many pages of this study the character of a phantasmagoria."

[40] Benjamin, AP, 902. Benjamin draws particular attention to Wagner's aesthetic modernity via a focus on Baudelaire's fascination with Wagner (AP, 895), and acknowledges Baudelaire's first letter to Wagner. Baudelaire says that in Wagner's *Tannhäuser*, *Lohengrin*, and *The Flying Dutchman* he finds not only "a spirit of order and division that recalls the architecture of ancient tragedies" but also a resemblance to "antiquity." AP, 237 [J5a,4 and 5].

[41] See Jean-Louis Baudry, "Ideological Effects of the Basic Cinematographic Apparatus," in *Film Theory and Criticism*, eds. Leo Braudy and Marshall Cohen (Oxford: Oxford University Press, 1999), 345–55. According to Jonathan Crary, the art theorist Paul Souriau was one of the first critics who characterized Wagner's work specifically as 'phantasmagoric': "Souriau noted the "absolute illusion" produced by the invisibility of the orchestra at Bayreuth, and noted that the inability to localize the origin of musical sounds enhanced their magical and hypnotic effects." Jonathan Crary, *Suspensions of Perception* (Cambridge, Mass.: The MIT Press, 1999), 254.

[42] Benjamin, "The Exposé of 1935," in AP, 11.

[43] T. W. Adorno, *In Search of Wagner* (London: New Left Books, 1981). Adorno states that this analysis is intimately bound up with Max Horkheimer's 1936 essay "Egoism and the Movement for Emancipation: Towards an Anthropology of the Bourgeois Era." As Gyorgy Markus reveals, the idea of a musical monography of this type occurred to Adorno partly as the result of his fiercely negative reaction to Kracauer's book *Jacques Offenbach und das Paris seiner Zeit* (1937). See Gyorgy Markus, "Adorno's Wagner," in *Thesis Eleven* vol. 56 (February 1999).

[44] Adorno, *Wagner*, 86.

[45] T. W. Adorno, "Fragmente über Wagner," in *Zeitschrift für Sozialforschung*, 8 (1939), 48. For a more detailed analysis, see Max Paddison, *Adorno's Aesthetics of Music*

(Cambridge: Cambridge University Press, 1993), 243–46.

46 For instance, Adorno suggests that the effect of "loudness from afar" is created through the use of the high woodwind—especially the piccolo—and through omitting the bass instruments. See Paddison, *Adorno's Aesthetics of Music*, 245–46.

47 Adorno, *Wagner*, 97

48 Andreas Huyssen, *After the Great Divide: Modernism, Mass Culture and Postmodernism* (London: MacMillan, 1986), 38.

49 Adorno, *Wagner*, 89.

50 Ibid., 91.

51 Crary, *Suspensions of Perception*, 250–51.

52 Ibid., 253–54.

53 Adorno, *Wagner*, 90. Emphasis added.

54 Ibid., 90. Emphasis added.

55 Adorno, letter to Benjamin, November 10, 1938, in *The Complete Correspondence*, 283.

56 For a more detailed analysis, see Gillian Rose, *The Melancholy Science* (London: Macmillan Press, 1978), 37–40.

57 Ibid., 40.

58 Adorno, letter to Benjamin, February 1, 1939, in *The Complete Correspondence*, 300.

59 *Aesthetics and Politics*, ed. Roland Taylor, 102–3.

60 Adorno, letter to Benjamin, November 10, 1938, in *The Complete Correspondence*, 281–82.

61 Adorno, letter to Benjamin, August, 2–4, 1935, in *The Complete Correspondence*, 106.

62 Adorno, *The Culture Industry*, ed. J. M. Bernstein (London: Routledge, 1991), 33.

63 Ibid., 34.

64 Markus, "Adorno's Wagner", 42.

65 In light of Adorno's critique of the 1935 exposé, Benjamin only modified the structure of his piece by omitting the second part of the first version (II. Daugerre, or the Panorama). See Benjamin, letter to Adorno, December 9, 1938, in *The Complete Correspondence*, 290.

66 Benjamin, AP, 466 [N4a,6]. Emphasis added.

67 Charles Baudelaire, *The Painter of Modern Life* (London: Phaidon, 1995), 12.

68 David Frisby, *Fragments of Modernity: Theories of Modernity in the work of Simmel, Kracauer and Benjamin* (Cambridge: Polity, 1985), 13.

69 Benjamin, AP, 476 [N11,4]. Translation modified and emphasis added.

70 Benjamin, "On the Concept of History," in SW 4, 390

71 Benjamin, AP, 463, [N3,3].

72 Ibid., 460, [N1a,8].

Images of the Aura

Some Motifs in French Modernism

Beryl Schlossman

Tout à l'heure, comme je traversais le boulevard, en grande hâte (...) mon auréole, dans un mouvement brusque, a glissé de ma tête dans la fange du macadam.

(Charles Baudelaire)

The concept of aura is featured in Benjamin's theory of modernity and in his interpretive readings of modern culture. aura appears at the crossroads of literature, painting, photography, philosophy, and modern subjectivity. Within a precise configuration that includes the trace and the aura's decay, Benjamin uses the concept of aura to articulate a shift that occurs in the mid-nineteenth century, when the subjects of High Capitalism become the subjects of modernity. In the transition from romanticism to modernism, a break occurs that transforms vision, sensation, and the perception of experience. Aura enters Benjamin's writing from his reading of Charles Baudelaire, and especially Baudelaire's *Les Fleurs du Mal* (*The Flowers of Evil*).

Baudelaire dramatizes Art and Love in urban scenes, 'tableaux' or pictures. Benjamin reads Baudelaire through Parisian streets, and in the allegories of woman, death, and the city that give those streets a new poetic form. Engaged in thought, mourning, and memory, the subject of desire walks through Paris.[1]

In Baudelaire's theater of poetry and in Benjamin's critical responses to Baudelaire, time and space shape the images of modernity: the manifestations of aura are temporal and spatial constructions, projections, visions, and illusions. Aura can fill the atmosphere with a golden haze or with the wind that blows us around in the storm of history. Benjamin evokes aura as a mode of being in the world of appearances.

Paris is the capital of the nineteenth century: Baudelaire is the artist who emblematizes Parisian modernity, and his writings circulate in Benjamin's text-city, the Arcades project. Benjamin theorizes aura as a dialectical concept of authenticity and plenitude, associated with Baudelaire's correspondences (*Korrespondenzen*) and Benjamin's term of *Verschränkungen*. Baudelaire's prose poem entitled "*Perte d'Auréole*" (Loss of the Halo) plays a central role in Benjamin's elaboration of the aura in modernity. Benjamin's concept takes root in the arcades, where Baudelaire reshapes Nature into the public gardens and theaters, the alleys and boulevards, of his new Parisian poetics. Steeped in literature, the city emerges from Baudelaire's poems.

The last sections of Benjamin's "On Some Motifs in Baudelaire" develop a theory of the correspondences and of the aura. The final section of the essay gathers together Baudelaire's motifs to focus on the prose poem "*Perte d'Auréole*." The poet's halo or golden crown is evoked in the context of its loss; similarly, Benjamin's concept of aura is elaborated in the conceptual framework of its decay. 'Aura' relates to the poet's '*auréole*' in the context of the shattering effects of modernity on the poet and on lyric poetry.

Spectral Images

In Latin and French, aureole appears as a diminutive form of aura. The terms play distinct roles in theological writings and in iconographic representations of sainthood through the seventeenth century.[2] The vocabulary of aura and aureole includes elements of visible and invisible sensation, emanation, atmosphere, and something that is difficult to define... a kind of otherworldly presence. Aura and aureole are simultaneously visible and invisible, alive and spectral. Benjamin's term of aura formulates a concept that is essential to his reading of modernity. It is steeped in Baudelairean (and Proustian) resonances that leave their traces in Benjamin's written works and in his translations of French modernist texts. Benjamin's search for the literary and cultural constructions of modernity leads him to the discovery of the arcades in his most ambitious project. The unfinished Book of Arcades is their translation into written form. He commands his Parisian arcades like the disguised regiments of Blanqui's invisible army, he organizes them like the streets of a city, and he looks at them with the double gaze of the modern.

This inhabitant of urban modernity (*der Moderner*) looks back at Nature, tradition, and the feast days of cultic worship. Benjamin sees the modern man as someone who laments the lost world of the past and proclaims it as irretrievable. Benjamin consecrates this double gaze in the nineteenth-century Grenoble bar named "*Au Temps Perdu*" (The Place of Lost Time) that appears in his essay entitled "Toward an Image of Proust." He commemorates the occasion by taking a literary snapshot of Proust. In the vocabulary of Benjamin's writing on photography, he encodes the image of an invisible photograph. He takes the stance of the Modern for whom, in spite of the power of painting and the complicity that Benjamin demonstrates between the art of painting and the creations of involuntary memory, the photographic image captures the violent and instantaneous power of resurrected time: "*Wo das Gewesene im taufrischen 'Nu' sich spiegelt, rafft ein schmerzlicher Chock der Verjüngung es noch einmal so unaufhaltsam zusammen* [...] *Aber eben diese Konzentration, in der, was sonst nur welkt und dämmert, blitzhaft sich verzehrt, heißt Verjüngung.* [Where that which was is mirrored in the dewfresh instant, a painful shock of rejuvenation irresistibly takes it up once more (...) But this very concentration, in which that which otherwise only wilts and flickers in twilight, is consumed in a lightning flash, is called rejuvenation.]"[3] Framed between the clasping of time and the similarity of the correspondences, the rejuvenating power of involuntary memory recalls an entire life in a single explosive instant that restores its clarity.

Benjamin's mirroring image occurs *im 'Nu'*, in an 'instant' or in a flash of lightning, like a snapshot (aptly named in French an *instantané*). This lightning flash or shock consumes a life in an instant; it marks the site of photography. In *The Arcades Project*, Benjamin quotes a description of

281

photography from an anonymous account of an exhibit of the graphic works of Constantin Guys in 1937: *"L'humanité a aussi inventé, dans son égarement du soir, c'est à dire au dix-neuvième siècle, le symbole du souvenir; elle a inventé ce qui eût paru impossible; elle a inventé un miroir qui se souvient. Elle a inventé la photographie.* [In its nighttime madness, i.e. in the nineteenth century, humanity also invented the symbol of memory; it invented that which would have appeared impossible; it invented a mirror that remembers things. It invented photography.]"[4] This commentary sounds as if Baudelaire had written it.

The Hall of Mirrors

In Webster's rather poetic definition, aura is "an invisible emanation or vapor, as the aroma of flowers." In the doctrines of the occult, it designates a halo seen only by initiates. In the figurative usage that the *Robert* dates as 1923, aura connotes an atmosphere that surrounds a being. The Latin word *aura* (air) derives from the Greek form, to breathe or to blow. The definition of 'aura' as a sensation of a current of air preceding an attack of epilepsy or hysteria occurs in the medical vocabulary of the 1840's. Although the term of 'aureole' sounds like another version of 'aura' and is related to it, its Latin source is different: the Old French *auriole* comes from the ecclesial Latin term for the halo or crown of gold (*corona aureola*) painted around the heads of Christ, the Virgin, and the saints. The word also is defined as a luminous circle that the eye perceives around an object, e.g. the Moon or the Sun. The resonances of the aura echo and mirror Baudelaire's term of the Poet's aureole in the essay "On Some Motifs in Baudelaire," when the two terms converge. The confrontation between Nature and the City that supplies the decor and the images of Baudelaire's writings shapes Benjamin's theory of modernity.

In "On Some Motifs," two poems in particular lead Benjamin into the hall of mirrors called aura: the sonnet *"Correspondances,"* with its enigmatic temple of Nature, and *"La Vie Antérieure"* (Anterior Life) with its arcade-like constructions of grottos and porticos. A third poem that plays an important role for Benjamin's reading of Baudelaire is *"A Une Passante"*

(To a Woman Passing By), discussed in chapter five of "On Some Motifs" and in the "Flâneur" chapter of *Charles Baudelaire: A Lyric Poet in the Age of High Capitalism*. "*Le Cygne*" (The Swan), arguably Baudelaire's most important poem for Benjamin, is evoked in the "Flâneur" chapter and in many passages of the Arcades project. Like "*A Une Passante*," "*Le Cygne*" is one of the "Parisian Pictures," and it is one of two long poems dedicated to Victor Hugo in exile. Because of its political resonances, as well as Benjamin's valorization of the poem in a theoretical context, "*Le Cygne*" has become an emblematic text of modernity.

These poems dramatize the subject of modernity who succumbs to sensuality and the shock waves of modern life without forgetting the loss that shines secretly and intimately in images of the past. Temporal frames shift forward and back in anticipation and longing, landscapes alternate with cityscapes, but the evocation of aura—the plenitude of experience, in Art and in Love—is central to each of these poems. Baudelaire's taste for artifice may be related to the important place of melancholy in his writings: beginning with Dürer's famous allegorical image of Melancholia, melancholy is related to the powerful impact of aura on Baudelaire's subject and especially to the pain of loss. Melancholy enters the scene of aura at the moment when the illusion of plenitude and authenticity is dispelled: the past cannot be recovered, the woman passing by disappears into the Night. The sorcery of art and the pleasures of the senses are all that remain when the illusions of aura have vanished into thin air.

In the language of Baudelaire's poetry, modernity—the latest thing—encounters the archaic forms and types of the past: correspondence imaginatively reshapes the old within the new. Style is at the heart of this imaginative transformation. Benjamin recalls Jacques Rivière's quotation from Paul Claudel: "Claudel said that Baudelaire's style 'is an extraordinary combination of Racine's style and the journalistic style of the period.'"[5] Claudel's remark captures the poetic tension that Benjamin interprets through the theoretical and textual effects of the correspondence of modernity and antiquity. Benjamin explores this combination in Baudelaire's style, "the baroque of banality" (...) "the realm of language

283

in which the fashionable word encounters the allegorized abstraction (Spleen and Ideal)."[6]

Melancholy increases the sense of isolation that afflicts the subject of modernity, but like the lover, the melancholic seeks lyric to appease the subject's lonely suffering. Jean Starobinski refers to the character of Jacques in Shakespeare's comedy, "As You Like It." Longing for harmony and filled with dissonance ("compact of jars"), the exiled melancholic Jacques anticipates Baudelaire's types in his blackest poems, as well as the elegiac Narrator of "*Le Cygne.*" Benjamin's vision of Baudelaire as angry and bitter, ironic, misanthropic, asocial, and unfit for love implicitly takes up the type that Jacques represents. The singing that Jacques longs to hear increases his melancholy.[7] Jacques is an exile who has his place in the Duke's community of exiles until love officially enters their world; at that moment, he turns his back on the community. Except for lyric, correspondence (and the similitude at its origin) holds no appeal for Jacques. Closer to Baudelaire, who was familiar with the rich iconography and the literary tradition of Melancholia, his friend Gérard de Nerval uses images from antiquity and the Renaissance to combine the poet's music with the black sun of Melancholy in the opening poem of his "*Chimères,*" entitled "*El Desdichado*" (*The Unhappy One*).

It is perhaps in response to Baudelaire's poetic use of correspondence that Benjamin theorizes the concept of aura and the trace, its antithesis. Because Benjamin sees Baudelaire's relation to Nature as one of renunciation, Nature poses an initial problem. Allegory gives evidence of that renunciation, but Benjamin begins his accounts of the work of translation as well as the aura with reference to trees and mountains. These pointed references to "Nature" in Benjamin's writings over many years point back toward the *Ähnlichkeit* or likeness, resemblance, that is at the origin of correspondence. But Baudelaire takes a baroque position on the split between the senses and the spirit or the mind; his aesthetic and the figures that he coins for it are not synthetic—they display rather than hide their contradictions and paradoxes. Baudelaire does not seek to reconcile the plenitude of correspondence and the infinitely empty abyss of allegory.

The aporetic figure of the oxymoron is one of Baudelaire's stylistic trademarks; he does not ask how the two terms of his oxymorons—including light and darkness—can be reconciled. His most perfect account of the correspondences, in the sonnet that takes its indefinite title from them, distances itself from theology. Similar to Poe's exposition of the detective's use of Analogy in "The Purloined Letter," Baudelaire's correspondence is suggestive of aesthetic perception and poetic practice.

Like Baudelaire's images of light and darkness in "*Correspondances*," allegory and correspondence secretly unite. Nature is inhabited by the artificial time and space of allegory: it is filled with secrets, memories, and suffering. In Baudelaire's paired opposition of Spleen and Ideal, the subject of beauty and evil/suffering uses the artifices of Allegory to infiltrate nature. For this reason, all of Baudelaire's seascapes contain sailing ships; his poetic landscapes are secretly shaped by the eye of an architect; forests turn his imagination to cathedrals, and public gardens represent nature in the city. Lost forever, the garden of Eden and the natural world of the golden age form the decor of original sin. Nature has become a text or a set of images. Rousseau's Nature is denounced as an illusion: the Nature of the naturalists is a resource for poets in search of allegorical materials (or abstractions). For Baudelaire, Nature is monstrously grotesque or sublimely beautiful; it appears only in the context of original sin and its consequences. Like Edgar Allan Poe, Thomas de Quincy, Gérard de Nerval, and even the painter Eugène Delacroix, Baudelaire subordinates Nature to the fictions of Art.

In Baudelaire's concept of art in modernity, beauty is shaped by artifice and *le Mal* (evil and suffering) is the effect of original sin. Melancholy and allegory detach (or estrange) the subject from nature, from the present time and place, and potentially from a sense of reality. As sensory perception (or at a second level, among art forms), correspondence posits a plenitude that artfully combines the raw materials of Nature but that cannot be attributed to Nature. For Baudelaire, correspondence is like a painter's palette of colors: it relies on artifice and produces art. Baudelaire reshapes correspondence by subtracting from it the original reference to theology; the echoing and mirroring effects remain. After the sonnet entitled *"Correspondances"* marks the descent from the spirit to the senses, correspondence enters the intersections and crossroads of city streets, like Poe's convalescent rushing out of the cafe to follow the crowd. The transports of correspondence enter modernity and mingle with the personifications and abstractions that characterize allegory; perhaps the transports of the *sens*–translatable as sensory perception and intellectual meaning–are the secrets that dwell within the allegories.

The Poet's Crown: the Twentieth Century

A century after Baudelaire, the impact of Baudelaire's written account of auratic experience is illustrated in a French modernist novel that takes up the secular and comic overtones of *"Perte d'Auréole."* In *Guignol's Band,* Céline discreetly alludes to the French Romantic poetic tradition that leaves its traces in Symbolism and in the art and writing of Surrealism. A passage from the novel gives an enlightening account of the traditional aura as a mystical halo or crown that suggests spiritual properties.

Toward the end of *Guignol's Band,* Ferdinand meets a man in Chinese robes named Hervé Sosthène de Rodiencourt. Sosthène proclaims himself an authority on the occult and describes his noble background and his cult of the dead. Ferdinand brags about his experiences in the cavalry, in the hopes that Sosthène will take him on an expedition. Sosthène names him his squire (*écuyer*) and proclaims the sudden appearance of his halo, a symbol of supernatural vision:

– *Vous êtes coiffé!*
J'avais pas de chapeau.
– *Coiffé! Coiffé du Destin! Parfaitement! Et là! L'Aura! là! je la vois!... Cette bonne surprise! Ne bougez plus!*
Il me la voyait! Il me la décrivait dans l'air! un petit cercle autour de ma tête!
– *Quelle destinée!... quel symbole!... Oh! Vous ne sauriez comprendre! Evidemment! Opaque! Opaque! mais rayonnant!*
Ah, je le deçois encore un coup! Ah, il en était excédé de voir de si beaux dons perdus, gaspillés sur une tête si sotte!...

[–You're coiffed! I wasn't wearing a hat.–Coiffed! Coiffed by Fate! Most certainly! And there! The Aura! there! I see it!... What a wonderful surprise! Don't move! He saw me in it! He drew it in the air! a little circle around my head! What a destiny!... What a symbol!... Oh! You couldn't understand! Obviously! Opaque! Opaque! but radiant! Ah, I disappoint him again! Ah, he was beside himself to see such beautiful gifts lost, wasted on such a stupid head!].[8]

The 'aura' or aureole seems to arouse the attention of others, possible spies who are listening to them and watching them. Sosthène says: "*Chutt! Halte-là! Il me semble qu'on nous écoute! Qu'on nous épie tout alentour!* [Hush! Stop right there! I think someone is listening to us! Someone is spying on us all around!]"

Sosthène thinks that he perceives some other person, but the perception of otherness or of another time, blown toward us and exhumed from the past in an instant, approaching us like the air of an unfathomable breeze, is itself an auratic effect. Sosthène's perceptions of the presence of the aura and the suspicion that it arouses in him recall Gérard de Nerval's poem, "*Vers Dorés*" (Golden Verse). A line of the poem indicates what is at stake in the Aura that combines the perception of intimate otherness in the image of a glance or a gaze. Intertwined nearness and distance produce the uncanny traces of lost Time in the form of Aura: Baudelaire's "familiar glances" reflect the looking/being looked at of "Man." These gazes or glances are familiar–empty of content, empty of identity, but known, or rather recognized as the unknown and unknowable object of loss, the irretrievable object that Baudelaire (and Proust after him) calls "*l'Inconnu*." Proust will add a feminine ending to turn the unknown one into a woman, "*l'Inconnue*." Mysteriously, the allegorical image of the Unknown casts familiar glances.

Nerval's scene seems to anticipate the "forests of symbols" with their strange "familiar glances" in Baudelaire's poem, "*Correspondances*." The speaker in Nerval's "*Vers Dorés*" begins the poem with an apostrophe to "*Homme, libre penseur* [Man, free thinker]!" The speaker exhorts him: "*Crains, dans le mur aveugle, un regard qui t'épie* [Fear, in the blind wall, a glance that spies on you]." The sonnet ends with these lines: "*Souvent dans l'être obscur habite un Dieu caché;/ Et comme un oeil naissant couvert par ses paupières,/ Un pur esprit s'accroît sous l'écorce des pierres* [Often in the obscure being a hidden god dwells; And like an eye born covered with its lids, a pure spirit grows under the bark of stones]!"[9] The eyes in the forest of symbols look at Man with the same sharp and covert glances (the "*regards familiers*") of Nerval's walls and stones where spirit takes the form of a new eye that grows and opens. In Nerval's Pythagorean Nature, the uncanny eye of God emerges to observe Man; in Baudelaire's temple of Nature, Man passes by, observed with "familiar glances" by forests of symbols. Baudelaire's "*Correspondances*" reshape Nature into an uncanny space filled with enigmatic glances and the anonymous fleeting appearances of figures passing by, in flight. Although Nerval's Nature remains within the parameters of romanticism, the poet transforms a common claim for the presence of God in the creation into a command to fear the eye of God: the blind inanimate stone (*pierre*) can see. It is watching him with the eye of God. The phallic resonance of the sonnet indicates that this version of aura might be a deadly one: the evil eye threatens the free-thinker with castration, paranoia, madness. Nerval turns his back on the inventions of modernity and crafts a short series of poems that ostensibly celebrate the auratic powers of Pythagorean mysticism; he combines the pagan and the Christian elements of a fictional antiquity. But the glance that strikes the man in the golden verse of aura is a menacing one; pushing against the tide of modernity, it is fighting the crowd.

The uncanny eye of God observes Man in Nerval's poem, but the uncanny glances of Baudelaire's "*Correspondances*" emerge from the forests of symbols and their pillars to enter the temple of allegory, the temple of 'Nature' with a capital letter. God is absent from this temple, and the *esprit* of the last line of the sonnet leaves Nerval's divinity behind, with the other gods of Romanticism. In Baudelaire's poem, the spirit is drawn into a celebration of aura: Nerval's uncanny God is replaced by the murmured words and the symbol forests of allegorical images. The auratic

looking of the first stanza prepares the sensual transports of the correspondences that dominate the artful ending of the sonnet. It concludes
with the perfumes of aura: emanation, vapor, or invisible atmosphere,
the golden crown or halo of verse. Found and lost, aura enters the romantic
terrain of Baudelaire's writing: the shattering of aura transforms
Baudelaire's romantic inheritance into an aesthetic of loss. *"Perte d'Auréole"*
finds its ultimate translation, in Benjamin's words, as *"Der Verfall der Aura*
[The decay of aura]."

Halos, perfumes, and emanations are visible only to the initiates who
celebrate them in a new cult of the dead, that Proust, taking his cue from
Baudelaire, will call the search for lost time: *A La Recherche du temps perdu.*
Aura and its decay form a range of phenomena and effects, a continuum
of darkness and light that Benjamin associates with the early development
of photography. The reproduction of Nature occurs through the new
powers of artifice: the machine alters Nature irrevocably, and the human
face stares out of the early photographs as a sign of that alteration. They
form a kind of visual telegram that transmits the messages of aura and
its decay. They bear the message that the human presence portrayed in
them is disappearing into the darkness and light that their image pours
into our mortal gaze.

In *The Arcades Project*, Benjamin mentions Delacroix's opinion that a
human face could not possibly be recorded by a machine.[10] The theory
of the daguerreotype that Balzac proposed in *Le Cousin Pons* and that
Nadar adopted focuses on the unresolved body of the baroque in its
most modern form: the *"spectre saisissable* [palpable spectre]" revealed by
the new invention. An uncanny compromise between the material world
of objects in Nature and the spiritual world that transforms time produces
the form, trace, or image in the atmosphere. Balzac writes: *"les corps se
projettent réellement dans l'atmosphère en y laissant subsister ce spectre saisi par le
daguerréotype qui l'arrête au passage* [bodies are projected as real bodies in
the atmosphere by allowing to remain in it the specter caught in passing
by the daguerreotype]."[11]

In Balzac's descriptions, atmosphere seems to reserve a place for the aura. Benjamin records the passage in his notes without indicating its remarkable context: in Balzac's novel, daguerreotype is evoked at a moment of suspense that decides the death of the protagonist, a talented musician. Pons's concierge visits her neighborhood psychic, an old woman with a truly visionary gift for seeing into the future.[12] Her auratic powers offer a model to an early form of photography: like Balzac's view of the writer, the visionary captures reality itself. The photographer catches the aura for an instant in the same way that the speaker of Baudelaire's "*A Une Passante*" catches the eye of the woman dressed in mourning, in a widow's veils, as Benjamin reads her. Balzac emphasizes the uncanny spectral impact of vision, while Baudelaire emphasizes the erotic quality of the gaze that leads into the future.

In Nerval's poem, an unmistakeable threat represented in the spying glance gives an account of the shattering experience of aura and its loss. Nerval's attraction to cult and ritual repetition at the source of authenticity could not protect him from the threat of destruction that led to the mysterious and lurid circumstances of his death.

But Nerval's account of the all-powerful spying glance inscribed in the blind stone may indicate that his mystical tone is a cover-up for the predicament of the modern. The dispossession of his melancholy figure of the poet as the disinherited subject named "*El Desdichado*", the title of the first of the "*Chimères*," is closer to the mood of modernity that Benjamin detects in Baudelaire's poems about love and memory. Like "*El Desdichado*," the poet in Baudelaire's "*Perte d'Auréole*" emerges from the mysterious underworld of experience to proclaim his loss of prestige and authority. The poet enters the crowd, or goes underground: a new anonymity afflicts the trans-romantic poet.

"*A Une Passante*" also tells a story of a subject caught at the crossroads, but its effects are different. While "*El Desdichado*" offers the poetic experience in the form of rebus and enigma, Baudelaire's auratic moments and correspondences connect the reader with the Unknown. In "*A Une Passante*," the unknown element appears as a sensual, melancholic, and anonymous woman in flight. Her fugitive form glimpsed in a moment is all that Baudelaire can say, forever and ever, about love. Mourning and celebration, loss and the magical possession of love are mysteriously reconciled in Baudelaire's poetry. The voice that sings the transports of the spirit and the senses shapes its celebrations within an aesthetic of loss. In the violent terms of unbearably intense and sudden sensation that Benjamin evokes as 'shock,' he describes the experience evoked in Baudelaire's poetry. The experience of shock destroys aura: the conceptual path that leads Benjamin beyond the merely registered experience of *Erlebnis* to the auratic experience of *Erfahrung* includes a paradoxical complicity with the shattering of aura. Benjamin names this terrible complicity as an affirmation or an acceptance, as *Einverständnis*. Baudelaire's *Einverständnis* with the shattering of aura is played out in *"Perte d'Auréole,"* where he undercuts the cultic role of the Poet and renders him anonymous; Baudelaire casts his shining crown into the mud of the streets of Paris. Benjamin ends "On Some Motifs in Baudelaire" with the remark that Baudelaire's poetry *"steht am Himmel des zweiten Kaiserreichs als 'ein Gestirn ohne Atmosphäre'* [stands in the sky of the Second Empire like a planet/star without atmosphere]." The atmosphere around Baudelaire and his poetry has been emptied of aura: the planet is without an atmosphere, the poet is deprived of air, and the eyes that cast their familiar glances on the subject who speaks in these poems are empty. The air of aura does not blow any more; adorable Spring has lost its perfume. Suddenly invisible, the uncrowned Poet slips into the crowd and wanders in search of pleasure, forgetting, and the images of artifice.

Notes

[1] Quotations from Baudelaire's works refer to Claude Pichois's edition of Charles Baudelaire, *Oeuvres complètes* (Paris: Gallimard, 1975 and 1976), in two volumes, indicated as OC1 and OC2. For an introduction to some major works of criticism

of Baudelaire, including the well-known essays by Gautier, Valéry, Proust, Auerbach, and others, see *Wege der Forschung: Baudelaire,* ed. Alfred Noyer-Weidner (Darmstadt: Wissenschaftliche Buchgesellschaft, 1976), vol. cclxxxiii. On Baudelaire and Benjamin, see Rainer Nägele, *Echoes of Translation* (Baltimore: Johns Hopkins University Press, 1997); by the same author, *Lesarten der Moderne* (Eggingen: Edition Klaus Isele, 1998); and by the same author, "The Poetic Ground Laid Bare (Benjamin Reading Baudelaire)" in *Walter Benjamin: Theoretical Questions,* ed. David S. Ferris (Stanford: Stanford University Press, 1996), 118–38. On Benjamin, see Rodolphe Gasché, "The Sober Absolute: On Benjamin and the Early Romantics" in Ferris (ed.), 50–74. On Baudelaire, see Hans-Jost Frey, *Studies in Poetic Discourse: Mallarmé, Baudelaire, Rimbaud, Hölderlin* (Stanford: Stanford University Press, 1996); Paul de Man, *The Rhetoric of Romanticism* (New York: Columbia University Press, 1984); Ross Chambers, "'Je' dans les Tableaux Parisiens de Baudelaire," in *Nineteenth Century French Studies* vol. 9 (1980–81), 59-68; by the same author, "Baudelaire's Street Poetry," in *Nineteenth Century French Studies* vol. 13 (1985), 244–59; by the same author, *Mélancolie et opposition: les débuts du modernisme en France* (Paris: José Corti, 1987), 167–86; Jean Starobinski, "Sur quelques répondants allégorique du poète," in *RHLF* vol. 67, (1967), 402–12; by the same author, a series of essays on melancholy that includes "Le Regard des Statues," in *Nouvelle revue de psychanalyse* vol. 50 (1994), 45–64; by the same author, "L'Immor-talité mélancolique," in *Le Temps de la réflexion* vol. 3 (1982), 231–51; and by the same author, *La Mélancolie au miroir* (Paris: Julliard, 1989).

2   Edwin Hall and Horst Uhr, "Aureola and Fructus: Distinctions of Beatitude in Scholastic Thought and the Meaning of Some Crowns in Early Flemish Painting," in *Art Bulletin* vol. lx (1978), 249–70; by the same authors, "Aureola super Auream: Crowns and Related Symbols of Special Distinction for Saints in Late Gothic and Renaissance Iconography," in *Art Bulletin* vol. lxvii (1985), 567–603.

3   Benjamin, "Zum Bilde Prousts," in GS II, 320.

4   Benjamin, *Das Passagen-Werk* in GS V, 841 [Y8a,3].

5   Jacques Rivière, *Etudes* (Paris: n.e.), 6e ed, 1924, quoted by Benjamin. See note below.

6   "Kurz, ich möchte noch einmal ausziehen, um es zu versuchen, jene sprachlichen Bereiche zu betreten, in denen das Modewort mit dem allegorisierten Abstractum (Spleen et Ideal) sich begegnet." Benjamin discusses Baudelaire's "Barock der Banalität" in a letter to Hugo von Hofmannsthal, January 13, 1924. (*GS, Briefe,* vol. 2, 391–4).

7   Shakespeare, "As You Like It," Act I, scene x. The connection with Baudelaire is made by Jean Starobinski, *La Mélancolie au miroir,* 33.

8   Louis-Ferdinand Céline, *Guignol's Band* (Gallimard, 1951, folio), 321-22.

9 Gérard de Nerval, "Vers Dorés," in *Oeuvres* (Paris: Garnier Frères, 1966), 709.
10 Benjamin, *Das Passagen-Werk* in GS V, 832 [Y4a,4].
11 Benjamin quotes this passage in GS V, 840 [Y8a,1].
12 Honoré de Balzac, *Le Cousin Pons* (Paris: Livre de Poche, 1965), 135.

Contributors

Graeme Gilloch is Senior Lecturer in Sociology at the University of Salford and a former Humboldt Foundation Research Fellow at the Johann Wolfgang Goethe University of Frankfurt am Main. His main publications include *Myth and Metropolis: Walter Benjamin and the City* (1996) and *Walter Benjamin: Critical Constellations* (2002). He is presently writing an intellectual biography of Siegfried Kracauer.

Tara Forrest teaches Film and Cultural Studies at the University of Technology, Sydney, and is currently completing a Ph.D. on the work of Walter Benjamin, Siegfried Kracauer, and Alexander Kluge at the University of New South Wales. Her work in this area has been published in a number of journals, and is forthcoming in Gerald Hartung and Kay Schiller (eds.), *Weltoffener Humanismus. Philosophie, Philologie, und Geschichte in der deutsch-jüdischen Emigration*.

Dag Petersson is senior researcher at the Royal Library, Denmark and adjunct at the University of Copenhagen. He is the author of *The Art of Reconciliation: Photography and the Power of Dialectics in Benjamin, Hegel and Derrida* (forthcoming) and numerous articles on photography, digital visuality, archives, history and time.

Catherine D. Dhavernas is assistant professor of French Literature (19th & 20th century) and literary theory at Queen's University, Kingston, Canada. She is author of *Les lieux de l'histoire: l'individu à l'ère de la planéité moderne* (forthcoming), and several articles on Benjamin, Literary Theory, the "Nouveau Roman," Avant-Garde film, painting and literature, Marguerite Duras, Margerite Yourcenar, Marcel Proust, Francois Rabelais, Gerhard Richter and Lars von Trier. She is currently at work on a book-length study of cross-overs between medicine and the humanities.

Claus Krogholm Sand, Ph.D., is associate professor and director of Danish studies at Aalborg University. His research interests include the Swedish author Per Olov Enquist, modernism, modern Danish literature and film studies (in particular David Lynch and David Cronenberg). Among his resent publications are "Holy Shit! Quentin Tarantino's Excremental Aesthetics" (2003) and "Utopi og auto-geografi–Per Olov Enquist og modernismen" ["Utopia and Autogeography–Per Olov Enquist and Modernism"] (2004).

David Kelman is a doctoral student in comparative literature at Emory University. His publications include *"Diversiloquium, or, Vico's Concept of Allegory in the New Science"* (*New Vico Studies*, 2002) and "La pereza como resistencia en 'Vuelva usted mañana' de Larra" (*El Cid*, 2003). He is currently working on a study of the literary biography as genre.

Peter Fenves, Joan and Sarepta Harrison Professor of Literature at Northwestern University, is the author of *A Peculiar Fate: Metaphysics and World-History in Kant* (1991), *"Chatter": Language and History in Kierkegaard* (1993), *Arresting Language: From Leibniz to Benjamin* (2001), and *Late Kant: Towards Another Law of the Earth* (2003). He is also the editor of *Raising the Tone of Philosophy: Late Essays by Kant, Transformative Critique by Derrida* (1993), the co-editor of *"The Spirit of Poesy"* (2000), and the translator of Werner Hamacher's *Premises* (1996). Among his current projects is a monograph entitled *The Messianic Reduction: Walter Benjamin and the Abstention from Philosophy*.

Mikkel Bruun Zangenberg, Ph.D. is Assistant Professor at the University of Copenhagen, and the author of *Romanens medierende mellemrum* (Århus, 1999) on Joyce's "Finnegan's Wake" and *Beckett's Ontic Space* (2001, Ph.D. dissertation) on literature and philosophy in early Beckett. He has written numerous articles on problems in literary theory, the ontology of fiction, the European avantgarde and on various authors, e.g, Blanchot and Gombrowicz. He is currently working on a large-scale study of the relation between politics, aesthetics, violence and democracy in the Twentieth Century, from Italian futurism to the war in ex-Yugoslavia, as well as contemporary forms of terrorism.

Henry Sussman currently serves as a Professor of Comparative Literature at the University at Buffalo and a Visiting Professor of German at Yale University. He has been working on problems of literary exegesis, critical theory, modernity, modernism, postmodernism, psychoanalysis, and religion over the past thirty years. Among his self-authored books are *The Aesthetic Contract* (Stanford: Stanford University Press, 1997) and *Afterimages of Modernity* (Baltimore: Johns Hopkins University Press, 1990). He has just completed a study entitled "The Poet, the Philosopher, the Reader and the Critic: Discourse and Religion."

Erik Steinskog is Dr. art. in musicology with the dissertation *Arnold Schoenberg's 'Moses und Aron': Music, Language, and Representation* (Norwegian University of Science and Technology, 2002). He is associate professor at the Grieg Academy, Department of Music, University of Bergen. Publications include: "Being Touched by Art: Art and Sense in Jean-Luc Nancy" (in Per Bäckström & Troels Degn Johansson [eds.]: *Sense and Senses in Aesthetics* [2003]), "Meaning, Message and Medium: Arnold Schoenberg's *Moses und Aron* and the Question of Mediality" (in Joyce Goggin & Michael Burke [eds.]: *Travelling Concepts II: Meaning, Frame and Metaphor* [2002]).

Jae-Ho Kang is an Alexander von Humboldt Research Fellow at the Institut für Sozialforschung, J.W.Goethe-Universität Frankfurt am Main. He is currently completing a manuscript called *Walter Benjamin and a Critical Theory of Media* based on doctoral research at the University of Cambridge, England. He has published a number of articles on the critical theory of Georg Lukács, Siegfried Kracauer, T.W. Adorno, Herbert Marcuse and Jürgen Habermas. His research includes studies of mass culture, film theory and political communication.

Beryl Schlossman is the author of *Joyce's Catholic Comedy of Language* (University of Wisconsin Press), *The Orient of Style: Modernist Allegories of Conversion* (Duke University Press), *Objects of Desire: The Madonnas of Modernism* (Cornell University Press), and *Angelus Novus*, a book of poems published by *Editions Virgile*, Fontaine-lès-Dijon, France. She teaches literature, cinema, and the arts in society at Carnegie Mellon University.